DEMOCRACY
AN ALTERNATE VIEW

DEMOCRACY
AN ALTERNATE VIEW

John Riser

Problems in Contemporary Philosophy
Volume 58

The Edwin Mellen Press
Lewiston•Queenston•Lampeter

Library of Congress Cataloging-in-Publication Data

Riser, John.
   Democracy--an alternate view / John Riser.
     p. cm. -- (Problems in contemporary philosophy ; v. 58)
   Includes bibliographical references and index.
   ISBN-0-7734-6439-5
   1. Democracy. I. Title. II. Series.

JC423.R525 2004
321.8--d22

                                                        2004040341

This is volume 58 in the continuing series
Problems in Contemporary Philosophy
Volume 58 ISBN 0-7734-6439-5
PCP Series ISBN 0-88946-325-5

A CIP catalog record for this book is available from the British Library.

The Edwin Mellen Press   The Edwin Mellen Press
          Box 450   Box 67
   Lewiston, New York   Queenston, Ontario
    USA 14092-0450   CANADA L0S 1L0

The Edwin Mellen Press, Ltd.
Lampeter, Ceredigion, Wales
UNITED KINGDOM SA48 8LT

Printed in the United States of America

Dedication

To my wife, Janice Devlin

CONTENTS

PREFACE

Unlike many other defenders of democracy, John Riser explicates a form of democracy that he thinks cannot be instantiated by the modern state. This form of democracy is characterized by the practice of positive rather than negative liberty, a practice in which each participant is cooperatively empowered. For Riser, democracy at the national level can only be "a kind of quasi-democracy, adversarial in disposition, socially contractual in strategy, limited in effective popular participation, often elitist in governance, and much more likely to generate forms of satisfied accommodation than creative empowerment." There is much to recommend Riser's account here. Take the ideal of friendship. Sometimes the state is characterized as a form of civil friendship. But surely this can only be the case if the state is taken to be some form of quasi-friendship. True friendship in its most ideal forms can only exist among small groups of individuals, and maybe, in its most ideal form, true friendship can only exist between just two individuals. Civic friendship among citizens must then be only a pale reflection of true friendship.

Nevertheless, one reason Riser has for separating his more ideal form of democracy from other forms that he thinks can be instantiated in the modern state is that his ideal form of democracy is characterized by the practice of equal positive liberty whereas a modern state can be characterized, at best, by a practice of equal negative liberty. However, if an ideal of negative liberty can be shown to entail the same practical requirements as an ideal of positive liberty, then their corresponding forms of democracy would turn out to be more practically equivalent than we would otherwise have thought. Riser would still be right that it is very difficult to achieve a large-scale instantiation of democracy in the form that he so admirably characterizes in this book. It would just be the case that we would have a more broadly shared justification for instantiating democracy in all its desirable forms insofar as possible in our lives. Having that sort of justification would surely contribute to Riser's project as well.

Professor James Sterba
Department of Philosophy
University of Notre Dame

CHAPTER 1

INTRODUCTION

From the standpoint of both political philosophy and political practice, especially at the present historical conjuncture, democracy represents a standard and a project of paramount importance. Yet, whereas the virtues of democracy are advertised and celebrated in very different social systems, there is typically little substantive agreement as to what democracy is or entails. Thus, in the work at hand, I am concerned primarily with an attempt to identify and explicate what, in my view, are several essential components of a relevant conception of democracy. Although reference to these components, which I consider minimally defining criteria of democracy, can be found here and there in the literature on democratic theory, the particular meanings and roles that I attribute to them and, correlatively, the overall interpretation of democracy are, I believe, rather different from much of what is customary. Often minimized or even disregarded in democratic theory, such components are manifested in the following theses: (1) Democracy is not just a form of state; it is a form of human activity appropriate for manifold social groupings, both large and small; (2) Positive freedom, inherently comprising negative freedom, is crucial for democracy; indeed, democracy may be succinctly defined as the empowering practice of positive freedom oriented on humanistic values; (3) A cooperative model of democracy is more to the point than either unitary, adversary or deliberative variants of democracy, even though adversary quasi-democracy is likely to be unavoidable for large-scale social contexts.

My analysis does not claim to provide the "correct" or only intelligible definition of terms such as 'democracy', 'positive freedom', 'cooperation', the 'political', and so on. Instead, the definitions may be deemed stipulative, though I believe they are not at all arbitrary, since they are consistent with one another, coherent with my own proposed model of democracy, and not puzzlingly idiosyncratic with respect to ordinary usage. Reference to others' use of these terms is made in order to clarify, often by contrast, my own use of them. Additionally, I try to explicate and integrate a number of other ideas that relate to my conception of democracy. These include representation, elitism, preferences, interests, the common good, human needs, human rights, justice, equality, difference, majority rule, obligation and loyalty. Beyond this, I offer some reflections on the differences between, and the respective defects of, capitalist democracy and socialist democracy. Finally, I attempt to address problems concerning my own model of democracy.

While I argue that certain concepts and criteria are essential when talking about democracy, I do not pretend to delineate the characteristics of a putatively "full" or "perfect" democracy. The concepts and criteria emphasized are markers of the singularity of democracy, not elements of some end-state that might, in general, be attained. Moreover, democracy is not an "all or nothing" situation, but one that is "more or less". Democracy is always, socially and historically, a matter of degrees, from which it follows that it is very misleading to designate this or that country as a democracy. It is, simply, more or less democratic.

In that my aim is primarily focused upon conceptual clarification and normative assessment, I do not undertake the task of proffering detailed institutional mechanisms and procedures that would most effectively support and develop democracy. I am more concerned with the substantive nature of democracy than with procedural conditions for democracy. However, recognizing that the feasibility of practice is a test of, and a constraint on, theory, I take the possibilities of practice into account, in order to clarify and amplify theory, thus helping to demarcate my own view of democracy from alternatives. Lacking blueprints or recipes, I am satisfied with suggesting guidelines for the democratization, where possible, of human life.

Furthermore, I abjure any so-called "empirical" study of democracy, conceived as regulative, not only because, as mentioned, my object is analytic and evaluative but also because this kind of study tends rather palpably to beg the question of what 'democracy' means. That is, instead of merely describing and explaining how a society operates in a manner that the commentator prefers to designate as democratic, the society is assumed to be a normative paradigm of democracy.[1] Thereby, the general contours of the status quo are given sanction. Incidentally, this is not to say that I will not adduce a variety of facts about society, politics and life. For example, Chapter Ten will critically assess two historically influential models of democracy.

In addition, I do not seek to "justify", in some strong sense of that term, either democracy itself or my conception of it. This is not at all because I do not consider democracy to be reasonable and valuable. Rather, it is because my conception of democracy presupposes certain (humanistic) values that, metaethically speaking, cannot themselves be finally justified but only affirmed in theory and practice. From this ethically naturalistic perspective, one may give reasons for endorsing democracy; but the reasons will be only as compelling as the values that undergird and motivate them.

The literature on democracy is enormous, and it expands with remarkable celerity. I neither aspire, nor could I hope, to do anything beyond canvassing a very limited portion of it, in particular that which serves as comparison and contrast with the content of my own discussions. Accordingly, I do not intend to furnish detailed analyses, exegeses or evaluations of a large array of works in democratic theory, including many perhaps considered canonical. My principal objective, for whatever it may be worth, is to present and elaborate some ideas of mine on democracy, not to pass judgment, except where it seems useful, upon the

4

ideas of others. Clarification of the concepts and ideas I employ – whether or not the conclusions incorporating them are persuasive – is, I believe, pertinent and worthwhile, for, often, sophisticated and otherwise luminous discussions of democracy fail to make clear just what is being said.

In disconnecting democracy from its paradigmatic association with the state, it is necessary to rethink the meaning of the "political" (as do feminists), as well as to reconsider the distinction between the public and the private. An analysis of representation is carried out and its connection with elitism is examined. Problems with the representation of preferences are discussed, for example, the tendency toward a consumerist understanding of democracy along with certain difficulties brought out by social-choice theory. Moreover, the idea of a general interest is argued to be vacuous; and a common good is replaced by common goods, seen as a function of common needs. This leads to an explication of human needs and their role as a basis for the justification and specification of human rights. Preparatory to articulating my own model of democracy, the conception of positive freedom is fleshed out and its importance is accentuated. In addition, the notions of justice and equality are explored, with attention to their interrelationships. Further, the relevance for democracy of "difference" and "identity" is interrogated.

While advancing a critique of some other models of democracy (mentioned previously), I also develop my "cooperative" model, in the process differentiating between social cooperation and communal cooperation. This model, emphasizing mutually beneficial empowerment oriented on humanistic values, is something more than a mechanism for "participation" in collective affairs or a set of manageable procedures for conflict resolution, the balancing of interests, and so on. It is, in various ways and in different dimensions of human activity, a form of life. Correspondingly, I conceive of democracy not so much as a formula whose basic configuration is already largely in place but a task that remains to be carried out.

5

Subsequently, the significance for democracy of legitimacy, obligation and loyalty is elaborated. In order to give the idea of democracy historical context, an analysis of defects in both capitalist democracy and socialist democracy in the contemporary era is undertaken. Finally, I address various problems with my conception of democracy and attempt to evaluate realistically prospects of its implementation.

I gratefully acknowledge the influence of others (though I have not always agreed with them) upon the development of my thinking on democracy. My reading of their work has served constructively as a stimulant, sometimes a challenge, to my reflections. Especially, I am indebted in this regard to the writings of Ellen Wood, Anne Phillips, Nancy Fraser, Iris Young, C. B. Macpherson, Jane Mansbridge, Carole Patemen, Carol Gould, Jürgen Habermas and Roy Medvedev. As is de rigueur to declare, I alone am responsible for what I have made of any of this. Further, I have benefited to a considerable extent from various conversations dealing with the illusions and defects of capitalist democracy, on the one hand, and of socialist democracy, on the other, the latter discussions occurring primarily in the Soviet Union and the German Democratic Republic. Finally, the person who has been the greatest help to me is my wife, Janice Devlin. She has steadfastly supported me in this endeavor (sometimes at inconvenience to herself), has been, when necessary, a strict yet beneficial critic, and has, as an incomparable companion and friend, ensured that living and working are sources of deep satisfaction.

NOTE

1. It may not be amiss to suggest that bestowing peremptory status upon "empirically" existing democracy in Western countries is analogous to the former Soviet practice of honorifically designating its social system as "existing socialism" or "real socialism".

CHAPTER 2

THE SCOPE OF DEMOCRACY

It is instructive that a variety of influential political theorists, dispersed widely over time and disparate in ideology, have explicitly identified democracy as a form of state. Such an identification is probably based on at least three assumptions: the state is that arena in which all citizens are involved, more or less indirectly, in the process of decision-making about affairs of general interest, a process for which democracy is supposed to be singularly germane; democracy is a specifically political structure/process, and the state is a prototypical embodiment of politics; and democracy has to do with "public" activities and interrelationships – such as those conspicuously exemplified in the state – a category to be distinguished from what is "private".

These three assumptions I wish to question and substantially qualify. First, democracy as such should not be construed primarily as a mechanism for decision-making, as an arbitrational technique for adjudicating between competing claims or agendas, as a device for selecting among alternative individuals, proposals or policies. Procedures are certainly required for rendering decisions consistent with what I take to be the proper function of democracy, namely, the mutual empowerment of individuals (or, in my terminology, the communal practice of positive freedom), supported by cooperation and oriented upon humanistic values enhancing the creative meaningfulness of life; and to the extent that individuals efficaciously participate in making decisions, they are, in that kind of activity at least, so far forth empowered. But empowerment is much more than the prerogative to articulate choices. It relates to the ability (and opportunity) to exercise power in a variety of social contexts, not just that of the state. The word 'power' may appear inordinate, but I use it in the sense of the capability, knowingly, to control; and democratic control is over outcomes, not "over" people, a collaborative activity that eschews all types of exploitation, domination, and so on.[1] This cooperative activity is entirely appropriate, and more feasible, in social contexts of less scale and complexity than the nation-state. Yet this hardly derogates from its value in those contexts.

Second, although it may be convenient to associate "politics" with governmental entities, the term 'political', understood as referring to the presence and exercise of power, that is, influence and control, in the dynamics of interpersonal relationships, may be used, non-invidiously, with respect to situations in general where individuals seek intentionally to manage common problems, concerns and tasks. Political phenomena within the state may well be phenomenologically and operationally unlike those found elsewhere; but if the latter reflect interpersonal relationships wherein decisions are made and carried out in some sort of interactive concert and wherein factors of influence and control are at work, that is, power relations, then the interactions exhibit distinct characteristics of the political.[2] What is important, I think, is not to cavil at this use of 'political' but to be specifically concerned with whether its presence, in whatever context, is humane, cooperative, mutually empowering, thus democratic.

That the (inter-) personal is political, that is, it is a domain of relationships involving the exercise of power, does not imply the converse, namely, that the political is personal, since power relations obviously exist in domains other than the more closely personal. To be sure, public political power (for example, that of the nation-state) impacts upon persons and their relationships, not infrequently in a prejudicial manner for women and minorities. However, this influence is not what is implied by "the personal is political".

Third, traditional distinctions between the public and the private (for example, between state and civil society), while analytically intelligible, have not been innocuous. The state has been deemed the sphere within which political relations and processes are evident; and other spheres, usually the economy and, almost always, marriage and the family, have not been so categorized. Concomitantly, democracy has been regarded as pertinent for the former sphere, where its members are viewed, in one way or the other, as citizens, but not generally for the latter, in which individuals have different roles and status. To be sure, democratization of economic power, a theme conveying different meanings to different people, has been advocated, in this or that form, for some two centuries; but its internally inadequate inauguration and subsequent deterioration in the twentieth century has understandably occasioned a prevailing skepticism about its feasibility. In addition, for almost as long a time, many feminists have insisted upon the democratization of gendered relationships in personal and domestic life; but, though much has been achieved, it is difficult to be particularly sanguine here.[3]

That government is held to be in the public sector and the economy and various personal relationships in the private sector is due basically to historical causes and ideological reasons.[4] The public sector is that in which, ideally, all members of the relevant public participate in constituting its nature and direction (and, presumably, benefit from doing so) and in which publicity is rightly maximized (in other words, its activity is "made public"). By contrast, the private sector is customarily seen as self-selecting and as properly removed from undue public intervention or scrutiny. Yet, all human interrelationship and interaction involve some kind of "public", from a minimum of two individuals to many millions; and it is my contention that democratic practice, to whatever degree practicable, is appropriate for any "public" context. Not every "public" has the same scale of publicness or the same expectation of, or need for, publicizing what it does; but for its own members, openness is important.

There is, therefore, not the public domain but a variety of public domains – and of conventionally private domains also. Public domains differ in size, structure, complexity and the types of activity that take place in them. A given public domain is inclusive with respect to its own membership but exclusive, that is, particularizing, with respect to specific tasks, interests, problems, etc., associated with it. The nation-state is an obvious example here; yet, so is marriage. There may be good reasons to make some public domains "private", that is, relatively immune to, or impenetrable by, other public domains. If so, the reasons are basically normative, ideological or sociological. Something of an empirical hierarchy of public domains exists, such that some, overlapping, as it were, with others, are more extensive in range of actions and effects and more capacious in commonalities and obligations. To place a "public" domain in a/the "private" sector says nothing, as such, about the scale and scope of the former; rather, it attests to the fact that prerogatives and control within the latter are supposed to be reserved to those whose membership status is defined by factors such as voluntary commitment, ownership of the means of production, tradition or "difference". For example, the first factor applies to marriage, the second to the capitalist economy, the third to religious associations, the last to groupings based upon varied collective identities. Typically, collectivities with expanded commonalities are more likely to be designated as "public".

The preceding observations on 'public' and 'private' are not intended to be an idiosyncratic exercise in terminological revisionism. Rather, recognizing that the conventional demarcation of "private" domains from "the public" domain has often ostensibly justified and reinforced the belief that public criteria such as justice, equality, rights, etc., apply to individuals only qua members of the public polity, but not necessarily or at all in other roles they may have, I wish to challenge the use of 'private' as a device for exempting marriage, family, assorted social collectives and the economy from those criteria and, most generally, from the requirements of democracy itself.[5]

It should be recognized, in light of important commentary by Jean Cohen, that the category of the private is not coextensive with that of privacy. Whereas characteristically "private" domains, sectors or groupings (that are actually public in structure and performance) may claim and maintain "entity privacy", persons may avow specifically individual privacy, presupposing a (public) social background but not necessarily involving at all times public performances, a privacy often associated with the possibility of decisional autonomy and appropriately protected by privacy rights.[6] To designate something as private is to demarcate, functionally, boundaries and margins. To appeal to privacy is to claim a zone of properly protected identity formation.

As the centralized monopolization of state power is incompatible with democracy in a standard political sense, so the concentrated monopolization of economic power is incompatible with democracy in a broader social sense. In the cases of both state and economy, oligarchic dominance is adverse to democracy, understood in these contexts as comprising the extensive sharing of power, a guaranteed "stake" in the system, strict accountability of the "rulers" to the "ruled", conformity of all to collectively established rules, and the formation of "rationality" and "efficiency" according to humanistic ends.

It should be noted that the centralization of functions is not equivalent to the monopolization of power – although the former can lead to the latter, if there are not structural safeguards against this eventuality. The relevant aim, then, is not routinely to "decentralize" democracy (for example, in the context of national parameters) but to extend it to multiple areas of human life. In fact, decentralized decision-making regarding the national society and its problems is not necessarily more effective;[7] and however satisfying participation in small-scale contexts might be, it usually does not translate into large-scale influence. Yet, even if local control has minimal effect on national politics, it nevertheless can embody democracy in a manner and to an extent not possible at the national level.

Furthermore, the patriarchal, gender-biased marriage, like the (perhaps benevolently) despotic state, is objectively antagonistic to democracy, not only because a conjugal grouping so structured impairs the freedom (including empowerment) of all its members but also because the dynamics of this kind of relationship are a potent factor in helping to preserve other non-democratic institutions in society. In general, elitist supremacy found in a "private" context tends to inhibit the practice of democracy in contexts marked by more conventionally "public" activity. This interdependency, as Okin points out, is obscured by the arbitrary "dichotomizing of public from private spheres".[8]

Associating democracy paradigmatically with the state is, more often than not, connected with an electoral interpretation of democracy. Democracy is construed as a rule-governed procedure by means of which, at the most basic level, citizens select those who will allegedly represent them by selecting, in turn, programs, policies, and other representative figures. While this construal of democracy is prevalent and probably reassuring in its apparent valorization of the average citizen, it faces some serious questions and criticisms even in its own terms. For example, voters are equally authorized to exercise the power of choice with regard, say, to candidates presented to them. However, by and large, citizen voters, who exercise this power only intermittently, possess negligible control over who those candidates will be in the first place. It may be argued that public opinion significantly shapes the viability of potential candidates. No doubt this factor plays some role. Yet, in my opinion, opportunism and ideological cautiousness mean that predominating options will fall within restricted parameters, reinforced by the underlying imperatives of the socioeconomic system. Furthermore, the ability of voters to control the activity of those selected – at least until it is time for the latter, possibly, to start "running" for election again – is exiguous (certainly by comparison to the influence of lobbyists, major campaign contributors, political party operatives, etc.).[9] In addition, the equality of voters is formal. One way to put this is to say that though each vote is equally counted, each vote does not count equally, namely, in the sequel. Whereas elections may be decided by slender margins – as recent history attests – the votes (and voters) of some constituencies resonate with influence, more than do others, in the interval between elections.

Although it is questionable whether the public of (potential) voters would even want to exercise substantive control over those elected (assuming effective mechanisms were in place), in view of the considerable demands that this control would place on the time, attention and deliberations of the public, the collective decision-making procedure of voting itself might be improved by a more egalitarian distribution of non-procedural resources, thereby rendering the decision-making process associated with voting more equitably participatory.[10]

This is not to deny any value to elections. Although, as I see it, electoral procedures do not at all define democracy, they are, on the one hand, more or less effective means for supporting a kind of quasi-democracy in those large-scale contexts, such as the nation-state, where competitive, adversarial dynamics can be dislodged only by a stultifying conformity. On the other hand, participation in voting is an expression of empowerment, however modest, that goes to the heart of what democracy does mean. Hence, the most important reason for popular voting, as I see the matter, is not that people's choices somehow express a collective "wisdom", not simply that it is fair for those affected by decisions to have some role in selecting those who make the decisions (though even when "consent of the governed" is voluntary, it is often not informed), and not that majority rule legitimizes (in some obscure normative sense) the outcomes of voting, but that participatory procedures such as voting, which encourage deliberation, can embody, within definite limits, an empowering exercise of positive freedom.

II

The problematic concerning electoral democracy raises an important additional issue, namely, whether democracy is to be understood more in terms of procedure or in terms of result. Incidentally, it is worth noting that crucial emphases of this presumptive dichotomy are parallel to ones obtaining in the distinction between justice in procedures and justice in results. For some, democracy is, essentially, a set of procedures.[11] This would, surely, comprise elections, the enactment of legislation or other prescriptions, judicial review, and so on. Whereas it should be granted readily that the fairness and integrity of rule-governed procedures, with regard to both formulation and application (since unjust rules may be applied equitably and just rules may be applied inequitably), are necessary for democratic practice, I maintain that a merely proceduralist interpretation of democracy is inadequate for at least two reasons. In the first place, procedures and the rules governing them make sense only in terms of purposes to be promoted, possibly realized. Of course, it is possible to determine whether one is following, that is, conforming to, a given rule without knowing what the purpose of that rule might be. Moreover, it may be that one is conforming to a rule for the sake of a purpose entirely different from that for which the rule was designed in the first place (roughly put, one may do the right thing for the wrong reasons). Nevertheless, there is a point to the rule, however well or ill the rule is formulated; and this point is delineated in the purpose the rule is intended to serve. It may be that some rule-governed activities are aimless with reference to outcomes. Perhaps this applies to some kinds of play – but certainly not to democracy as activity. Purposes, for their part, are directed toward results, outcomes, that is, ends treated seldom as final but, rather, as temporary, provisional and corrigible. Accordingly, the conception of democracy as essentially procedure is, if not disingenuous, substantively incomplete, because the purposes, hence, goals/ends, of the implicated rules must be specified.[12]

In the second place, the goal of democracy, its ever-recurring, never fully realized end, is, I suggest, the mutually beneficial empowerment of individuals, their engagement in the practice of positive freedom (about which more later), that is, the development and enhancement of capabilities, whose exercise avoids exploitation, domination, oppression, and any other anti-humanistic behavior and which materially facilitates the prospects of a creatively meaningful existence. 'Empowerment' refers to the enabling power of those capabilities, some of which are rooted in natural endowments (that nonetheless require social support for their activation and development), while others derive primarily from environments of learning (in a generic sense). Although, for its development and exercise, empowerment necessarily requires a favorable social context, it is nonetheless individuated. Hence, vicarious or heteronomously subordinative participation and self-exaltation in the power of something other, for example, the nation-state, is not what I have in mind by the practice of positive freedom. I prefer 'empowerment' to 'self-fulfillment' or 'self-realization', since the latter two terms may mislead by connoting not only that there is some ontological self that is at work here but also that 'fulfillment' and 'realization' indicate processes that can be brought to fruition, that is, that one can realize a project of self-fulfillment or self-realization. Furthermore, both terms tend to slight the fact that individuals are inherently social beings; who they are is constituted, to a very significant degree, by the interrelationships in which they stand with others. A further consideration: empowerment is the capacity (ability and opportunity) to act, not action itself, a difference corresponding to the distinction between positive freedom and the exercise of it. In addition, being empowered does not entail that what one can thereby do will not be personally harmful or socially injurious. Consequently, stress is placed upon empowerment in accordance with humanistic values and goals.

It may be objected that the kinds of humanistic values presupposed here – specified negatively as avoidance of exploitation, domination and oppression and positively as creatively meaningful existence in the context of socially cooperative activity – are, at best, "ideals" incapable of realization and therefore of only very limited use as guides to action. Moreover, it may be averred that antifoundationalism "removes the authority from supposedly fundamental humanist ideals".[13] Both objections miss the mark. With respect to the first, the humanistic values assumed are <u>not</u> construed as ideals but as tasks or projects whose implementation is relatively more advanced in some democratically relevant contexts than in others – normally least of all in large-scale, adversarial contexts such as the nation-state. Regarding the second, so-called humanist "ideals" do not have "authority", certainly not in or of themselves. Rather, they have (individually authoritative) value insofar as they are affirmed and (social) effectiveness insofar as people are committed collectively to them.

Democracy is not an end-in-itself. Instead, it is, so to speak, a way of life, a social task, a praxis, which, one hopes, will both serve and be an expression of the humanistic enrichment of human life. In the activity that is democracy, various procedures will prove to be more efficacious than others in the face of typical exigencies such as informing, deliberating, choosing and implementing. But which procedures are more effective for sustaining and strengthening democracy, which are more reliable inducements to a democratic mentality and culture, which are more practicable for this or that sphere or scale of democratic activity are matters that can only be determined experimentally, that is, empirically. The larger rationale for democratic procedures is not to guarantee certain transient results but to maximize ongoing involvement in the practice of positive freedom, that is, empowerment. To put it differently, the point is not so much to enable people to <u>have</u> more as to <u>do</u> more, although the former is generally a necessary condition for the latter.

Voting is usually touted as an exemplary type of participation in democracy as conventionally understood. To be sure, participation, in principle, exemplifies the commonly constructive activity that is essential to democracy. The concept of participation, however, is rather amorphous; and, especially in large-scale contexts, its practice is subject to considerable constraints. Theoretically, participation is a form of action that amounts to "taking part" in something. In unpacking this conception, obvious questions emerge: what kind of part does one have (that is, with regard to what does, or should, one's participation make a difference) and how much of a part does one have (that is, is one's role actually effective or is it more frequently a perfunctory routine that at least makes one feel that one has played a part)? [14] If participation is to be more than just "going through the motions", it must involve an efficacious degree of continuing influence on matters of common relevance. As with voting in traditional "political" contexts, this participation is likely to be episodic and detached from many of the more crucial structures and processes of power in those contexts. [15] Participation – except in the kinds of cooperatively communal groupings that will be addressed later – is therefore uncertainly conjoined with control. Correspondingly (hardly a revelation to most observers), the formula that democracy is "rule by the people" is vacuous, in practice, in most polities. Leaving aside the issue of who "the people" might be, [16] their "rule" (control) tends to be exceedingly marginal. One formulaic pronouncement is the following: "Democracy means people's rule, i.e. participation of the people in government." [17] Asserted by a Bulgarian Marxist ideologist when "existing socialism" still existed, this statement is particularly revealing in light of its general political background. Thus, in the countries of more or less developed "socialism", including the USSR and the GDR, the level of citizen participation, for example, in (routine) discussion groups and in voting was quite high, much more so than in Western countries. With respect to the GDR, as a case in point, it has been remarked that some 98-99% of citizens participated in elections to the *Volkskammer.* [18] Whatever the motivation for doing so, it shows that participation, while imbricated with rule, is assuredly not coextensive with it. Participation, though necessary for rule (control), is not at all sufficient for it. Participation may be guided by deception, manipulation, even intimidation. [19] Moreover, people will sometimes affirm (and reaffirm) authoritarian power over them. [20] Assessing the factors that may be at work here – the relative security of conformity, the phenomenon of the "happy slave", the politics of envy and revenge that see the authoritarian power as a vengeful instrument of retribution on the people's behalf, chauvinistic nationalism, or simply masochism – is beyond the scope of this book, as well as beyond the competence of its author. The fact remains that people normally participate, not in directing those who have power over them, but in sanctioning, hence legitimizing, the holders of power and their actions. The fact manifests the very substantial difference between collectively selecting policy decision-makers and collectively making policy decisions.

Participation, in short, should be a form of collective control by members of a group over what that group is involved in doing. At the same time, it can be a means of enhancing individual growth and mutual empowerment. Admittedly, participatory control is more feasible in smaller groupings, such as marriage, family, work and other social collectives, together with "chosen" communities in general, than in those of major scale, such as the nation-state. The former tend to be those of one's *Lebenswelt*, in which one's daily life is more directly implicated, those in which the practice of democracy can be more readily evident and fruitful. And the value of this practice therein is not diminished by the tenuousness of its existence in large-scale contexts of quasi-democracy. Participation in conventionally political decision-making is thus not the only, and perhaps not always the most important, context for the exercise of positive freedom.

In smaller groupings, members can participate more thoroughly as equals, that is, they can not only equally participate but also participate equally, since the distribution of power, hence control, is more likely to be equalized. Joshua Cohen proclaims that an equal right of participation involves an "equal opportunity for effective influence".[21] This formulation is ambiguous. Does it mean an equal opportunity for equally effective influence or does it mean an equal opportunity for some, quite possibly differentially, effective influence? In addition, the formulation is vague, because of the unanalyzed term 'opportunity'. Later, in Chapter 7, I will attempt to make the concept of opportunity relatively precise.

For the present, I will simply remark that an opportunity is only a possibility, which may or may not be actualizable under the circumstances.

For large groupings, such as the nation-state, members, although quite possibly having a normatively articulated status of equality, do not participate equally, in view of considerable disparities in power/control, and, for that matter, do not equally participate, because, for example, of personal disinclination, supersessive responsibilities or exclusionary practices.[22] Individuals or organizations in these latter kinds of contexts can hardly possess equalized power; but legally enforceable arrangements can be put in place to inhibit the exercise of dominative, oppressive and exploitative power, and abuses of power can, and should be, contested vigorously by both official and unofficial means.

Regarding the disinclination to participate, it is worthwhile to consider the "trade-off" problem outlined by Thomas Christiano. He observes that "it is possible for there to be a trade-off between the freedom that is had in participation and the freedom that can be experienced in the pursuit of one's personal projects".[23] It might be that one of the reasons for such a trade-off is recognition that being free to participate is not the same as participating freely, in view of the fact that the latter is often constrained by an unempowering imbalance of resources. My own response to the trade-off problem is that such trades-off are acceptable, so long as personal projects do not involve exploitation, domination, oppression, and so on, and do not interfere in an egocentric manner with collective projects. It is no doubt true that, for many people, their participation in individual projects or in those of groups with which they are more personally associated is preferred to participation in political activities of larger-scale significance. Nonetheless, it should be remembered that the social conditions for the viability of personal projects are themselves generally dependent upon the propitious results of forms of collective, cooperative participation.

20

NOTES

1. Control can be exercised not only by means of coercion or prohibition but also by withholding requisite resources or through disadvantageous exchanges. The authoritarian socialist state utilized widely the former ("What is not permitted is prohibited"); the autocratic capitalist economy puts the latter to use, where its substantial control over the social means required by individuals for acting can affect their choosing and, in particular, their doing. An additional point: Carole Pateman has insightfully argued that exploitation is based upon, and made possible by, subordination, rather than the converse [see The Sexual Contract. Stanford: Stanford University Press, 1988, pp. 8 & 149, for example].

2. Relevant here is Susan Okin's explanation that to say the personal is political means "what happens in personal life, particularly in relations between the sexes, is not immune from the dynamics of power, which has typically been seen as a distinguishing feature of the political" ["Gender, the Public and the Private", in Political Theory Today, ed. David Held. Stanford: Stanford University Press, 1991, p. 77].

3. Indeed, Pateman declares, "For feminists, democracy has never existed." ["Feminism and democracy", in Democratic theory and practice, ed. Graeme Duncan. Cambridge: Cambridge University Press, 1983, p. 204]. A poignant example of the obstacles facing those who have struggled to extend democracy to "civil society" is found in the largely unknown activity of Alexandra Kollontai during the early years of Bolshevik rule. Although a hardworking Party member, her support for democracy in the workplace was sharply criticized by Lenin and others; and her even more sustained advocacy -- employing analyses and arguments that are remarkably timely today -- of cooperation, consideration and fairness between men and women was regarded as unnecessary or premature by many women, most men and virtually the entire Party membership [see Alix Holt, ed. Selected Writings of Alexandra Kollontai. London: Allison and Busby, 1977]. The claim that attention to gender discrimination and related problems is premature during a period of fundamental social change characterized not only emerging socialist societies but also developing post-socialist societies as well. In this regard, Peggy Watson quotes a relatively recent statement that "women's issues can be addressed only once the democratization process is completed" ["The Rise of Masculinism in Eastern Europe", New Left Review, March/April, 1993, p. 73], an attitude that has reinforced "the selective political empowerment of men" [ibid., p. 72]. However, the democratization of society without a thorough democratization in society, including gendered relationships, is impossible. Related to this is Pateman's assertion that "A despotic, patriarchal family is no school for democratic citizenship." {The Disorder of Women. Stanford: Stanford University Press, 1989, p. 130].

4. "The boundaries between public and private ... have been shown to be conventional rather than natural, as are the cultural codes that assign specific roles and places to different genders." [Jean Cohen, "Democracy, Difference, and the Right of Privacy", in Democracy and Difference, ed. Seyla Benhabib. Princeton: Princeton University Press, 1996, p. 209]. In passing, I will mention that my differentiation of the "public" and the "private" is different from that suggestively put forward by John Dewey in The public and its problems. Athens: Ohio University Press, 1954. There the distinction depends upon the differential consequences of the actions of participants,

where what is "private" comprises consequences primarily affecting only those participants directly involved, but what is "public" contains consequences indirectly affecting others as well [pp. 12-13].

5. As Zillah Eisenstein rightly avows, "Democratic societies need democratic families <u>and</u> democratic economies, and democratic sexual and racial relations." ["Eastern European Male Democracies: A Problem of Unequal Equality", in <u>Gender Politics and Post-Communism</u>, Nanette Funk & Magda Mueller, eds. New York: Routledge, 1993, p. 306]. A major part of the problem here has been, as Pateman points out, that liberal democracies have viewed social inequalities as not relevant for political equality. She emphasizes, in addition, that liberal individualism has involved a "practical contradiction between the formal political equality of liberal democracy and the social subordination of women, including their subjection as wives within the patriarchal structure of the institution of marriage" ["Feminism and democracy", pp. 204 & 208; see also <u>The Disorder</u>, pp. 120 & 129]. This point is amplified by Anne Phillips in her comment that the distinction between public and private spheres has contributed significantly to patriarchal political thought, in that women, "having been subordinated to men in the private sphere ... were then subsumed under men in the public" [<u>Democracy and difference</u>. University Park, PA: Pennsylvania State University Press, 1993, p. 63].

6. See "Democracy", pp. 194, 195 & 202.

7. See Sheldon Wolin, "Fugitive Democracy", in Benhabib, <u>Democracy</u>, p. 34. Moreover, relatively autonomous local groups and associations may not be especially sensitive to society-wide issues of social justice; and relations of inequality and injustice can exist within and among these groups [see Iris Marion Young, <u>Justice and the Politics of Difference</u>. Princeton: Princeton University Press, pp. 233 & 249-250].

8, <u>Justice, Gender, and the Family</u>. New York: Basic Books, 1989, p. 23. Interestingly, Pateman argues that the slogan concerning the political nature of the personal "not only explicitly rejects the liberal separation of the private and the public, but also implies that no distinction can or should be drawn between the two spheres", where 'private' typically denotes the family sphere with its sexual division of labor [see <u>The Disorder</u>, p. 131]. My own view, described previously, is that every set of continuing interpersonal relationships constitutes a "public" sphere, which can, for better or worse, be privatized operationally.

9. Some time ago, Karl Popper argued that democracy is a form of government in which bad rulers can be dismissed, without violence, thereby preventing them from doing too much damage [see <u>The Open Society and its Enemies</u>. New York: Harper & Row, 1963, I, pp. 121 & 124]. Although this is salutary, it neglects the fact that bad rulers can instigate policies, programs and commitments that wreak "too much" damage before the rulers can be removed -- and sometimes after their removal as well. Besides, social damage does not always derive only from elected rulers but also from non-elected authorities or from recurring types of institutionalized oppression both within and outside government.

10. This point is made by Thomas Christiano in "Social choice and democracy" [<u>The idea of democracy</u>, David Copp, Jean Hampton & John E. Roemer, eds. Cambridge: Cambridge University Press, 1993, p. 183]. However, whether more equitable participation would also be more informed and thoughtful is likewise questionable, in view of P. H. Partridge's claim that "voting can be as much a matter of following custom or codes absorbed through the processes of 'socialization' as other forms of behaviour are" [<u>Consent and Consensus</u>. New York: Praeger Publishers, 1971, p. 43].

11. Thus, Barry Holden avers that "in a democracy 'the rules for conducting business' are the basic features of democracy itself " [The Nature of Democracy. New York: Barnes & Noble, 1974, p. 188].

12. My argument presupposes the priority of good over right, not conversely. This argument is grounded in epistemological and psychological considerations and has nothing to do with any metaphysical "first" principles. Stated simply, what is right is so in accordance with rules, which are intelligible only in relation to purposes the rules are designed to serve; and purposes themselves are specified in terms of ends, that is, results assessed as good or worthwhile in some respect.

13. See Phillips, Democracy, pp. 142-143.

14. Frank Cunningham has helpfully singled out various dimensions of the difference that participation is supposed to make, namely, the aggregative influence (or control) by participants, the range of factors that participants influence (control), and the importance of these factors for democratic purposes [see Democratic Theory and Socialism. Cambridge: Cambridge University Press, 1987, pp. 26-27]. Incidentally, having an equal "say" in matters under discussion or in dispute does not mean that persons say what they say equally well or equally effectively or that equal consideration is given to what is said.

15. Wolin has reminded us that "The demos has no effective voice in what the President does, yet once the election is over their mythical act is carefully preserved as ritual and invoked whenever a President feels the need of courting public support." ["Fugitive Democracy", p. 34].

16. This will depend, in large measure, upon whether the grouping is "found" or "chosen". On this distinction, fraught with multiple relevancies, see the valuable discussion by Marilyn Friedman in "Feminism and Modern Friendship: Dislocating the Community", Ethics, 99, January 1989.

17. See Assen Kozharov, Marxism and Pluralism in Ideology and in Politics. Sofia: Sofia Press, n.d., p. 193.

18. See David Childs, The GDR: Moscow's German Ally. London: Unwin Hyman, 1988, pp. 130-133.

19. Intimidation can be prominent and persuasive without being solely decisive. For example, Roy Medvedev has declared that "It would ... be a mistake to reduce Stalin's regime merely to political terror and violence. Stalin relied not only on force and deception; he also fed parasitically on the faith put by the majority in socialism and the Communist Party -- a faith that had resulted from the social reforms carried out after the October Revolution." [On Socialist Democracy. New York: W. W. Norton, 1977, p. 342]. For the possibilities of sociopolitical deception and manipulation in the United States, see, among others, Michael Parenti, Democracy for the Few, Fifth Edition. New York: St. Martin's Press, 1988; G. William Domhoff, The Powers That Be. New York: Random House, 1978; and Domhoff, Who Rules America Now? Englewood Cliffs, NJ: Prentice-Hall, 1983.

20. Regarding the Stalinist Soviet Union, see Roy Medvedev, Let History Judge. New York: Columbia University Press, 1989; and for Nazi Germany, see Ian Kershaw, The Hitler Myth. Oxford: Oxford University Press, 1989.

21. See "Procedure and Substance in Deliberative Democracy", in Benhabib, Democracy, p. 106

22. Pateman claims that a major cause for non-participation is the belief, corroborated by empirical findings, that "the benefits of participation tend to go to the better off", so that "working-class citizens reason that it is not worth being active" and "women can perceive that participation

helps men more than women, so that it is rational for them to abstain from political activity" [see The Disorder, p. 7]. Her claim, though argued more than twenty years ago, is probably still substantially true.

23. See "Freedom, Consensus, and Equality in Collective Decision Making", Ethics, 101, October 1990, p. 163.

CHAPTER 3

REPRESENTATION AND ELITISM

I

It has been claimed that extensive participation by the citizens of a society is not necessary for democracy, so long as "the leaders are more or less responsive to the preferences of non-leaders".[1] Later, I will argue that democracy should be focused primarily upon needs rather than preferences; but, for now, I wish to examine the dialectic of representation and elitism. The discussion that follows pertains essentially to possibilities in the nation-state. For smaller scale contexts, such as marriage, worker organizations and voluntary associations, wherein direct communication is feasible and each can be heard by all, views and preferences can be "represented" without mediation -- though hegemonic elitism can still exist.

The role of representatives, as I see it, is to "re-present" (in some forum) that which reflects the needs, interests, preferences, or otherwise of those represented. Immediately obvious questions are how representatives know, and, if they do, whether they are disposed consistently to advocate, those needs, interests, etc. In what is customarily called liberal (capitalist) democracies, with their competition among political parties and interest groups, the first question is resolved, in particular, by pragmatic attention to these parties and groups and to the balance of power among them. It is interesting to note, by contrast, that putative representatives of the people in the erstwhile socialist countries professed to have relevant knowledge by virtue of their privileged conversance with the implied requirements of a unitary "science" of history and society. In addition, this "ideological monism" was utilized, at the level of theory, to justify rejection of any political pluralism in ideology. The second question is answered, for liberal democracies, by ascertaining whether conscientious advocacy comports with fundamental socioeconomic postulates and also redounds to the benefit of personal political careers. For socialist countries, there was a persistent desire by Party elites, including the *nomenklatura*, to keep things in place for both social and personal objectives, along with an attempt to identify themselves as, after all, one with the popular masses.

Further, just what is a representative supposed to know that is relevant for those represented and how much independence of judgment may a representative properly claim to possess? With regard to the latter, independence tends, ceteris paribus, to be correlated positively with the "distance" between representatives and the represented. For some, the distance is neutralized by their ability to access representatives directly whenever it is useful; but for the vast majority of citizens within the nation-state, they can only hope that someone "up there" is listening. Nor do the represented instruct their representatives, for the latter are not delegates constrained by specific mandates from the former. With respect to the issue concerning that which representatives might know that will be of benefit to those represented, there is an obvious difference between more or less enduring goals (ends), together with the values that invest them with normative content, and the means by which these ends might be realized. As I will elaborate the argument later, the recurrent, presiding end ingredient in democracy is the mutual empowerment (practice of positive freedom) of as many individuals as possible, in accordance with humanistic (humane) values oriented upon the communal enrichment of human life. The substance of that end is marked out by those values, which are actualized and sustained, on one hand, by individuals who commitedly affirm them and, on another, by the prescriptions of human rights enactments that emphasize positive rights (coordinate with positive freedom) as much as negative rights (coordinate with negative freedom). This is not to say that personal commitments and political enactments of these sorts are likely to command significant assent in our world, including the United States. For this reason, I think the most that can be attained, especially in large-scale contexts such as the nation-state, is some kind of quasi-democracy (perhaps, more accurately, pseudo-democracy), which serves certain useful organizational purposes and is, if one lowers one's expectations, generally good enough.[2]

Returning to the distinction between ends and means, those who function as representatives should attend, by and large, to means rather than ends. If one accepts the communal empowerment and enrichment of human life (cognitively, emotionally and otherwise) in line with humanistic (non-exploitative, non-dominative, non-oppressive) values as summing up the end of democracy, that is, democratic life, then the central (complex and difficult) task remains of discerning and instituting appropriate means. It is this task that should be taken on, provisionally and with modesty, by assorted representatives, "experts" and "authorities". Their role, properly, is to advise, and consult with, the people concerning what ought to be done to approximate democratic goals in particular circumstances. In this regard, I believe it is singularly presumptuous – though, of course, understandable as an expression of special interest – for national political leaders to declaim about what constitutes the "national interest". If it is in the national interest to promote democracy, then typically what has passed for this interest has been either a means for preserving the possibility of democracy (as in WW II) or a spurious substitute for it.

In an enlightening essay on the "politics of presence", Anne Phillips argues persuasively that the process of representation would be improved by integrating the politics of ideas with the politics of presence. Liberal democracy, she notes, has traditionally accepted difference and diversity within society, but primarily with respect to ideas, beliefs and opinions.[3] "One consequence for democracy is that what is to be represented then takes priority over who does the representation."[4] From the standpoint of the politics of ideas, any person, even if outside a group, is adequate as a representative so long as the ideas of the group are conscientiously represented.

Yet, as Phillips rightly insists, "Where policy initiatives are worked out <u>for</u> rather than <u>with</u> a politically excluded constituency, they rarely engage with all relevant concerns." [5] The implication here, I think, is that, however well intentioned they may be, representatives of marginalized, oppressed or excluded groups are not likely to be able to represent those groups adequately if the representatives do not know (not only by description but even more by acquaintance) what a <u>difference</u> it makes to belong to such groups. The particular character of the experiences, needs and interests of members of these groups can best, often only, be presented by those members themselves, but not simply re-presented by others. In addition, there is always the possibility that representation (of ideas) will be conjoined with elitism, especially when representatives (of ideas) believe themselves to have distinctively superior cognitive and verbal skills, able to think "impartially" and to speak in elegant and polished cadences. Admittedly, there may be some kinds of excluded groups whose members cannot, literally or figuratively, speak for themselves; but, in any case, their presence in society should be acknowledged, comprehended (so far as possible) and meliorated.

A caveat to this type of argument is, nonetheless, timely. Carol Gould remarks, quite appropriately, that it is not the case that "<u>any</u> member of a group can equally well represent <u>all</u> members of a group".[6] Empirically falsified essentialism should caution us against any assumption that groups possess undifferentiated differences internally. Gender, racial, ethnic and cultural groups, in general, contain both arch reactionaries and "flaming" radicals. What the politics of presence requires is that representatives be able, knowledgeably and forcefully, to present what a humanistically informed public policy would consider <u>relevant</u> differences, which, by the way, may well be of a singularly constructive nature, not just imprints of oppression and exploitation.

Representational mechanisms are not infrequently conjoined with elitism, and this conjunction is not altogether adventitious. Partly this is due to the tendency of such mechanisms, especially where they involve hierarchical, centralized structures, to become bureaucratized, a tendency reinforced by the activity therein of egoistic, self-aggrandizing individuals or groups. Partly it is due to the tendency of some representatives to become alienated from those whom they ostensibly represent, a situation compounded by the ambition of the former or the indifference of the latter, or both. And partly it is due to the fact that skilled representation does require some amount of expertise, a capability that may appear to function more "efficiently" in the absence of complicating popular, that is, democratic, controls. A danger in all of this is that acting on behalf of others may, for all practical purposes, verge into thinking for them as well, a scenario endorsed by the kind of government that says to the people: "You will work well, and we shall govern well." [7]

It is by no means sufficient for a government to be for the people; it is necessary for it to be, as comprehensively as possible, by the people as well.[8] Even authoritarian governments can claim, consistently and without disingenuousness, albeit falsely, to be acting for, that is, on behalf of, their citizens. Should legitimation devolve not from citizens upon government but, instead, from government upon citizens, the people would be deputies of governing power rather than conversely, thus rendering the people theoretically replaceable, an eventuality caustically delineated by Bertolt Brecht in his poem, "The Solution":

> After the uprising of June 17 / The Secretary of the
> Writers Union had / Leaflets handed out on Stalin Avenue /
> On which one could read that the people / Had lost the trust
> of the government / And only through redoubled work /
> Could it be won back. Would it / Not after all be simpler
> if the government / Dissolved the people and/
> Chose a different one? [9]

Perhaps what is involved here is an ironically inverted revolution that would entail, not the replacement of the state, but the dissolution of the people.

II

Often it is argued that the superior knowledge and insight of some warrant their peremptory authority in decision-making. Whereas I reject this authoritativeness in the matter of democratic goals (ends), I am willing to acknowledge that some people, sometimes, are better able to identify, clarify and direct the implementation of means for these goals. However, this is not at all to grant that such people should have a privileged status as arbiters of the public good or as decision-makers transcending popular initiative and control. There is, of course, the ideological tradition of privileged status associated with elitism, according to which "rulership should be entrusted to a minority of persons who are specially qualified to govern by reasons of their superior knowledge and virtue", a situation seen further "as the inevitable and/or desirable response to the incapacity of the masses to cope with ruling complex modern societies".[10] The acceptance or tolerance by the masses of elitist rule has, undoubtedly, multiple causes: "strong socialization and ideological persuasion", along with apathy based upon a belief that participation is not really effective.[11] Additionally, it may be due to a generalized indifference, so long as one's actual or anticipated life-style is not adversely affected, or to a disinclination to expend the effort required for anything more than merely formal, routine "democratic" participation. Perhaps some of these factors might be linked with a politics of distraction, where the average citizen, except for occasional "pep rallies" around poll time, focuses predominant attention, understandably, upon the need to make a living, and attendant diversions are often satiating or enervating. All of this activity is rather time-consuming. Moreover, if the aggregate affluence of a society conveys the impression that there is no necessity to fix what is not broken, one may engage one's "spare" time with "circuses and consumerism".[12] Fixated concern with these two activities can deflect any interest and awareness requiring more than a short attention-span from political structures and processes that appear, for example, exasperatingly complicated and elusively arcane.[13]

Moreover, it may well be that most people esteem what is called "democracy" more in terms of the personal material benefits, economic well-being, etc., purportedly flowing from it than in terms of expanded possibilities for mutually beneficial empowerment as creative individuals and for cooperative control of common processes and tasks. It is revealing that politicians in this country, in order to persuade voters to prefer them, sometimes employ (either as celebration or as criticism) the question whether the voters are now "better off" than before, leaving aside the question whether the country itself is better, that is, more democratic, humane and just, than before.

It is instructive to realize that elitism has been substantiated, not simply in some Platonic fashion according to which an invincible segregation of human competencies dictates that the brightest and best alone should rule, but by its being fully compatible with democracy itself. [14] For example, John Stuart Mill's scheme of weighted voting implied that those exhibiting greater knowledge and diligence should play a more substantive role in democratic participation, thereby helping to neutralize any effects due to the ignorance of the masses. Max Weber, recognizing that many citizens are politically passive and that such indolence undermines the prospect of developing a broadly based model of political decision-making as rational and deliberative, advanced the model of "competitive elitism", where potential leaders compete to establish who is most competent to rule. This standpoint is summarized by Held in the following manner: "Far from democracy being the basis for the potential development of the citizens, democracy is best understood as a key mechanism to ensure effective political and national leadership. In serving a selection function, and in legitimating the selected (via elections), democracy is indispensable." [15]

Similar was the standpoint of Joseph Schumpeter. Believing that "excessive" participation by average citizens, who are intellectually limited and emotionally immature, as well as subject to irrational prejudice and impulse, would have destabilizing consequences for society, Schumpeter advocated "leadership democracy" rooted in "competitive elitism".[16] For both Weber and Schumpeter, "elitist democracy" is not a contradiction in terms, since, "while power is always held by an elite (or elites), the choice of which elite(s) shall hold political power for a certain period remains in the hands of the whole people" [17] – or at least in the hands of appropriately qualified people.

The people may have, to be sure, a not negligible influence upon which elites, in some categories and on some occasions, exercise power. Two considerations, however, should not be overlooked: not all political elites who hold and exercise significant power are chosen, or otherwise certified, by the people; and the alternation or replacement of elites does not necessarily modify the kind of social power which facilitates their being taken to deserve the cachet of elite status. Furthermore, to say that the people choose (periodically) between elites is to acknowledge that their so choosing does not itself confer that status upon elites but represents both a more or less willing acceptance of the reality of elitist status and a disposition to choose elite overseers who will purportedly support their (the people's) interests. This sometimes suspicious, sometimes cynical acquiescence in elitism assists in translating the personal authority of (presumed) expertise into the social authority of legitimized power.

A remark in passing concerning the "ignorance" of the masses: apart from the fact that, as I see the matter, it is more desirable to remedy the political ignorance of the masses than to cordon it off (an "ignorance" that is sometimes rather astute and perceptive), satisfaction of the needs of the people should not have to rely wholly upon flawed outcomes turning upon the intentions of elites who may be kindly disposed (to some of the people) for whatever reason, but upon the requirements of legislated human rights that, in accordance with humanistic values, strengthen the positive freedom of all citizens – a point that will be developed more fully later.

Elitism also surfaces in the political arrangement of consociationalism, where different, possibly antagonistic groups (usually demarcated culturally, that is, ethnically, linguistically, religiously, and so on) share in a corporatist-type distribution of power and resources at the national level, so as to maintain social stability by obviating disruptive competition among different groups and by avoiding the problem of a majority rule that recycles the power of dominant groups. [18] However, power and resources are allocated via political parties ostensibly representing disjunctive groups, parties that are typically managed by elites. In light of this, "consociationalism is not so much about democracy as about accommodation between political elites". [19]

Elitist rule or guardianship is likely to be, at best, paternalistic and patronizing and, at worst, imperious and domineering, neither situation being consonant with a humanistic outlook that cares about others in solidarity. Perhaps those attitudes are fitting, respectively, toward small children and toward anti-social personalities. In any case, they are inappropriate for individuals for whom democracy can be knowingly, voluntarily a serious concern and task.[20] It may be asseverated – as it has been more than once – that the (elite) expertise of political rulers is required for the same kind of reason that one expects it from, say, physicians, engineers, ship captains, and other specialists whose skills are crucial. The relevance of expertise for many contexts and situations cannot be gainsaid; but the pertinent question for the present discussion is: for what purpose is it employed? The expertise of non-political experts is instrumental, a special competency to formulate, and direct the implementation of, means on behalf of certain ends. Those ends need not be – and usually are not – determined by those "elites" of knowledge and skill. Physicians qua physicians do not validate the claims that health ought to be maintained and/or recovered or that life ought to be saved; they accept these claims. By and large, engineers do not decide whether it is good that some bridge be built (though given certain normative assumptions, they may recommend that it ought to be built, just as certain technical considerations may dictate that it ought not to be); and ship captains "steer" a ship but do not valorize its destination. In summary, then, there is an important categorial difference between the determination of (facilitating, expediting) means and the determination of (presiding, orienting) ends. Whereas experts may often be utilized unobjectionably for the former purpose, I wish to reassert that the latter purpose falls within the purview of single or associated individuals. For the nation-state – at least on my own interpretation of democracy – proper ends are not substantiated by their being discerned or created by elite experts but by their being implicitly affirmed consistently in the interrelated activities of citizens, however diverse they might otherwise be in attitude, commitment and world-outlook, and explicitly instantiated, so far as possible, in the regulatory and enabling prescriptions of human rights enactments. Admittedly, I cannot refute the objections that, on the one hand, many or, quite possibly, most people would not actively endorse, in principle or in practice, the kind of humanistic values that justify a conception of democracy as the empowering exercise of positive freedom or that, on the other hand, it is improbable, even in "liberal democratic" societies, that the provision of positive (social, economic) rights would materialize. It is for these reasons that I have said that what does, or could, obtain in the nation-state is, at best, a type of quasi-democracy which, while failing conspicuously to meet a variety of genuine human needs, at least militates against a variety of human excesses. At the same time, the real prospects for a humanistically empowering democracy in other contexts, which prominently define one's life-world, are as valuable as ever.

The desirability of elitism may be backed up by appealing to the inevitability, in many contexts, of hierarchy. It is probably the case that, for the sake of organizational coherence, instrumental rationality, and non-redundancy, hierarchy will be an accompaniment of virtually any moderately complex grouping of appreciable size. Yet, there is no need for a sociologically necessary hierarchy to engender and sustain a psychologically and morally invidious elitism.

Hierarchy, not oppressive or obnoxious in itself, when it is simply a form of a non-exploitative division of labor based upon sincere interests and demonstrable qualifications, becomes so when it is a counterpart of elitism, with its concentration of power, its self-reproducing character, its merely formal accountability to those "below" it, and its arrogation of special privileges. Effective measures to forestall a hierarchically sanctioned elitism are not easy to come by. Arrangements such as those put in place by the Paris Commune of 1871 are most likely not practicable for the large, modern nation-state. I can only recommend, however inadequately, greater efforts to inhibit bureaucracy and careerism in political life, more manifest accountability to the people by the de facto political elite, less obsequious reverence for "experts" and other denizens of upper strata (this should not become a form of anti-intellectualism), and an unrelenting struggle to democratize society whenever and wherever possible. For hegemonic dominance, whether in economic activity, gendered relationships or elsewhere, is often cognate with elitist arrogance.

A further observation here on elitism. In the state sector, elitism can often become embodied in the activities of bureaucracy, where managers treat their positions as private property, as something they own. This phenomenon was reflected not only in the former Soviet Union, where public ownership was in practice displaced, to a considerable degree, by bureaucratic control, but also in the 1990s in Russia, when, with the sanction of Western-oriented "reformers", influential public figures converted political power into economic power, that is, major bureaucrats became prominent capitalists. Under capitalism, elite managers, composing a significant segment of the bureaucracy of corporations, cannot treat the corporations as their own private property, although, as it turns out, they are able, by devious and dishonest machinations, to manipulate finances and profitability to their own private benefit.

36

NOTES

1. Holden, The Nature, p. 186. Contrary to this, it has been maintained that "Democratic societies are populated not by freely acting individuals but by collective organizations that are capable of coercing those whose interests they represent." [see Adam Przeworski, Democracy and the market. Cambridge: Cambridge University Press, 1991, p. 12]. Furthermore, it is frequently the case that "representation" is not a way of incorporating citizen power, even if indirectly, but of filtering it out, of occluding the untoward consequences of "too much" democracy. [See Ellen Meiksins Wood, Democracy Against Capitalism. Cambridge: Cambridge University Press, 1995, pp. 216-217].

2. The kinds of problematic representation that are dictated by the size and complexity of large-scale contexts such as the nation-state may be a necessary evil; but "representation" that takes place among members of small-scale groupings may also be hegemonic, an unnecessary evil.

3. See "Dealing with Difference: A Politics of Ideas, or a Politics of Presence?", in Benhabib, Democracy, pp. 139-140.

4. Ibid., pp. 140-141.

5. Ibid., p. 147.

6. See "Diversity and Democracy: Representing Differences", in Benhabib, Democracy, p. 184.

7. Statement by Edward Gierek in 1970, quoted by Rudolf Bahro in his Ich werde meinen Weg fortsetzen, excerpted in Roger Woods, Opposition in the GDR under Honecker, 1971-1985. New York: St. Martin's Press, 1986, p. 4.

8. This principle was vigorously expounded by Anatoly Butenko in "Marksistsko-leninskaja ideja samoupravlenija naroda i ee istoricheskoe razvitie", Sovetskoe gosudarstvo i pravo, 3, 1986, and in Vlast' naroda posredstvom samogo naroda. Moskva: "Mysl' ", 1988.

9. Gesammelte Werke in acht Bänden. Frankfurt am Main: Suhrkamp Verlag, 1967, IV, pp. 1009-1010.

10. The first quotation is from Robert A. Dahl, Democracy and Its Critics. New Haven: Yale University Press, 1989, p. 52; the second is from Holden, The Nature, p. 137. An interesting example alleged by Boris Kagarlitsky comes out in the fact that, in the early 1990s, Westernizing "reformers" in Russia relied "on the old Byzantine principle according to which power in society must be concentrated in the hands of the possessors of 'knowledge', or as it has been put in more recent times, the 'enlightened classes' " [The Disintegration of the Monolith. London: Verso, 1992, 42].

11. See Carol C. Gould. Rethinking Democracy. Cambridge: Cambridge University Press, 1988, p. 296. Milton Fisk has discerned another cause: "To increase chances of winning disputes, groups will grant enormous power to their elites." [The State and Justice. Cambridge: Cambridge

University Press, 1989, p. 324]. Within the framework of adversarial politics, this strategy may well be sound.

12. I have adopted this phrase from J. F. Brown, who, in his Surge to Freedom [Durham, NC: Duke University Press, 1991], notes that an adroit use of "coercion, circuses, and consumerism" enabled the Czechoslovak regime in the 1970s to be relatively successful [p. 167]. On the other hand, David Held points out that Herbert Marcuse's critique, in One Dimensional Man, directed against capitalist society asserts that "the cult of affluence and consumerism ... creates modes of behavior that are adaptive, passive and acquiescent" [Models of Democracy. Stanford: Stanford University Press, 1987, p. 227]. It is my opinion that much of the disillusionment that grew in socialist countries was fueled, not by a paucity of "circuses" (which were usually quite grand), but by failure to satisfy the consumer needs and sustain the political hopes of their citizens.

13. According to Partridge, most people are absorbed in their own particular interests and activities, and political participation is not a continuing priority: "it is not realistic to expect that a very large proportion of citizens will pay more that intermittent and somewhat remote attention to political questions" [Consent, p. 149]. Besides, many people are uneasy about the possibility of public political confrontations or problematic social experiments. In response to crises, government, according to Held, characteristically develops "strategies that disperse the worst effects of economic and political problems onto vulnerable groups while appeasing those able to mobilize claims most effectively" [Models, p. 240]. On the other hand, when political issues bear significantly upon international relationships connected with actual or assumed foreign enemies, with the intention to maintain hegemonic status in the world, with the desire to coerce recalcitrant nations, and so on, citizens can be quite enthusiastic and engaged, an orientation facilitated by the reduction of complex questions to a matter of good (us) versus evil (them).

14. In Models, Chapter 5, Held canvasses some of the more influential and typical versions of "elitist democracy". One variant that he does not consider is that which has been attributed to Friedrich Nietzsche by Lawrence J. Hatab in A Nietzschean Defense of Democracy. LaSalle, IL: Open Court, 1995. Although "Nietzschean democracy" is, in my judgment, oxymoronic, Hatab does his best to diffuse the contradiction, an endeavor that I have criticized elsewhere.

15. Models, p. 158. It seems to me that there is some degree of analogy here to the free enterprise doctrine that quality will win out in the competition of the market.

16. Ibid., pp. 166-170. Others have argued that equally important is a consensus among elites, which "is a necessary condition for the relatively stable, peaceful working of the democratic machinery" [Partridge, Consent, p. 116]. Reinforcing this stability, it is claimed, is the political apathy of the people [see ibid., p. 133].

17. See Holden, The Nature, p. 156.

18. See Phillips, Democracy, pp. 17-18 & 152-156.

19. Ibid., pp. 152-153

20. For such individuals, those attitudes would be at odds with the value of autonomy (which properly is integrated with society or community). Both capitalist elitist "democracy" and socialist vanguard "democracy" (also elitist) detract from that value.

CHAPTER 4

PREFERENCES, INTERESTS AND
THE COMMON GOOD

I

Mentioned earlier was the claim that democracy is not curtailed so long as leaders/rulers are responsive to the preferences of non-leaders/non-rulers. Preferences are known most reliably by those who have them and are made known to others through overt pronouncements and behavior. Leaders/rulers do not so much represent the preferences of citizens as respond to them in one way or another – except in the sense that the selection of leaders/rulers "represents" what citizens prefer.

In now defunct socialist societies, ruling elites occasionally sought to ascertain the preferences of citizens, not primarily so that those preferences might be incorporated explicitly in the construction of policy, which was determined preemptively by a "scientific ideology", but, in effect, so that the trends of public opinion might be made more evident. Thus, I think it is fair to say, political practices there, such as referenda and discussions (sometimes on a nation-wide scale), were actually sociological exercises in polling the sentiments of the people, as well as techniques for embellishing citizen "participation".

In existing liberal-democratic societies, as C. B. Macpherson has made plain, preferences (alternatively, "utilities") of citizens are, more often than not, construed as those of "political consumers", for whom preferences compose "a bundle of appetites demanding satisfaction".[1] On this model of "democracy", aspiring political leaders "sell" themselves and their promissory wares -- making use, where possible, of increasingly expensive (and effective) advertising -- to citizen-consumers who attempt to "buy" favorably disposed leaders by out-bidding, with their votes, other "consumers". Here, by contrast to the situation that was typical of socialist societies, concern with "sales" prompts relatively serious attention to the electoral purchasing power of citizen-consumers. [2] Within this political market, however, preferences are subject to being fostered (even introjected), manipulated and re-directed by means of the skillful practices of political operatives. Even if democracy as political free market should be noticeably responsive, in general, to the preferences of citizens, this market, on the one hand, will respond more readily and steadily to those who display greater "buying" power and, on the other hand, will frequently accommodate to preferences that are egoistically adversarial, exploitative, domineering, crass, and so on.

Often, discourse about interests substitutes for that about preferences. An "interest in" perhaps conveys something more intentional and thoughtful than an emotivistic "preference for". Wanting hints at a stronger, more complex disposition than liking. Be that as it may, the issue is complicated by an apparently real difference between "subjective" interests and "objective" interests. One way of making this distinction is to say that subjective interest indicates that one has a conscious interest in something, is interested in it, wants it, desires it, etc. Objective interest refers to something's being for/to the interest of something else, to the benefit of it, etc., particularly insofar as benefit can be determined factually according to scientifically creditable criteria. Subjective interests are held only by "subjects"; objective interests apply to anything that can be benefited in one way or another. For example, one may have a subjective interest in seeing a certain film or eating at a certain restaurant. In contrast, it is for the objective interest (in effect, good) of crops that there be enough rain but no freezing weather. As I am using the terms, 'subjective interest' signifies something psychological, connected with wants and desires; 'objective interest' signifies something causal, connected with beneficial outcomes. Human beings are aware of their subjective interests, while, of course, plants are not aware of what objectively is in their interest as living things. For that matter, human beings may be aware not at all, or only dimly, of what objectively is in their own interest.

The upshot of this (somewhat cursory) discussion is that subjective interests tend to be assimilated to preferences, and objective interests, in the case of human beings, are understood to be identical to that which purports to be demonstrably good for them. Noted above are some of the issues related to the representation, as well as marketing, of preferences (now "subjective interests"). Moreover, it is implicit in the previous remarks about elitism that elites, in professing to know what is best for the lower strata, thereby claim to know what is really in/for their objective interest.

Much of the commentary about interests in democracy has to do with what I have called "subjective interests". People themselves may be the most accurate judges of what they are, in fact, interested in; but it does not follow that they are the best judges of how some of these interests can be most relevantly or adequately implemented. It is one of the roles of political leaders in a conventionally representative liberal democracy to offer such judgments. Another task for liberal democracy is to accommodate and, frequently, adjudicate disparate, conflicting interests. One regulative presupposition advanced is that there should be equal consideration of interests, since democracy can be fully effective "only if people generally relate to each other as equals and with respect for each other's individual differences and interests". [3] Leaving aside the murky conception of "respect" – Is this particular notion psychological, moral, juridical, or all of the preceding at once? – I will address the issue of equally taking into account conflicting interests stemming from individual differences. Now, just what is it for diverse interests to be equally considered? Sometimes it seems that this means the interests are equally recognized by those with power to do something about them – and, subsequently, differentially ignored. Even if there is some effort to implement the differing interests, the attempt may prove intractable when interests are incompatible. Two issues, in particular, present themselves. Implementing the interests of some individuals may occur only at the patently detrimental expense of other individuals. In addition, some interests, from the standpoint of humanistic values and democratic aims, ought not to be given equal consideration, much less implemented. These overlapping problems call attention to the fact that the interests of some individuals (or groups) are prejudicial in intent, domineering in manifestation, and exploitative and inhumane in results. As far as I am concerned, there is no reason to "respect" such individuals (or groups) or to accord them anything but disdain and resistance. Surely, for example, the (subjective) interests involved in brutality directed against children, in sexism and racism, in piratical capitalism, in the despotism of some political rulers, in the actions of those who are inveterately cruel, deserve no less.

In passing, I may take note of a somewhat related problem articulated by Cunningham, namely, that democracy and morality can conflict, since "democratic tolerance" for individual preferences (that is, "subjective interests") can fail to support a "good society".[4] Democracy should indeed exhibit tolerance for (non-oppressive, non-exploitative) individual preferences; and these preferences may well have nothing to do with constituting a "good society". However, the point of democracy is not, as such, merely tolerance, but, in particular, empowerment designed to promote lives in society that have enriched, distinctively humanistic meaning -- and this, I maintain, is "good".

Divergent interests may be tolerated, even encouraged, so long as they do not, as indicated above, conflict with humanistic values and democratic aims. The situation is more problematic, however, when the interests conflict with each other. For an adversarial, competitive model of democracy, this conflict is part and parcel of its inner logic and dynamics. Later, I will argue explicitly that adversary democracy, though in some contexts the only viable option, is a very

43

flawed, deficient type of democracy and I will, concomitantly, argue for something different. At present, however, I wish to observe that if the problem of conflicting interests is not resolved by those who have the preponderance of power/control – as it is, more often than not – it may be resolved, theoretically, by relocating deciding criteria under the aegis of "objective" interests or by essaying to locate "common" interests that will take precedence.

A singular, and seemingly intractable, problem with regard to the collective representation and implementation of preferences ("subjective interests") is that, according to public (social)-choice theory, there is no way rationally to aggregate from individual preferences to a collective preference ordering that could orient public policy. [5] There are, according to Hardin, several important consequences of this situation. First, majoritarian democracy is conceptually flawed.[6] Second, alternative social-choice procedures will normally include "nondemocratic, coercive, and deceptive moves".[7] Third, it is questionable whether "the outcome of democratic voting procedures is a coherent mapping of citizen preferences onto policies".[8] Fourth, "If we wish to justify particular practices for adopting and implementing policies, we must have recourse to extra-democratic values", such as social stability, resolution of disagreements, etc.[9] In addition, it seems to me, the intelligibility of an aggregative "general will" is called into question, even where the individual preference-inputs are determined by interpersonal consultation.

Christiano, for his part, has responded to the general problematic ventilated by Hardin. For example, he contends that majority-rule procedures should not be thought of as a function from individual preferences to a social preference. The route is more tenuous than that: "In actual uses of the majority-rule procedure, some decisions will be made if only to delay making a decision. More often, decisions are made in these circumstances because of the strategic manipulation of the agenda or the voting procedure by some or all of the members of the group."[10] Such manipulation (including vote-trading in certain procedural contexts) can mitigate Condorcet cycles and circumvent Arrow's Impossibility result. Further, Christiano insists, it is a mistake to view a specifically democratic procedure as a method by which outcomes are derived from (individual) preferences. Preferences can be manipulated, such that individuals do not vote their "real", that is, considered, preferences; individuals may be uncertain or confused about those preferences; or they may make mistakes in indicating preferences. The inference from all this is that voting is a procedure that goes "not from preferences to outcomes but from actions to outcomes".[11]

Although Hardin and Christiano identify somewhat different challenges and consequences of social-choice theory for democracy, they concur that political governance cannot be based in any straightforward manner upon citizens' expressed preferences. I find their arguments persuasive and, moreover, submit that democratic policy should attend more to the satisfaction of needs than to the satisfaction of preferences.

Deploying decision-making criteria under the heading of objective interests gives rise to the dual question of how this kind of interest is to be ascertained and who ascertains it. Given individuals may sometimes possess as adequate an awareness and understanding of what will "really" benefit them as do those with ostensibly expert cognition. However, there is an ambiguity here concerning 'benefit': it may refer either to beneficial (good/efficacious) means or to beneficial (good/valorized) ends. Identification of objectively good means is characteristically a "technical" question; and those with expert knowledge may well be more adept at it – in the sphere of political governance or elsewhere – than those untutored in such matters. Once again, though, I stress that expertise does not justify hegemonic and prejudicial elitism.

The determination of beneficial/good ends is, in my opinion, a philosophically more contentious issue. As I see it, there is no such thing as a "good-in-itself" or an "end-in-itself". An "end-in-itself" is actually either an unending end of surpassing value, a non-terminating state that normatively calls for continued reproduction, or else an end that ends, apparently once and for all, the striving either to realize some positively appraised condition or to terminate some condition negatively appraised. These kinds of ends are not without remainder: in the first case, there remains the unending project; in the second case, there remains the valued condition issuing, respectively, from realization or termination. A so-called end-in-itself is, in truth, an end-valued-for-itself, an open-ended end that can be reached but never completed and that is judged to be preemptively good. Such good is not a "good-in-itself", for to have value is to be valued; and something may be valued "for" itself, but it does not have value "in" itself. Thus, the question of "ultimate" values for human beings turns upon the nature of human beings, a nature understood not a priori or essentialistically but historically and functionally.[12] In view of the lack of fixity in those cognitive and emotional dimensions of human nature that bear upon evaluation, ultimate values tend to be not only diverse but also somewhat protean. Under these circumstances, it is to be hoped that humanistic values will become more prevalent and more compelling. Because of considerations such as the foregoing, I propose that, for the purposes of democracy, orientation upon interests (subjective or objective) be substantially, though hardly exclusively, superseded by emphasis upon needs – a subject to be dealt with soon.

II

In the meantime, I wish to deal with the other alternative mentioned above, namely, that conflicting interests should be adjusted in accord with "common interests". Jane Mansbridge has pointed out that common interests can exist for one or more of three reasons: an overlap or coincidence of individual interests, making the interests of others one's own, or adopting the interests of the whole group.[13] The commonality obtaining in the first case would most likely be due either to closely shared attitudes and outlooks on certain matters or to bargaining and negotiation; but either scenario would not necessarily render the interests identical, because those discussing/formulating policy on the basis of these common interests "would probably have different reasons for preferring the policy, be willing to incur different costs to gain their preference, and have different enlightened preferences about how the policy could best be implemented".[14] People sometimes are willing, in common, to accept a policy about which they, individually, have misgivings, an agreement grounded more in an interest in preventing destructive fractiousness than in convergent interests themselves. With respect to the second case, making others' interests one's own doubtlessly effects a type of commonality. However, there are radically, and significantly, different ways by which common interests may be attained in this case. If taking on the interests of others is based, for example, on genuine caring, a caring that is most vital and beneficial when mutuality does not eviscerate individuality, that is one thing; but accommodating to the interests of others out of egoistic, "cost-effective" calculation or in the face of superior, aggrandizing power is something else. Self-serving calculation may well "work" for all concerned, or it may be in one's pragmatic interest to accede (perhaps there is simply no other option) to the interests of those who wield decisive, unremitting power, hence control, over political circumstances. Neither alternative, though it may make for political stability and continuity, is an ingredient of democracy.

Adopting the interests of the whole group presupposes that the group can have its own interests as a group, since it is obviously not implied that everyone can share all the interests of everyone else. It will be useful to differentiate the interests of the whole group either as common interests or as general interests. General interests are aggregative and collective, instantiated in particular cases but transcending them logically. Common interests are distributive, shared by all particular cases and derived from them.[15] A troublesome problem with both kinds of interests lies in perspicuously and plausibly specifying them. Historically, it is not unknown for the alleged general interests of society to be, in a more or less dissimulated fashion, the extrapolated special interests of a limited segment of it.[16]

Sometimes, indeed, dissimulation may not even be put to use. Elitism, especially when bureaucratized, is an example already discussed. Social Darwinism, whether inside or outside the economy, furnishes another case in point. In view of the conceptual vagaries of "general" interests, I believe that an orientation upon "common" interests would be more fruitful.

Common interests, as subjective, tend to be present more readily in small groupings and to be relatively less prominent when the domain is of large scale. For the former contexts, any conflicts of interests can, given a sincere spirit of community, be negotiated dependably and fairly. For the latter, conflicts of interest can be rationalized, defused, sublimated, rearranged or, if necessary, suppressed. It may be noted that a voluntarily self-affirmed spirit of community, of communality, is more forthcoming in "chosen", mutually constructed communities than in social groupings in which one, willingly or not, "finds" oneself. Communitarians, who, correctly, appeal to important differences between societies and communities and, furthermore, point up the way in which one's identity is constituted, to a considerable extent, by the communities in which one lives and acts, are nonetheless prone to a combination of nostalgic fabrication of idealized community in the past and utopian wistfulness for imaginary community in the future, especially that which is supposed to be possible, because desirable, at the level of the highly pluralistic, typically atomistic nation-state. For communitarians, in effect, subjective interests should be aligned with the objective interests of the relevant community, where the latter interests are substantiated by their being directed toward the common good.

Much of the contemporary debate between liberals and communitarians deals with the question whether there is, or should be, a common good for different types of groupings, most contentiously with respect to the nation-state. For my part, I wish to begin by trying to make out what it might mean to say that there is a common good. A common good is not the collective, cumulative good of a society or community of which various individuals are members in common.

Rather, it is a good that is common to those members. In other words, it is a value, embedded, for example, in relationships, practices, policies, institutions or consequences, that is commonly good (good in common), although it may well be so in different ways and to different degrees for different individuals. Communitarians tend morally to hypostasize the common good, whereas liberals judge that it becomes substantively, though not procedurally, problematic for a pluralistic society of great diversity comprising both fundamental attitudes and comprehensive world-views and doctrines. A common good of sorts can be the result of imposition or indoctrination, or it can be due to a commonly accepted endorsement of the value of allowing, within limits, a multiplicity of personally relevant goods. With respect to the first case, a good of this sort is, humanistically speaking, not good. With respect to the second, toleration in the face of non-oppressive diversity and disagreement is assuredly good; but it is a good that lends support to negative freedom and a judicious, indeed fair, balancing of differences, not directly to positive freedom and democratic practice itself.

A common good founded on subjective interests is not likely to subsist except in small-scale groupings; and even here it may be fragile. [17] A common good founded on objective interests is, on the face of it, more precise and consistent in application; but a decision-procedure for identifying prima facie objective interests can sometimes be ironically and subversively subjective. Where it is not and where, at the same time, it is about commonly good (efficacious) means, there remains the question of the determination of commonly good ends. The intersubjective agreement of participants may determine a commonly good set of subjective interests; and the intersubjective agreement of those more knowledgeable and experienced may do so for objective interests as instrumentalities. Yet, what can be a decision-procedure for a commonly good set of ends? Before attempting to answer this question, I wish to reaffirm the position that there are no ends-in-themselves, which might be sanctioned by, or coordinated with, some good-in-itself (intrinsic good). The good is always instrumental; and the end which it serves is never a final end, but one which, as mentioned earlier, is recurring and magisterial. These assertions are made from the standpoint of what I take to be ethical naturalism, a standpoint that demurs at absolute values but accepts the possibility that some values may be affirmed with absolute conviction because one is absolutely committed to them. Something has value because it is valued, and some things are valued above all else (that is, "absolutely").[18] Of course, there is no way, logically or epistemologically, to justify, strictly speaking, definitive ends/goods viewed in this manner. One can only affirm in thought, attitude and practice the primacy of certain values. If this "existential" affirmation is shared by numbers of people and if, in particular, it focuses upon humanistically understood values of empowerment and enrichment in human life, then, so far forth, the democratic prospect is auspicious.

My suggestion, now, for operationally specifying the practical content of the common good within the context of the nation-state is to embody that good, namely, the humanistic value of democratic empowerment as the practice of positive freedom, in the legally enforceable prescriptions of human rights, both negative and, especially, positive (since the latter are customarily ignored altogether). The appropriate decision-procedure for this specification, I submit, is to coordinate human needs and human rights, that is, to base the directives of human rights upon the requirements of human needs. The satisfaction of human needs is a common good; it is a good, in common, for every individual. Moreover, common human needs can be identified by an intersubjective agreement that, when thoughtful, considerate, realistic and attentive to positive freedom, can avoid bogging down in querulous disputes regarding the boundaries between genuine needs and merely subjective preferences and interests. A further advantage of emphasizing the extant commonality of needs, rather than the fugitive coincidence of preferences or interests, is that, when enacted human rights mandate the satisfaction, so far as possible, of basic human needs, majority disregard for the empowerment of minorities is disallowed – a disregard more likely to obtain with the professed implementation of preferences or interests, where uneven relationships of power and control have their effect. In the next chapter, I will examine more closely the status of human needs and human rights, together with their proposed coordination.

51

NOTES

1. See <u>Democratic Theory</u>. Oxford: Clarendon Press, 1973, pp. 3-4. Such a construal is probably reinforced by a standard assumption in economics that self-interest maximization characterizes actual human behavior. Regarding this assumption, see Amartya Sen. <u>On Ethics and Economics</u>. Oxford: Blackwell, 1987, passim.

2. Supplementing this analysis is the view put forward by Wolin that the dominant powers which organize, operate and finance electoral campaigns see them as "investment opportunities" [see "Fugitive Democracy", p. 35].

3. See Gould, <u>Rethinking Democracy</u>, p. 257.

4. See <u>Democratic Theory</u>, p. 57.

5. For a clear discussion of the implications of Arrow's Impossibility Theorem for public choice, see Russell Hardin, "Public choice versus democracy", in Copp, <u>The Idea</u>.

6. <u>Ibid.</u>, p. 157.

7. <u>Ibid.</u>, p. 162.

8. <u>Ibid.</u>, p. 166.

9. <u>Ibid.</u>, p. 169.

10. See "Social choice", p. 175.

11. <u>Ibid.</u>, p. 179. Christiano's proposal for a democratic decision-making process is that it should be one in which people have the opportunity to participate equally with the help of equally distributed <u>non-procedural</u> resources [see pp.174 & 185].

12. This naturalistic axiology is somewhat similar to Mill's ethical naturalism, wherein the ends of conduct determine the criteria of morality. Nevertheless, I have serious reservations about his reliance upon the principle of "psychological hedonism". Furthermore, I am persuaded by Sen's emphasis upon the importance of consequentialist (but not necessarily utilitarian) reasoning: "Even activities that are intrinsically valuable may have <u>other</u> consequences. The intrinsic value of any activity is not an adequate reason for ignoring its instrumental role, and the existence of instrumental relevance is no denial of its intrinsic value." [<u>On Ethics</u>, p. 75].

13. See <u>Beyond Adversary Democracy</u>. New York: Basic Books, 1980, p. 27.

14. <u>Ibid</u>.

15. Similar distinctions obtain between "general" happiness and "common" happiness. In addition, any "general will" would not be, as such, common. It would probably be invoked in an attempt to portray a society as a community.

16. If Marx is right, this is so in "bourgeois" societies; and, contrary to his expectations, it became so in nominally socialist societies of the past century. When defining the values and standards of an allegedly impartial general interest, the standpoint of privileged strata may be cultural as well as political or social [see Young, Justice, p. 116].

17. Observing that "democratic institutions on a national scale can seldom be based on the assumption of a common good", whereas there usually exists in small-scale units "the actual greater coincidence of their members' interests", Mansbridge yet calls attention to the fact that these small units may preserve, even strengthen, inequalities of power and fail to protect individual interests equally [see Beyond Adversary Democracy, pp. 279-281, 287 & 295]. Small is not necessarily "beautiful".

18. It is my impression that things represented as intrinsically good within human experience are said to be so because they are valued without qualification and without exception. Thus, the "good-in-itself" is simply the "good-for-itself" for human beings.

CHAPTER 5

HUMAN NEEDS AND HUMAN RIGHTS

I

Human needs, I propose, establish the basis for the identification and justification of human rights. Human rights reflect claims concerning what is needed, at least to a considerable extent, for the democratic empowerment of human life and for its humane enhancement. That which is needed is what is necessary (as a means) for the realization of a continuing end; and the fact that it is necessary can be determined empirically, subject to correction. Assuming that there is overriding positive value in the humanization of human life, this "end" legitimizes the means, including human rights enactments, that further it. Human rights, conceived as general, basic and obligatory, declare what needs to be assured if humanistic values are to be secured and developed. Moreover, the commonality of needs underlies the equality implicit in the conception of general human rights.

It would be incorrect to say that one has a right to have rights. Rather, one ought to have rights because of their indispensable functionality for the sake of what one already always has, namely, needs; and if one values the satisfaction of (humanizing) needs, then one should valorize the enactment of (humanizing) rights. Concomitantly, an empowering, that is, enabling, allocation of resources, development of competencies, provision of opportunities, etc., is based, strictly speaking, not upon a "right" to any of this but upon a need for it, where the language of rights sanctions the importance and urgency of the needs. Thus, it may be said that the expression "welfare rights" is elliptical, since any right so designated is not to the welfare ingredients themselves but to the satisfaction of the need(s) that the ingredients are intended to make possible. I believe this way of interpreting the matter is preferable, on the one hand, because it grounds welfare in objectively discernible circumstances (of need), rather than in some more elusive notion of beneficence, and, on the other, because it exposes as petulant and mean-spirited the assertion that welfare is a "giveaway".

Human rights, I contend, cannot be justified by appeal to some ground independent of human agreement and commitment. Instead, they are justified by being shown to be instrumental with respect to the aims and values of democracy. Theoretically, human rights are validated only so long as, and only to the extent that, democracy is valorized. Practically, they are secure and effective only if there exists a continuing, conscientious commitment to democracy as the humanistic practice of positive freedom. An abstractly theoretical justification does not, as such, render them secure and effective. The fact that human rights can be violated demonstrates, correspondingly, that democracy can be debilitated or disregarded. Furthermore, basic human rights are "contestable" only in the sense that which (kinds of) rights genuinely promote the satisfaction of human needs (supporting empowerment) is contestable. However, if democracy, as practice, is established as an end/goal, then the relevance of human rights as a means is not contestable. To be told that this viewpoint does not furnish a solid enough foundation for human rights is, I submit, unpersuasive, since the preservation and implementation of human rights is only as strong as fidelity, individual and social, to them – whatever more allegedly objective, independent backing might be attributed to them. The provision of an irrefragable theoretical foundation for a doctrine of human rights may satisfy the need of theorists (including philosophers) for putting things neatly and authoritatively into place, but the provision of material foundations for satisfying the actual needs of those who have them, while facing obstacles of its own, is rather more urgent.

The justification of human rights on the basis of the "legitimacy" of satisfying genuinely humanizing needs is distinct from at least two other standpoints. According to one of them, human rights are derived from the intrinsic dignity, worth, and so on, of human beings. I must confess that I do not altogether comprehend what this kind of language means. If human beings have (possibly "infinite") worth because they are the children of God or for some other similar reason, then their value is clearly not "intrinsic". Further, it seems to me that the "intrinsic dignity" of many people is, ironically, rather well hidden. I submit that we do not value human beings due to their having some metaphysical dignity. Instead, we attribute "intrinsic" dignity to them, when we do, in order to affirm strongly that we value them.

Another quite different standpoint – which sometimes sanctions negative rights but not positive rights – is that wherein the satisfaction of needs, humanizing or not, is supposed to be primarily the project of individual initiative. This standpoint, in effect expressed in the views, for example, of Locke and Nozick, treats basic rights as authorizing the preservation and/or acquisition of, in a very generic sense, "private property" such as one's life, (negative) liberty and exchangeable property. That one needs something else or something more establishes no claim on it but only, if one has sufficient power or resources, a stimulus to action.

Often associated with this ideologically conservative standpoint – yet found, in its own way, in conjunction with a liberal orientation – is the view that if people do not have what they need, it is essentially due to some failing or deficiency on their part. This outlook corresponds closely with that characterized (and criticized) forcefully and insightfully by Michael Lewis in The Culture of Inequality.[1] According to Lewis, a "culture of inequality" in America has been rationalized by invoking an "individual-as-central sensibility" that "virtually ignores the impact of social structure upon personal achievement and mobility".[2] This sensibility, in its more conservative, moralizing form, ascribes disadvantageous inequalities to personal defects in character that render many individuals unfit for a more equal status in society. In its more liberal form, the sensibility emphasizes deficiencies in cognitive skills and in other competencies, including inculcated motivation. For this latter version, in contrast to the former, "Personal success and personal failure ... are matters not of moral superiority and inferiority, but rather of capacity and incapacity." [3] For each version, significantly, success and failure are individualized. Although, in response, conservatives and liberals endorse differing public policy proposals – the former sanctioning a prudent neglect; the latter, government programs to remediate deficiencies – both accept the individual-as-central sensibility with its implicit separability of personal destiny from social circumstance. In so doing, they tend equally to disregard the following considerations:

> that poverty and disadvantage (and therefore inequality) must more often than not be accounted for by unjust social and economic circumstances imposed upon those who appear to fail (the disadvantaged poor), and that freedom from poverty and disadvantage ("success", in varying degrees) must more often than not be accounted for by social and economic circumstances which at a minimum do not impede the realization of ambition and frequently guarantee a modicum of success irrespective of talent or intensity of ambition. [4]

An implication of the kinds of remarks made by Lewis is that empowering capacities integrally connected with democracy come into being and are developed only through the type of cooperative social practice that is seriously impaired by "unjust social and economic circumstances" which, in particular, institutionalize exploitation and the invidious fungibility of advantages.

A more recent work by William Julius Wilson in sociological analysis and interpretation essentially corroborates what Lewis has said. Looking at disadvantaged individuals in urban centers, he states that conservative ideology seeks to "shift the focus away from changing the environments of the minority poor to changing their values and behavior", [5] thereby downplaying the role of socioeconomic factors in producing that disadvantage. Apparently, the minority poor, disabled by deep-seated character flaws, need to be born again so as to rid themselves of certain "self-perpetuating cultural traits" and "deeply ingrained habits" [6] But, as Wilson notes, aspects of societal organization directly influence a group's cultural behavior, as well as its norms and values. Hence, the so-called "ghetto underclass" evinces "social isolation", not a "culture of poverty", where the former is a result of "structural constraints and limited opportunities" that compound an originally operative racial subjugation.[7] Liberal ideology (which, as Lewis noted, stresses defects of competence rather than defects of character) sometimes ignores the fact that, to use Wilson's words, "the effectiveness of training, education, and employment programs depends on a favorable economic climate". [8] This means favorable not only for those who can provide jobs but, in particular, for those who need them.

Substantive value in life materializes in the fulfillment of a complex of needs, a complex uniquely characteristic of the social, productive nature of human beings.[9] The related enhancement of life is valuable for itself or, to put it differently, it is the locus of those experiences of interest, satisfaction, creative effort, mutuality, social interaction, etc., that express and develop that (historical) human nature. The value in human life lies in its being lived, in the quality and quantity of experiences that manifest and reinforce satisfying purposes. Such valuable purposes, continually projected, appropriated and renewed, constitute meaning in -- indeed, the meaning of – life. It is my distinct impression that, whatever else human beings desire in life, they desire a life that is, in some way and to some extent, "meaningful". Of course, such a meaning may be, because of external conditions, minimal and, because of internal dispositions and affects, confused or self-destructive. However, I think it unlikely that individuals willingly and knowingly embrace utter hopelessness and crushing despair. For some, even self-annihilation has "meaning".[10] Within this general framework, human rights subserve, instrumentally, the project, at once social and individual, of humanistically meaningful existence. To be sure, human rights cannot

58

guarantee that meaningfulness; but they can substantially promote the implementation of the necessary conditions for a more realistic quest for that meaning.

Although the kinds of needs that I have in mind in this discussion are the needs (biological/material, cognitive, social, cultural, etc.) of individuals, where the needs are coordinated with rights understood as general human rights, the identification and the satisfaction of these needs are contextual, in that the social placement of the individual, including the individual's situatedness in this or that group, should be taken into account. For example, the specific needs of those in oppressed or marginalized groups will often be appreciably different from the needs of those in currently advantaged social groups. Again, though the categories of needs are common, the ways and means of satisfying the sometimes differentiated needs of women and men will thereby be particularized according to concrete contexts of residual patriarchalism, domination, and so on, affecting the former. As the category of the individual is not abstract, but socially situated, so is the category of need.

The humanistically meaningful enhancement of human life, whose conditions of realization furnish the rationale and focus for human rights, obtains along the lines of knowingly creative activity in accordance with social, productive human capabilities. Forms of satisfaction in life that derive from an exploitative, predatory individualism depend for their success upon the kind of society that tolerates, indeed encourages, egoistic aggrandizement and that poses an obstacle to democratic practice and empowerment. By contrast, forms of satisfaction deriving their power through a recognition of one's existence as social activity, as active self-production in cooperative social practice, dialectically strengthen the very conditions that enlarge opportunities for experienced meaning in life, as well as help to ensure that the democratization of social life is a viable project.

Consolidation and enhancement of the humanistic value of life – a goal/task that orients the practice of democracy – are not possible unless certain requirements are met, that is, unless, at least, certain human needs are satisfied.[11] Without the supportive institutionalization of human rights, the needed prerequisites are things that one is permitted to seek, though not things on which one can realistically rely; there occurs an emphasis upon the idealization (even mystification) of the possibilities of satisfying crucial human needs, rather than upon the actualization of those possibilities. The conception of human rights as social (including political) guarantees, where a wide spectrum of rights, both "negative" and "positive", corresponds to a substantial range of needs, does not imply that the realization of individual meaningfulness in life through the social practice of democracy can itself be guaranteed. Human existence is too "contingent" and "ambiguous" for that. What can be guaranteed (within limits) are the necessary conditions, including opportunities, that objectively facilitate, both individually and socially, that realization.

The interpretation of human rights as enacted entitlements to the means required for satisfying human needs may appear impractical when relevant means are scarce or, even more, unavailable. To this it may be rejoined, as Marx says, that "Right can never be higher than the economic structure of society and its cultural development conditioned thereby."[12] Definition and substantiation of human rights crystallize when there is shared concern for human life and perspicacious recognition of its needs. The actual implementation of human rights takes place to the extent that both the political and the socioeconomic structures of society can, and do, engender the means to make such implementation feasible within the framework of a regulative social equality. Constitutions and legal systems may articulate human rights in theory, but only the sociopolitical system can provide them in practice. Thus, in an authoritarian and/or economically impoverished society, human rights are, at most, "manifesto rights", functioning practically as demands on history. In a democratic society that is, at the same time, economically developed (or significantly developing), human rights can have the status of reasonably reliable guarantees, ensured by the joint capacity of the political and socioeconomic systems to provide what is needed. Admittedly, at the level of the nation-state, where the legal institutionalization of human rights can take place, it is exceedingly problematic, indeed rather unlikely, whether the range of rights envisioned above, comprising positive (socioeconomic, cultural) rights, would, in fact, be implemented in any contemporary society. However disappointing this might be, it simply attests, in my opinion, to the fact that democracy in the nation-state is severely, perhaps permanently, constricted and that the model of democracy I have been recommending must find its distinct embodiment elsewhere in contexts in which the concept of human rights can constitute a normative background, but not an actual energizing force, for empowerment.

II

Not only do the imperatives of human needs establish the rationale for the entitlements expressed in human rights, the identification of needs can serve as a decision-procedure for the specification of particular rights, where general human rights are a function of common human needs. I should emphasize, in passing, that human rights, as common rights applying to all individuals, are not collective rights in the sense of group rights. The latter often function either as internal restrictions for the group (and are not an unmixed blessing) or as external protections against the wider society. [13] The coordination of rights with needs has, I believe, the following considerations in its favor.

First, common human needs provide a point of reference for making sense philosophically of the generality and equality implicit in human rights. All people equally have various needs in common. More or less exigent, depending upon circumstances, their differential satisfaction is, equally for everyone, an essential element in sustaining and enhancing human life. To say that all people equally have needs is not to say that their needs are always equal, that is, equivalent. In general, an equal right to A is not the same as a right to an equal amount or degree of A. The point is that the satisfaction of genuine needs is equally important for everyone. To be sure, some individuals will need more of this or that, on some occasion or other, than will other individuals. Moreover, depending upon biological or social/historical factors, some categories of individuals will have needs singular in kind or duration. For example, human beings who are impaired physically or cognitively have special needs. One can, and should, advocate equally the development and exercise of capacities engendering (humane) meaningfulness in life for anyone who might so benefit. This advocacy follows from the conception of democracy as an activity of common empowerment motivated by common concern, however constrained this empowerment may be in the case of individuals with extremely limited abilities. On this conception, the special competencies of some individuals, by comparison to others, while perhaps relevant for the tasks of selecting or executing means necessary for democratic goals, are not relevant for substantiating the humanistic value of these goals themselves. Life can often be just as meaningful, in its own way, for those with limited abilities as it can be for those more favorably endowed. Surely, the value of a person's life does not lie primarily in that person's "use value".

A personal disability should not become a social disadvantage, that is, it should not operationally stigmatize a person as a disadvantage to society. Not only does the humanistic valorization of the satisfaction of genuine needs disallow this, it places the social value of people in their utility as instruments conducing to the general good, in contrast to the common good. A democratic society should empower everyone – as far as possible and consistently with humane values – not just those who can participate, perhaps excel, in a competitive version of social life. Even if the disabled usually could not compete successfully against those not disabled (who, strictly speaking, do not deserve or merit their advantaged situation as non-disabled), the former can, in most cases, "compete" successfully against the degree of their own prior attainments.

Another type of case has to do with those groups of human beings who have suffered the lingering consequences of racial or gendered discrimination, exploitation and oppression and who, therefore, have special needs for these consequences to be rectified through, among other things, what is known as "affirmative action". This necessarily "unequal", that is, differential, satisfaction of needs does not at all detract from the equal importance to human beings of that kind of satisfaction or from the equality of human beings as bearers of needs. Correspondingly, human rights, applicable, in principle, equally to everyone, are, in practice, implemented in different ways for different human beings in different contexts. What a right to education means for a child will differ in practical details from what that right means for an adult; and a right to medical care will obviously unfold differently depending upon the particular needs of individuals at particular times. Analogously, the ways in which, and the extent to which, individuals can be empowered, democratically, to realize a humanistically meaningful existence will be varied. Yet in all of this, a democratic outlook valorizes this kind of existence for everyone.

Second, distinguishing between fundamental, general human rights and derivative, contingent rights is coherently effected by means of differentiating between primary, common human needs and secondary, singular needs. A functional hierarchy of such primary needs can be delineated, wherein a need is ranked more or less basically according to whether its relative satisfaction is a precondition for the relative satisfaction of other needs. Schematically, one may so rank certain kinds of needs as follows: material needs, including food, health care, clothing, shelter; social needs, including meaningful activity and relationships; cognitive needs, including education and general mental development; cultural needs, including understanding of intellectual, emotional and aesthetic values. In this functionally lexical ordering, the most basic needs are principally relevant to the maintenance of human life. The less basic, but not less important, needs are more relevant to its enhancement, to the expansion and growth of distinctively human, and humanizing, qualities. Coordinate with this, an organic system of human rights can be formulated, corresponding to the complex of primary needs, such that the ranking of needs entails a concomitant arrangement of rights. Functional priority in needs yields strategic precedence in rights. Hence, with reference to conventional classifications, economic rights are the foundation for social rights; the latter undergird political and civil rights, which, in turn, by ensuring an "open" society, assist in giving substance to cultural rights.

A third consideration in favor of the needs-rights linkage is that needs are empirically identifiable and, consequently, appropriate rights are fairly clearly indicated. In order to obviate disputes about the genuineness of needs and to counter arguments that claims about needs may well be nothing more than dissembled representations on behalf of mere interests or preferences, it can be stipulated that "genuine" needs are those whose satisfaction sustains and develops the capacity of individuals to take part, in principle and, one hopes, in practice, in the empowerment of democratic life. Furthermore, the degree of progress in the implementation of human rights can be measured by the extent of satisfaction of human needs. Incidentally, it should be noted that genuine needs, congruent with humanistic values and democratic aims, can grow or evolve, and thus that the specific interpretation and implementation of this or that human right may vary over time.

Fourth, and finally, a foundation for human rights in human needs defuses any conflict or disparity between negative rights and positive rights, that is, between civil and political rights, on one hand, and economic, social, political and cultural rights, on another. If human rights theoretically express and confirm the practical demands of basic human needs, then arbitrary interference in the process of their satisfaction and deployment is proscribed and, at the same time, active and thoroughgoing support for this process is prescribed. One is obligated both to refrain from doing what hinders, and to participate in doing what promotes, the satisfaction of common (humanistically relevant) needs. The distinction between "negative" and "positive" bears ultimately upon the tactics, not the strategy, of human rights, which serve different, yet complementary, kinds of human needs.

In passing, it should be mentioned that making the satisfaction of human needs a function of legally institutionalized human rights prescriptions would help to lessen, but not completely eliminate, the "free rider" problem. Insofar as satisfaction (to the degree possible) of the basic needs of citizens would be a constitutional obligation, dictating budgetary allocations, no adult citizen would be exempt from supporting that obligation. At the same time, to be sure, to the extent that the assignment or the collection of taxes was skewed to the advantage of various categories of influential individuals, free riding would remain a problem.

The coordination of human rights with human needs and the resultant expansion of the scope of the former has the virtue that the nation-state, in its diversified, sometimes inconsistent policies and programs, should, however haltingly, adhere to the project of attempting to bring about the empowerment of citizens within the framework of democratically oriented practice. This "should", of course, is a hypothetical imperative, possessing only tenuous force in view of a present, and doubtlessly permanent, counterfactual willingness and ability of those determining national policy to implement that imperative. In other words, any legal institutionalization of the broad range of human rights, as conceived herein, is, to say the least, uncertain. But, as noted before, it is enlightening and useful to know the limits of democratization (due to the unrealizability of certain of its conditions), to know where it will work and where it will not. Normatively, democratic empowerment becomes a social, collective responsibility, mandated as a basic legal requirement. While there is no guarantee that the rule of law will always prevail over the "laws" of the rulers or that the evasion, desultoriness and carelessness of legal authorities will not have a baneful effect, at least the humanization and democratization of life might approximate the status of official political commitment (reinforced by the personal commitments of as many citizens as possible), a status that would protect these goals from the occasionally insensitive, discriminatory and ungenerous tendencies of majority rule.[14] In addition, the effectiveness of comprehensive human rights enactments would help to give meaning to the idea of the rule of the people, in that their genuine, extensive needs, reflected in those rights as enabling forms of social and political participation, would influence the content and direction of general government policy.

To be sure, much government policy of the nation-state will be directed to tasks other than the implementation of human rights requirements. A wide range of issues, both domestic and foreign, command attention; and, in resolving them, human rights mandates serve primarily as background presuppositions. Nevertheless, these mandates can establish an agenda of priorities, not to be abrogated in practice either by other programmatic undertakings or by routine tasks.

Underwriting the project of democracy with the prescriptions and controls of human rights also bestows substance upon the matter of accountability. Accountability, within this framework, is something more than responsibility. The latter, as "responsibility to", suggests an obligation to conform to the expectations or requirements of someone or something (a relationship that may not be recognized or accepted by the one so responsible). As "responsibility for", it indicates either a causal, moral or legal attribution of connectedness to some event or else an ascription of obligation to act on behalf of some purpose. For conventionally political contexts, those in charge often decide both how to communicate that they are responsible to the people and also how to demonstrate their responsibility for the public good. Accountability, by comparison, focuses upon the question of how to hold people responsible, that is, how to enforce, and measure the extent of compliance with, such responsibility. Some governing individuals treat accountability as requiring little more than "giving an account of" their activities, an account that may be incomplete, misleading or falsified. On an electoral model of democracy, popular voting furnishes a negative method of accountability, in that voters can pressure governing individuals to be accountable by means of electoral disapproval or rejection – but only uncertainly or intermittently. By contrast, enforceable human rights yield definite criteria by which the content and extent of accountability to the people and for the satisfaction of their needs can be determined. Public accountability thus becomes not a matter of announcements and pronouncements, but something that can be tested by perceptible improvement in the (humanistic) meaningfulness of life for as many people as possible.

67

NOTES

1. New York: New American Library, 1978.

2. Ibid., p. 8.

3. Ibid., p. 10.

4. Ibid., p. 13.

5. The Truly Disadvantaged. Chicago: University of Chicago Press, 1987, p. 148.

6. Ibid., p. 137.

7. Ibid.

8. Ibid., p. 132.

9. Gould describes this distinguishable human nature as "free agency and social individuality" [see Rethinking Democracy, p. 209]. This potential human nature, historically mediated and modified, is, admittedly, not always manifest and, in some people, never so. Nonetheless, it remains that which is (or can be) distinctive in human beings.

10. Nietzsche is correct, I believe, when he says that "it [the human will] needs a goal, -- and it will rather will nothingness than not will" [*Zur Genealogie der Moral, Dritte Abhandlung*, in *Werke. Kritische Gesamtausgabe* {WKG}, Hrsg. von Giorgio Colli & Mazzino Montinari, VI.2, S. 357. Berlin: Walter de Gruyter, 1967 -].

11. This rationale for satisfying needs of individuals as human beings is different from that which John Rawls urges in Political Liberalism for satisfying needs of individuals as citizens, that is, "so that they can take part in political and social life" [New York: Columbia University Press, 1996, p. 166]. Apart from the apparently more restricted scope of enablements associated with the need-satisfaction of citizens, his formula suffers from the vagueness of the expression 'take part'.

12. Critique of the Gotha Programme, in Karl Marx & Frederick Engels. Collected Works {MECW}, Vol. 24, p. 87. New York: International Publishers, 1989. It is frequently intimated, if not asserted, that the greater public expenditure necessary to implement socioeconomic and cultural rights, by contrast to civil and political rights, is an important consideration in favor of the latter, as opposed to the former. Yet, the economic costs to society of preserving (in distinction to improving) human life, of guarding (negative) liberty, which entails major outlays for both domestic "law and order" and "national defense", of maintaining representational and juridical systems, of compensating those who have a legal right to interest payments on the national debt, and of protecting the objectives of (frequently globalized) private property are indeed quite large. The argument against positive rights will also include ideologically motivated claims about the injustice of the "redistribution" of material values, the incompatibility between (negative) freedom and equality (the former deemed pre-eminent), the inefficiency of the inescapably bureaucratized

state, which works best when it has fewest responsibilities, the moral and practical superiority of charity over "welfare", and so on.

13. See Will Kymlicka, "Three Forms of Group-Differentiated Citizenship in Canada", in Benhabib, Democracy, pp. 159-161.

14 The points that I have stressed with respect to the status of human rights within the specific context of the nation-state are, I believe, consonant with the assertion by Przeworski that "The decisive step toward democracy is the devolution of power from a group of people to a set of rules." [Democracy, p. 14] Though his assertion is probably inspired, in particular, by the experience of Poland (and other formerly socialist countries, which were "guided" by the Party), it possesses general pertinence.

CHAPTER 6

NEGATIVE FREEDOM AND POSITIVE FREEDOM

In the Introduction, I stated that positive freedom, inherently comprising negative freedom, is crucial for democracy and that, indeed, democracy may be considered the empowering practice of positive freedom. Democracy is a form of life, in which individuals, interacting in some type of grouping and joined together by functionally significant common interrelationships, as well as by communal solidarity, cooperate on tasks and projects of collective relevance, in the process empowering the individuals more effectively and fully not only to participate, if possible, in the joint endeavors but also to derive meaningfulness in life in accordance with humanistic values.

The type of freedom typically considered necessary – and sufficient – for democracy is negative freedom, that is, the relative absence of constraints, in particular those humanly constructed, which disallow certain options for acting. Often disregarded as irrelevant, otiose or even pernicious is positive freedom, that is, the capacity, situated within limits and ordinarily in conjunction with other individuals, purposefully to control circumstances and outcomes. This capacity is constituted jointly by ability and opportunity, in other words, not only by cognitive, emotional and material resources, socially developed and sustained, enabling one to produce certain (types of) results but also by situated possibilities presented for the actual utilization of specific abilities.[1] Although positive freedom, as capacity or empowerment, and negative freedom, as absence of (humanly imposed) limitations on action, might be defined in terms of each other or, alternatively, in terms of some putatively more basic concept, so that neither is primary conceptually or programmatically, I attribute precedence to positive freedom for two reasons. [2]

In the first place, their relationship is not symmetrical, for the concept of positive freedom implicitly incorporates that of negative freedom, but not conversely. Implicit in positive freedom is the (relative) absence of humanly established impediments to the acquisition, development or exercise of capacities composing that freedom. By contrast, in situations characterized, for example, by powerlessness, extreme social marginalization or abandonment, negative freedom can exist (apart from positive freedom). "Freedom from" debilitating interference or encroachment does not itself ensure that "freedom to" achieve or attain something is real. One may be allowed, even encouraged, to do what one has neither the ability nor the opportunity to do. One may be in a condition of dis-ablement as much by either malign or "benign" neglect as by intentional coercion. Moreover, though the enjoyment of negative freedom can, in principle, be radically individualized, the exercise of positive freedom cannot, since the latter depends upon a social framework of interdependencies and mutually supportive interactions.

Nor does Gerald MacCallum's triadic analysis dislodge the asymmetry, [3] for the point here is not specification of the categories, respectively, of agent, constraint and objective but recognition of the difference between the way one is free from something and the way one is free to do something. Being "free from" involves absence of constraint, whereas being "free to do" involves, in addition, absence of deficiency, since otherwise the freedom to do is idle. Of course, deficiencies constrain and constraints reinforce deficiencies. Yet, the two are not the same, as can be noticed in the difference between removing a constraint and "removing" (that is, in fact, satisfying or making up for) a deficiency. Constraints can sometimes be neutralized by being disregarded; deficiencies cannot. Both constraints and deficiencies (or incapacities) constitute limitations; but they limit in different ways and their elimination proceeds differently. [4] To put the point alternatively, constraints defeating negative freedom restrict the range of application of 'can', while deficiencies/incapacities defeating positive freedom debar 'can' as such.

Associating (positive) freedom with control calls for consideration of two matters. Besides the fact that emphasizing control brings into relief the element of empowerment, it avoids the inadequacy of interpreting freedom as being capable of doing what one wants. If one wants simply to do nothing at all, then one will probably be capable of "doing" this, especially if nothing interferes with this mental torpor and/or physical quiescence. Whereas this might be an example of negative freedom, it is scarcely an example of freedom in the more robust (positive) sense, where this means capacity to control, not just an "ability" to do little or nothing. Of course, the capacity to control processes or outcomes does not itself ensure that they will materialize as intended – or even at all. Possessing the conditions or resources connected with the ability to control does not guarantee that one can also control the objective conditions requisite for the actual exercise of positive freedom. In this regard, it would be very misleading, indeed incorrect, to say that the possession of positive freedom means, for example, that one can "have one's own way", that one can engage in "self-rule", or that one can be the "author" of one's own life. One may, assuredly, develop, under favorable conditions, the decisional autonomy that the latter two situations ambiguously express. However, the freedom to choose or decide does not necessarily correlate with successful, productive actions that embody one's choices and decisions. In addition, (positive) freedom is not necessarily exemplified in cases where one's choices or actions are caused primarily by one's own desires, wants, etc. Such desires may be pathologically compulsive or obsessive. What is essential for positive freedom is that one's choices are controlled by one's deliberate, deliberative and knowledgeable reflections and that one's acts, consistent with such choices and empowered by socially facilitated capacities, more or less control intended outcomes. Parenthetically, I will mention that the social facilitation of capacities, including deliberated reflections, applies also to what is traditionally called "free will", in my judgment, therefore, a learned skill. [5]

The other matter requiring consideration is that both negative freedom and positive freedom can be employed for malevolent purposes, harmful to individuals and/or groups. To say that freedom is a good is to recognize its instrumental value independently of the kinds of ends envisioned. To say, without qualification, that freedom is good is to beg the question. The options allowed by negative freedom and the capacities of positive freedom can both serve exploitative, oppressive, destructive aims. That is why, in characterizing democracy as the empowering practice of positive freedom, I have regularly insisted upon its being oriented on humanistic values and goals. Dostoevsky's "underground man" should have confirmed for us that freedom can be used for egoistic, perverse, ultimately self-defeating ends. In a more contemporary fashion, Sen, noting that, according to standard economic theory, "rationality" resides in the internal consistency of choice together with the maximization of self-interest, has pointed out that one may consistently choose means that are counterproductive with regard to ends.[6] This may apply, as well, to self-interest, which can be misinformed and misdirected.

A second reason for attributing precedence to positive freedom is the following: if democracy involves social or communal control over affairs of common concern, it is the concept of positive, rather than exclusively negative, freedom that is uniquely important. Individuated positive freedom is measured by the extent of (socially developed) autonomous control. In a related manner, democracy is measured by the extent of social/communal, specifically cooperative, control directed toward deciding and managing policies and practices for groupings of individuals. The parallel is not fortuitous, for it is in the social dimension of positive freedom that the distinctively communal practice of democracy is grounded.

If negative freedom is given priority over, or at the expense of, positive freedom, there will be a tendency for freedom, generally speaking, to be viewed as possession of utilities and for democracy, in the context of the nation-state, to be construed as a type of political consumerism. A market model of democracy will predominate, with its own laws of supply and demand, wherein politicians function as entrepreneurs and voters behave as consumers. Under these conditions, democracy reduces to a "market equilibrium system",[7] which may facilitate, to an appreciable degree, both the satisfaction of citizens as consumers of political values as well as the hegemony of elites, who, controlling the production of these values, also substantially direct their distribution. However, if democracy implies a communal-type of self-regulation that is humanistically emancipating and empowering, then the market model is grievously inappropriate.

None of this is intended to impugn the importance of negative freedom. Justly distributed empowerment (which, though distributed equally, need not be equal in its distribution) within a society (or other grouping) cannot take place if some individuals dominate others, if social structures and procedures privilege some at the expense of others, if some people are coercively prevented from being in a position to be empowered. The claims of positive freedom (empowerment) are not satisfied, however, solely by an overall aggregation of capacities, however striking. Furthermore, if the normative value of negative freedom is in its proscription of domination and invidious coercion, then negative judgment should be pronounced not only on their state-political forms but also, for example, on their economic, gendered and racial forms, [8] remembering that one can dominate and coerce others by depriving them of what is needed, as well as by suppressing them.

It may be suggested that democracy can conflict with freedom (liberty), in that citizens can democratically restrict the range or the application of (negative) liberties. [9] Yet, establishing restrictions on what is socially permissible does not necessarily constitute an unjustifiable abridgement of the liberty to (seek to) act in whatever way one might wish, in particular when acts would be exploitative, oppressive, inhumane, etc. It is not sufficient to declaim that liberty is never "absolute". It is not, and would not be, even if there were no imposed restrictions at all; for one can only do what one <u>can</u> do. Besides, where democracy is the cooperative development and exercise of positive freedom, that is, empowered capacities, democracy does not conflict with the negative freedom that delineates the framework within which these capacities are furthered and can flourish.

In addition to the hypothesized conflict referred to in the preceding paragraph, it has been said that democracy might be incompatible with demands for efficiency.[10] There is no doubt that democracy, especially at the level of the nation-state, can be cumbersome procedurally and elusive substantively. Nevertheless, although an authoritarian regime may be more efficient in making the trains run on time, whether democracy is efficient or not depends very much upon what is meant by "efficient". As an instrumentalistic concept, efficiency is always "efficiency for" the realization of some purpose, task or goal. To say that something is efficient requires specification of that for which it is efficient as a means. Simply to announce, without further ado, that a procedure or arrangement is efficient is to leave open the question as to the end(s) for which it is supposedly efficient. These ends may be benign or malign, constructive or destructive, beneficial to some but decidedly not so to others, in other words, ends of the most diverse and disparate kinds. For example, one may be efficient in making a fool of oneself, or a country may be efficient in intimidating other countries. Determining whether democracy as the cooperative practice of positive freedom guided by humanistic values is efficient is clearly dependent upon whether the ends of this model of democracy are accepted (or at least are acceptable) and whether the experientially ascertained and empirically tested arrangements, prescriptions and procedures associated with this model do indeed promote its ends.

Apart from the theorized inefficiency of possible political arrangements and procedures, it seems to me that another reason not infrequently advanced for alleging a conflict or tension between democracy and efficiency is that some of the rules and regulations of the (quasi-democratic) state inhibit the efficiency (effectiveness) of operations in the capitalist economy, an argument that presupposes the priority of negative freedom. Assumed as virtually apodictic are the greater virtues of the "free enterprise" economy compared to the lesser virtues of the impositional state, as well as the irrelevance, indeed harmfulness, of any democratization of the economy.

A capitalist economy might be considered "efficient" in one or both of two senses: technical efficiency, which requires that "no more of any output can be produced without producing less of some other output"; and economic efficiency (identified with Pareto optimality), which requires that "no one can be made better off without making someone else worse off".[11] Instructively, Sen remarks that a society of either extreme wealth or extreme poverty could be Pareto optimal. [12] Doubtlessly, capitalist apologists would argue that the free enterprise system is not a zero-sum game but is (or can be) a positive-sum game, in which the rising tide of social wealth lifts not only those in yachts but also those in rowboats. Granted, substantial inequalities in the distribution of economic values may be consistent with increased utilities, as the aggregate of social wealth improves, for those at the lower end of the scale; but those individuals most likely will not experience any increase in their relative position on the social scale and, thus, any augmentation of their social empowerment in accord with democratic aims. The problem here of relative impoverishment in social power is analogous to that which obtains with Pareto optimality, where, as Sen explains, no attention is paid to "the distributional considerations regarding utility", that is, to interpersonal comparisons. [13]

Another metaphor which may be exploited is the one that says it is better to have a small piece of a very large pie that an equal piece of a very small pie. It can be admitted, on the one hand, that an equality of shared poverty and destitution is hardly a desideratum and, on the other, that (as discussed previously) the interests of many people may dictate preference for (the possibility of) enlarged economic utilities, whether or not there is an enhancement of democratic empowerment. [14] It cannot be proved that this kind of preference is either morally wrong or empirically unworkable. At the same time, if democracy is to be taken seriously, one must go beyond a consumerist model of predominantly self-interested well-being and look to a cooperative model that is oriented on the humanistic interests of everyone and that provides, so far as objective circumstances permit, empowered capacities appropriate both for agential "well-being", that is, productive meaningfulness in life, and for effectively shared participation in the resolution of common problems and the realization of common tasks. Even in a poor society or other grouping, democracy is possible, limited not by any inapplicability in principle, but by limitations on individual empowerment presented by the lack of material prerequisites. In an affluent society or other context, however, the presence of material prerequisites by no means ensures that there will be the common, cooperative concern for mutual empowerment, equally pertaining to each person, that is ingredient in democracy.

The theoretical and practical insufficiencies of merely negative freedom do not, as already acknowledged, deprive it of its own importance. Obviously, the empowered practice of positive freedom cannot exist in the face of gratuitous, inhibiting and debilitating constraints. Negative freedom is a defining condition of the "open society", which is not (yet) the democratic society. The negative freedom of the open society does not, as such, foster the development of democracy. Rather, it allows "spaces" within which the positive freedom of the democratic society can be nurtured and consolidated. Epigones of negative freedom often maintain that historical "advances in democracy" have been based upon opening up of possibilities associated with the dismantling of various political constraints. There is some truth in this, although the "advances" have been, more often than not, an untrammeling of capitalist objectives and ambitions. Capitalist ideologues of an earlier time thought that movement toward democracy could take place with the overturn of feudal economic relations, as socialist ideologues of the twentieth century believed that real democracy was forthcoming with the overthrow of capitalist economic relations. Doctrinaire capitalists have divorced the political "superstructure" from the social "base" (in theory, at least, but not in practice), whereas doctrinaire socialists have delimited the political superstructure in conformity with the social base. The former maneuver yields, at best, a kind of protodemocracy; the latter, a pseudodemocracy.

In closing this discussion on freedom, I want to express a reservation about Rawls's use of the term 'free' and what this use implies. He asserts that, with regard to individuals as citizens, they are free insofar as they can develop and pursue a conception of the good, are "self-authenticating sources of valid claims", and are capable of taking responsibility for the ends they hold. [15] Earlier, he had qualified the definition of free citizen slightly differently on the first two points: they have "moral power to form, to revise, and rationally to pursue a conception of the good" and "they regard themselves as self-originating sources of valid claims".[16] This definition of 'free' comports rather well with a perhaps Kantian understanding of an autonomous, self-legislating and responsible person with "free will". Yet, the individual who is free, in the context of my understanding of democracy, possesses more than mental powers to reflect, deliberate and decide on courses of action, along with responsibility to oneself and for one's ends and their related means. The free individual also possesses the socially developed capacities of positive (empowered) freedom that enable that individual to implement (within limits) those decisions and realistically to pursue those ends.

78

NOTES

1. The dialectic of ability and opportunity is fundamental here. Ability without opportunity is superfluous; opportunity without ability is empty. A question from Martin Luther King, Jr., quoted by Wilson, captures the latter situation in an eloquently simple manner: "What good is it to be allowed to eat in a restaurant if you can't afford a hamburger?" [The Truly Disadvantaged, p. 126] Together, ability and opportunity compose what might be called capacity, the essence of positive freedom. My use of 'positive freedom' is far removed from, even antipodal to, that which was elaborated, not altogether consistently, by Isaiah Berlin in Four Essays on Liberty [New York: Oxford University Press, 1970]. For example, my conception of positive freedom has nothing to do with a "higher self", with incorporation into a totalizing whole for the sake of "self-realization", with leading a "prescribed form of life", with being "forced to be free", or with ideals of social perfection and ultimate harmony. It is the case, to be sure, that something like the "positive freedom" depicted by Berlin has had its advocates, as attested by the following declaration: "the individual can attain his own true freedom only in the Party" [Arthur Kiss, Marxism and Democracy. Budapest: Akadémiai Kiadó, 1982, p. 300].

2. The first alternative has been defended by Joel Feinberg in Rights, Justice, and the Bounds of Liberty [Princeton: Princeton University Press, 1980, pp. 5-7], the second by Tim Gray in Freedom [Atlantic Highlands, NJ: Humanities Press, 1991, chapter 1].

3. See "Negative and Positive Freedom ", Philosophical Review, LXXVI, 1967.

4. The contrast, psychologically, between the status of forced subjugation (lack of negative freedom) and that of unimposed powerlessness (lack of positive freedom) seems to reinforce this difference. Subjugation issues, generally, in powerlessness; but the latter can exist in the absence of the former.

5. My emphasis upon the social sources of free will is perhaps parallel to that placed by Jean Cohen upon the conditions of decisional autonomy, which "could be said to presuppose the communicatively mediated processes of moral and ethical development that make practical reflection and reasoning possible" ["Democracy", p. 198].

6. See On Ethics, p. 13.

7. See Macpherson, Democratic Theory, pp. 78-79.

8. A reminder of the wider dimensions of negative freedom is evinced in the remark by Kagarlitsky that "The ability to resist fashion, to stand up to prevailing ideological trends and to the pressures of the market is no less important than a preparedness to stand up to the state." [Disintegration, p. 38].

9. This possibility is mentioned by Lawrence Crocker in Positive Liberty [The Hague: Martinus Nijhoff, 1980, p. 137].

10. See Mansbridge, Beyond Adversary Democracy, p. 299.

79

11. Sen, On Ethics, pp. 20-21.

12. Ibid., p. 31.

13. Ibid., p. 33. Additionally, the metaphor of a rising tide lifting everyone is specious. In the recent past in the United States, the average real income of the bottom twenty percent of the population decreased not only relatively but also absolutely [see David C. Korten, When Corporations Rule the World. San Francisco: Berrett-Koehler Publishers, 2001, p. 113].

14. I think that this latter distinction corresponds approximately to that made by Sen when he differentiates between "well-being" and "agency", where the first refers to personal advantage and the second to "achievements" [see On Ethics, pp. 43 & 59].

15. See Political Liberalism, p. 72.

16. "Justice as Fairness: Political Not Metaphysical", Philosophy and Public Affairs, Vol. 14, no. 3, 1985, p. 332

CHAPTER 7

JUSTICE, EQUALITY AND DIFFERENCE

I

In her valuable discussion of democracy, Gould asserts that "justice should be interpreted as a principle of equal rights to the conditions of self-development, or equal positive freedom".[1] There are a number of points here that are important: justice entails equal rights, such rights prioritize self-development (a better term than 'self-realization' or 'self-fulfillment'), and self-development is roughly equipollent with positive freedom. Previously, I have argued for equally applicable (human) rights to the conditions of positive freedom, that is, democratic empowerment. Now, I wish to consider, perhaps schematically, the concepts of justice and equality and their relationship with each other and with democracy.

Traditional wisdom has it that justice means treating equals equally and unequals unequally, in accordance with, and to the degree of, some relevant difference. The sense in which people are equal in a (stipulated) legal sense can be made sufficiently precise (though apparently some are "more equal" than others). However, what it means to say that they are equal in some other (non-trivial) sense is, in my opinion, disconcertingly vague. For example, reference may be made to people's being moral equals or having a status of moral equality. The problem here, I think, lies not so much with 'equal' as with 'moral'. If being a moral agent means that one can knowingly make intelligible and deliberative use of language incorporating conventionally moral terms and can understandingly accept responsibility for one's actions, then not everyone is

82

equally a moral agent. If being morally equal means having equal moral status, what kind of status is this? Is it an inherent or intrinsic status, whatever that might mean and however it might ostensibly be discerned? If it is an attributed status, then what is being attributed – and for what reason? It is my view that moral equality is an attributed status, established by human beings themselves in conformity with normative assumptions and designed to reinforce certain values.

Further, it is something of a commonplace to say that justice means getting what one deserves. The difficulty here is ambiguity more than vagueness. What is the criterion of desert? Is it what one is or what one does? For example, does a human being deserve respect simply by virtue of being human? Why might not other kinds of living things, as well as inanimate nature itself, deserve respect? If we give preference to human beings, I submit that it is not because they deserve it more. Respect, as special esteem, valorization or attribution of significance, has to do with particular regard for someone or something. Respect may be neither mutual nor of a moral type. When it is directed to human beings, it is not, I suggest, because of any inherent or transcendent value in them; for they are no more valuable in themselves than anything else in the universe. Rather, it is because of the surpassing value in our relationship with them. Accordingly, "moral respect" for persons exists because of our valued moral relationship with them, where 'moral' designates certain dynamic psychological/affective qualities of the relationship. In a genuine community with thoroughgoing mutuality and continuing solidarity, active moral respect, aligned with reciprocal trust, is possible. In the kind of society defined by the nation-state, moral respect among all members is overwhelmingly improbable and, in any case, not necessary, since the nation-state can function reasonably well if sufficient trust (however pragmatically motivated) is in evidence. This is so, because one can trust (perhaps cautiously) those whom one does not respect; but, I maintain, one cannot respect those whom one does not trust.

Perhaps the criterion of desert is what one does. Then, is the specific ("material") principle, for example, a particular kind of act, an achievement, effort, the social significance of an act, or some combination of the preceding? These types of criteria are fairly clearly indicated for the contexts of distributive justice and retributive justice, applying to both benefits and burdens (including punishment). As for compensatory justice, it is based upon what has been done to (not by) some individual or group, in an extended sense of 'done'.

These brief remarks are enough, I hope, to render plausible the claim that the category of justice which entails equal human rights is none of the three kinds mentioned in the foregoing paragraph. Although the assignment of (negative and positive) human rights may be formally similar to a distribution, it is not based upon individuals' "deserving" them. One does not, strictly speaking, deserve human rights, though one definitely ought to have them for the sake of (humanistically) empowered human life, itself implied by values that can be commonly affirmed. Thus, the category of justice embedded in my conception of democracy relates to the status of human beings as valorized by value-givers, who, in theory and in practice, attribute a normative (but not necessarily moral) status to human beings. I say "not necessarily moral", because I consider that which is categorized as moral to be different from what is categorized as non-moral, not by virtue of some unique conceptual, epistemological or ontological distinction, but by a difference in the kinds of purposes that they respectively serve.

In connecting justice with (equal) human rights to the necessary conditions for self-development, namely, the practice of positive freedom, justice is being taken in a substantive sense, that is, with regard to outcomes, not merely procedures. Democracy as mutual empowerment oriented on humanistic ends cannot be divorced from results, in particular that empowerment and those ends. To be sure, these results cannot be guaranteed; rather, what is guaranteed, so far as possible, is the social provision of relevant conditions by means of the satisfaction of relevant human needs, such that the prospects of obtaining those ends are optimized. Democracy is not a system and process that simply does things for people, but one wherein people are enabled to do things, together, for themselves. Conjoined with this substantive justice, and implicit in it, is the justice (fairness) of procedures that apportion the resources, etc., whereby needs can be realistically satisfied for each individual. Such justice in procedures is analogous in its logic to the procedural justice that should exist in contexts different from the satisfaction of needs in accordance with the prescriptions of rights. Not only does the substantive justice of the democratic project not guarantee particular or invariable outcomes, it does not try to ensure equal outcomes. Correspondingly, what justice requires is not material equality for all but material sufficiency for each. Justice seeks to ensure, under the objective conditions prevailing, that all equally benefit, to the extent possible, from outcomes, that no one is excluded, and that no one benefits at the expense of others. All equally benefit, in that enabling means and opportunities are made available to all; but what one does with these is another matter. Whereas one can be prevented from utilizing these means and opportunities for exploitative and oppressive purposes, one cannot be forced (or otherwise manipulated) to use them wisely or successfully, since force is incompatible with the kind of cooperative mutuality that democratic practice envisions. Incidentally, given that democracy is the practice of positive freedom, the preceding point affirms, in its own way, that a human being cannot be "forced to be free".

Democracy, then, focuses not only on the procedurally fair apportioning of means/resources that satisfy basic human needs but also on the equitably mutual empowerment that this satisfaction facilitates. It should be clear that the enabling satisfaction, equally, of individuals' needs does not mean that individuals have equal power but that they are, equally, empowered to the extent that their individual capacities allow. Since empowered individuals, exercising positive freedom, are thereby productive and creative in both individual and collective activities, it is perhaps not far-fetched to denominate the justice that embodies recognition of this status as "productive" justice (or justice in production) by contrast to the distributive justice that bears upon the means for empowerment.[2] In an important sense, distributive justice emphasizes "having", while productive justice emphasizes "doing", the latter a distinguishing feature of (humanistic) meaningfulness in human life.[3]

Democratic equality of persons is, as mentioned above, an attributed status that mandates how they ought to be viewed and treated. Accordingly, perhaps it is more precise to say, not that individuals are equal members of some society or community or that they are equal citizens, and so on, but that they are equal as members or as citizens, that is, they are equally members, citizens, etc. This adverbial construction may be extended: not equal power but equally being empowered, with respect to engaging in democratic projects and in creating a meaningful life.[4] As remarked already, democratic empowerment is always situated within the framework of real possibilities of both abilities and opportunities. It is not unjust for some to have and to do more than others, provided the having and the doing of the former are not at the exploited expense of the latter and do not prevent them, in principle, from having and doing enough themselves.

With respect to these issues, it is understandable that Rawls would want to stress, in line with a political conception of justice and a non-metaphysical conception of the person, a cognate conception of the equality of individuals as citizens, according to which "citizens are equal in virtue of possessing, to the requisite minimum degree, the two moral powers and the other capacities that enable us to be normal and fully cooperating members of society".[5] These powers and capacities comprise "a capacity for a sense of justice and for a conception of the good", together with "judgment, thought, and inference connected with these powers".[6] Citizen, that is, political, equality consequently appears to involve possession, to an equally minimum degree, of capacities that would enable an individual to be a "fully cooperating member of society".

The conceptions that Rawls advances are, it is obvious, carefully thought through. There is recognition of the relevance for the role of citizen of what might be construed as a basic competence. If an individual, as citizen, is to be a fully cooperating member of society over a lifetime, an individual who, acknowledging relationships of reciprocity, engages in the deliberations of "public reason", then certain powers and other capacities are not only desirable but necessary (to the requisite minimum degree). However, apart from the fact that some citizens will not, sometimes or most of the time, actively participate in sustaining the collective political institutions and procedures of society, other citizens simply <u>cannot</u> do so. Appreciably incapacitated citizens, who do not possess competencies to "the requisite minimum degree" and therefore cannot participate in the collective project that is political society, can nevertheless participate in the personal project that is life. Moreover, such citizens are not likely to be part of an "overlapping consensus".

For Rawlsian liberal democracy, fair conditions for political participation are crucial, as are reasonable and conscientiously cooperative participants. With respect to the tasks and processes of democratic governance, such conditions are indeed essential. Yet, if democracy is something more, namely, the activity of common empowerment motivated by common concern, designed to enable individuals to participate more fully in life itself, then, while the participatory prerogatives of citizens may be properly based upon competencies, their human needs, whose satisfaction is necessary for whatever degree of individual empowerment may be possible, are equally compelling, independently of those competencies. "Public reason" and its deliverances may plausibly be the privilege of legally competent adults, who discuss and debate about "constitutional essentials and matters of basic justice"; but these issues bear upon the means for facilitating something like democracy in a particular kind of setting, that is, the nation-state, not upon the ends of democracy germane to any kind of social context.

To be sure, the entire logic of Rawls's argument regarding justice, his view that the domain of the political (consisting of qualified citizens) is different from those of (voluntary) associations and ("affectional") personal relationships, [7] his view that constitutional foundations engender a consensus that "establishes democratic electoral procedures for moderating political rivalry within society", [8] his appeal to "our considered convictions", "basic intuitive ideas" and "public traditions" adjusted by "reflective equilibrium", [9] and so on, make clear that, insofar as he is concerned with democracy, it is conceived as a form of the nation-state. Given what he declares is the basic problem of political liberalism, namely, "How is it possible that deeply opposed though reasonable comprehensive doctrines may live together and all affirm the political conception of a constitutional regime?", [10] this focus upon a national society is cogent. Specifying how a just society can accommodate reasonable (and inescapable) pluralism is something Rawls carries out with insight and analytical acuity. However, if the conception of democracy applies equally (indeed more promisingly) to contexts other than the nation-state, and if this broadening of the conception entails a rethinking of numerous principles and concepts, then, in my opinion, Rawls's standpoint is defective because incomplete. In addition, if one takes into account various feminist criticisms (considered later in this chapter on "difference"), his interpretation of pluralism is one-sided and his expectation of consensus is implicitly hegemonic.

Furthermore, Rawls's use of a social contract model to explicate the principles of justice (and, by extension, democracy) would not likely be applicable to contexts for democracy other than the nation-state. For example, is the heuristic of a social contract relevant for marriage, family, various voluntary associations, etc.?

Indeed, Pateman contends that theorists of the social contract, including Rawls, typically ignore the sexual contract between men and women, especially husbands and wives, that functions characteristically to the subordinated

88

disadvantage of the latter.[11] Forgetting or obscuring patriarchal relations of domination and subordination in the contexts of sex and/or marriage is facilitated by focusing primary attention on the public sphere of national society and the nation-state in which, as for Rawls, a social contract model is germane. Interestingly, Pateman disagrees with those who believe that, "if contract is extended into the private sphere, inequalities of status between men and women in marriage must disappear".[12] In her view, dimensions of patriarchy will endure within a private social contract applied to marriage, for example, since the concept of the contracting "individual", who is formally and procedurally an ostensibly sex-neutral and genderless entity, will be understood largely in masculinist terms. [13]

Moreover, Pateman, responding to Rawls's A Theory of Justice, argues that it is most questionable whether the interchangeable deliberators of the original position, construed as a "device of representation", are able to take relevant sexual differences into account. [14] Again, since Rawls's social contract is intended to apply specifically to the conventionally understood political realm that reflects a constitutional regime, he would probably reply that he is not proposing contracts for such "affectional" relationships as marriage. Insofar as individuals in Political Liberalism are seen essentially as citizens, not as metaphysical selves -- or as embodied selves, for that matter [15] -- this limitation of the social contract has its own logic, reinforced by the outlook that parties behind the veil of ignorance do not know, among other things, the sex and gender of the people that the parties "represent".[16] However, even if one methodologically restricts the discussion to the nation-state, thereby disregarding the contexts of "private" life, where considerations of democracy and justice are equally, if not more, important, Rawls's principle that the veil of ignorance is designed to inhibit any tendency to propose, or to expect others to accept, conceptions that favor one's own actual or anticipated social position [17] explicitly requires, if Pateman is right about endemic patriarchalism, that sex and/or gender be taken into account -- something difficult, furthermore, for contractually undifferentiated, intersubstitutable individuals behind the veil of ignorance.

In addition, do our "considered convictions" speak unequivocally about justice and democracy in economic arrangements, not to mention, among other things, gendered or racial relations? To be told that the contract-generating "original position" is simply a device of representation is, in my opinion, not altogether helpful. Since the parties in the original position do not necessarily exhibit the "moral psychology" of actual persons, [18] it appears that the contractors only represent what (ideally) reasonable people, prepared to cooperate, would agree to. Of course, reasonable people do what is reasonable; but is this conceptually pleonastic? Even if it is not, there remain two issues. First, what reason is there to believe that the contractors in the original position would agree on the two principles of justice that Rawls announces? Second, what reason is there to assume that "actual persons" would comply willingly with those principles once established? [19] For my part, I would argue that the basic rights and liberties of the first principle are focused on negative rights and liberties to the derogation of positive ones. Further, while granting that social and economic inequalities attached to offices and positions may appropriately issue under conditions of fair equality of opportunity, I contend that such inequalities often render the opportunities themselves elusive for many people.[20] Furthermore – though what I will say may be both unduly terse as well as based on a misreading of Rawls – I submit that, with regard to the least advantaged members of society, the point is not merely to compensate them for their disadvantages but, in particular, to neutralize, so far as possible, the negative social effects of any disadvantage. This latter principle, it seems to me, is a counterpart to the discounting of non-deserved advantages in Rawls's original position.

Returning to the main discussion, to treat people justly is to treat them as equal in some relevant respect(s) or to treat them as unequal according to some relevant difference(s). In her exposition of justice and difference, Young shows that "equality as the participation and inclusion of all groups sometimes requires different treatment for oppressed or disadvantaged groups".[21] It remains, in order to give suitable orientation to this equalization of equality, to furnish plausible normative and descriptive criteria for identifying such groups. Although there will be ongoing debate about which groups fall within these two categories, I do not think that, if humanistic values are assumed, the task will be unusually problematic, in spite of the fact that some oppressive groups claim to be oppressed themselves and numerous individuals and groups who have benefited from previous advantages at others' expense allege that a loss of these socially preferential advantages means that they are now "disadvantaged". For her part, Young characterizes an oppressed group as one that has been subjected to exploitation, marginalization, powerlessness, cultural imperialism and violence.[22] Her analysis of equality is more nuanced and unambiguous than is that of Benhabib, who avers that impartiality requires considering "the best interests of all equally".[23] However, as Young argues cogently, equal treatment requires giving special consideration to certain types of difference, a point accentuated also by Phillips, who maintains that concepts such as equality call for a gendered interpretation. [24] A relevant example of this is set forth by Fraser, who asserts that equality between women and men requires, among other things, dismantling of the existing gender division of labor, which substantially disadvantages women. [25] In general, equal treatment often consists in the equalization of the (prospectively) favorable results of such treatment. Differential means are utilized to promote the equality of ends. As for impartiality, it may well be unfair sometimes to be impartial – a point that I will try to develop in a later chapter.

To treat people equally, <u>simpliciter</u>, may well be unjust. Clearly, the (procedurally) equal application of a (substantively) unjust rule is itself unjust. Does this mean that the fair, non-discriminatory (procedurally just) application of an irrelevantly discriminatory (substantively unjust) rule is conceptually contradictory? Not necessarily, I suppose. People may be treated equally badly in anti-democratic contexts. For example, they may be equally oppressed and subjugated under authoritarian or totalitarian regimes. It will be said – and rightly so – that an unjust (discriminatory) rule, even if applied equally, fails normatively insofar as it is based upon an irrelevant difference. The question of what renders a difference relevant is complex and contentious. For the purposes of democracy, differences can be relevant in the specification of means but not in the prioritized prescription of ends. Thus, the satisfaction of needs will, perforce, take into account differences in their kind and extancy; but there are no relevant differences among human beings that would discountenance this satisfaction, in principle, for some of them. Democratic justice presupposes commonality and mutuality, an inclusiveness that willingly accepts differences in "identity", so long as these differences are expressed within the framework of humanistic values.

In my view, the substantive justice of a rule (prescription, etc.) has to do with the pre-eminent good that the rule is designed to serve. For democracy, this orienting good, not as such proved (or validated) but consistently affirmed (thus valorized), is the commonly empowered practice of positive freedom in line with humanistic values promoting individual and social meaningfulness in life. An alternative view is that justice is substantiated by appeal to the concept of right rather than the concept of good. [26] On this account, an unjust rule cannot be consistently universalized. If this is a psychological assessment, then it is surely false, if, that is, the attitudes of martyrs or masochists can be deemed probative. A stronger claim, reminiscent of Kant, would be that universalization of an unjust rule would be logically self-defeating, analogously to the putative non-universalizability of principles that permit exceptions to truth-telling or promising. Admittedly, to formulate and articulate a rule that allows carte blanche exceptions is to stultify that rule. However, some plausible "exceptions" can be built into the rule, constituting a more complexly qualified rule than one without the "exceptions"; and the more qualified rule can be, in principle, just as universally prescriptive as any other. No one can guarantee always to tell the truth, in part because one may not know the truth or because one is "honestly" mistaken. At most, one could always <u>attempt</u> to tell the truth, a situation that might or might not be reassuring to auditors. Again, one may make a promise in good faith. Yet, one cannot categorically promise to keep a promise, because one cannot always control the conditions under which it might be kept. Even Kant recognizes that "if one ought to, one can". Hence, if one cannot, objectively, keep a promise or if keeping the promise would conflict with another, equally imperative "ought", then the obligatoriness, however "categorical", implied by that act of promise-making is defeasible.

Democracy need not involve the unqualified universalization of principles on the grounds that the logic of "right" requires it – though principles/rules are properly universalized qualifiedly for this or that context ("universe" of application). If anything, what is important is the "universalization" of "good", that is, the widest possible realization of (humanistic) values defining and directing the aims and tasks of democratic practice. The value imperative central to democracy is indeed "hypothetical"; but this only implies that the commitment to democratic aims and practice can be ignored, treated in a desultory manner or abandoned. So long, however, as the commitment is intact and effective, that imperative and that practice are organically and integrally linked. [27]

Contrary to the insights of some people, I find no antinomy, in democracy at least, between equality and freedom (liberty). The case for an opposition between them takes on some plausibility only by an unacknowledged truncation of their respective meanings. Freedom (liberty) is construed solely in the negative sense, and equality is taken to mean the (doubtlessly coerced) equalization of results. The argument then appeals to the fact that freedom, the absence of involuntarily incurred restrictions/constraints of a social or political kind, will normally lead to significant differences in achievement, acquisition, performance, etc., by those who operate under its protection. Given these inevitable and legitimate inequalities, the demand for equality in, that is, for equalization of, results unjustifiably calls for a realignment in these results, perhaps by a redistribution of material values, positions or other advantages. Thus, equality can be established only at the expense of freedom, and freedom can be preserved only by discounting equality. Conservative ideologues, as well as some liberals, are especially fond of this argument. In its own terms, the argument has a certain logic. However, it is well known that one can argue validly from false premises; and, in this argument, the premises incorporate definitions of 'freedom' and 'equality' that distort what these terms can, and should, mean, thereby rendering the premises spurious. From the standpoint of democracy, I submit, freedom is empowered practice consonant with the solidarity of cooperation and oriented on humanistic values. Creative achievement rather than predatory acquisition, along with production of deeds rather than accumulation of things, are what are essential here. A freedom that sanctions and/or protects exploitation, domination, and so on, is not democratic freedom. Equality, for its part, is, on one hand, the equality of humanistically valorized and attributed status and, on the other, the equality of consideration (treatment) regarding the application of rules and procedures concerning, for example, the satisfaction of basic human needs. Differences in social/political standing, material possessions or accumulated advantages are compatible with democracy, so long as they are neither derived from the exploitation or oppression of anyone nor used for purposes of exploitation or oppression. Under democracy, it is not expected that all will have equal endowments, equal achievements or equal successes; but it is expected that the endowments of each equally will be developed, that each equally will be enabled, so far as possible, to achieve personally satisfying results (consistent with humanistic values), and that each equally will be successful (to the extent that "fate" permits) in constructing a cooperatively meaningful existence of not insignificant proportions. In this process, unequal capacities can be, equally, fostered and sustained. [28] To any charge that such expectations are utopian, I would reply that they identify and give orientation to tasks for democracy but do not, to be sure, constitute promises made on its behalf. In brief, democracy is a

94

continuing project, never a consummated state of affairs.

The uses of terms such as 'freedom', justice' and 'equality' are manifold, labile and sometimes obliquitous. Robert Dahl states that he finds a paradox in the fact that Americans, by and large, endorse the ethos of egalitarianism, yet willingly tolerate significant inequalities in actual practice. [29] To the extent that this is true, I believe that it reflects a rather persistent tendency to limit the application of equality to opportunity, but not to enabling conditions and resources. "Equal opportunity" has become an estimable ideal and standard. It is a value integral to freedom and, hence, to democracy. There are, though, at least two problems related to its use. The first has been noted already: the emphasis on opportunities, completely appropriate in context, often occurs to the neglect of enabling powers, needed resources, etc., without which one cannot "take advantage" of opportunities. The other problem has to do with the very meaning of 'opportunity' itself, in particular the sense of "having" an opportunity. Hoping to avoid too much in the way of "hair-splitting" analyses, I will limit myself to the following general comments. An opportunity is a "circumstantial" possibility that is normally viewed as desirable or worthwhile. To "have" an opportunity is to be in a position, such that, if one knows about the possibility, one can voluntarily seek to realize it. I say "voluntarily", since the notion of an opportunity's being forced on someone seems Pickwickian. Further, one strives to make use of an opportunity to do something or for something, in that, in the absence of constraints inconsistent with the opportunity, one attempts to obtain what the opportunity presents. In short, roughly speaking, to say that one "has" an opportunity is to say that one can (or could) attempt to realize the possibility that it represents. The point of all this for Dahl's remark is that "equal opportunity" usually means simply "equally available possibility", where the possibility is not constricted by discriminatory or other irrelevant deterrents, arbitrarily instituted. An opportunity is thus a reflection of negative freedom. That people accept, and may well energetically endorse, equal opportunity suggests two considerations. In the first place, there is the attitude that differences in outcomes are primarily an individual's own doing. This individualization of success and failure (see Michael Lewis again) means that the belief in egalitarian opportunity comports nicely with the acceptance of inequalities of outcomes. In the second place, there is the associated belief that ensuring equal opportunity (as distinct from empowerment) is sufficient as a collective social/political responsibility and, therefore, that it is enough to avoid interfering, officially or unofficially, with others in their attempts to avail themselves of opportunities – but not necessary collectively to ensure their feasible empowerment, so that the attempts might be, so far as possible, realistic. It might be objected that the principle of equal opportunity implies something stronger, namely, "equal access". In reply, I would argue that the former principle does not imply the latter, although the converse is valid. Equal access involves more than equal possibility to attempt. It includes, as well, equally making available the means whereby the attempt can be at least minimally practicable.

Equal opportunity, then, is necessary for democratic justice, but not at all sufficient. Frequently, moreover, it is invoked abstractly by disregarding pertinent historical background. Apropos here is the observation by Wilson that programs based upon principles of equal [negative] rights or equal opportunities are inadequate "because they are not designed to address the substantive inequality that exists at the time discrimination is eliminated" [30] Wilson proposes, instead of equality of opportunity, a different focus, namely, an "equality of life chances" that recognizes a serious obstacle for many individuals in the paucity of "the competitive resources associated with their economic-class background". [31] To the extent that one's "life chances" are involved in some form of "competition", it is surely fair not only to apply the "rules of the game" in an equal manner but also to equalize, to the extent that one's competency and motivation allow, the resources with which the game is played. Such is a competitive model of social justice. My concern regarding the important context of "life chances" is that, often in a distinctly competitive milieu, not only are there "winners' and "losers", but losers "lose out", perhaps permanently, as well. For social life, in general, there may be an appropriate competition for positions, benefits, rewards, recognition, etc.; but matters like the satisfaction of basic needs, the development of empowering capacities, and the attainment of humanistic meaningfulness in life should not be subject to a competition that leaves some advantaged at the expense of others disadvantaged.

II

One of the most complex and contentious issues connected with the theory and practice of democracy is it relationship to "difference", that is, to individuals and, especially, groups who define their identities in specific ways and who want both to preserve and to express their difference within the context of a democratic polity. Difference, in the context of the nation-state, is sometimes seen as, at best, a relatively innocuous manifestation of a group's distinguishing, perhaps anomalous, character, displayed most appropriately in the spaces of non-public life. Alternatively, difference may be viewed as, at worst, a divisive, even repugnant, expression of antagonism, separateness and intractability. Difference is constituted differently, that is, there are different kinds of difference: it may be based upon gender, race and/or ethnicity, nationality, language, life-style, cultural heritage, or other factors. In light of the ascendancy of cultural politics and the general disregard of, and disdain for, a socialist type of politics, difference based upon class does not play a prominent expository or explanatory, much less normative, role. [32] In remarking the change in focus from class difference to differences, say, of gender, race and ethnicity, Phillips brings out a most significant consideration: whereas, previously, the aim was to achieve a type of equality by dismantling, hence overcoming, (class) difference, non-class differences of gender, etc., cannot be similarly eliminated; instead, inequality must be overcome by means of a type of equality that contains and preserves difference itself. [33]

The question obviously and insistently arises concerning what is to be done about difference from the standpoint of the ostensibly democratic nation-state, which purports to consider individuals (and, by extension, groups) equally. Refined and benevolent references to the importance of "appreciating" multiculturalism are not sufficient here; for the point is not merely the sophisticated awareness of difference but its explicit incorporation into the unsettled and unsettling processes of social and political contestation. [34] Some may hope (and believe) that otherwise disruptive and discordant difference can be overcome either through bargaining and compromise, by analogy to what is supposed to ensue from the contestation of political parties – a type of "difference" with which liberal democracy is comfortable – or through some sublation (*Aufhebung*) of differences in a higher synthesis. The foregoing analogy is flawed, however. Political parties are, with some restrictions and exceptions, authorized to act in the political arena. Cultural difference groups are usually merely permitted to act therein, if that. The two major political parties in the United States disagree primarily about means, not ends. Difference groups often have disparate ends compared to one another. Whereas political parties give consent, difference groups are limited to giving advice. On the other hand, any synthesis of deeply instantiated difference – in the absence of a spurious unity grounded in coercion – is exceedingly unlikely in fact, as well as objectionable, humanistically speaking, in principle.

If difference is here to stay, the democratic task is to integrate it constructively. Integration, it should be recognized, is not at all the same as assimilation. Concomitantly, equality is not the same as similarity. Integration is a structure and dynamic in which difference is preserved, accorded "voice" and worked into coordinated activity on projects of common concern and value. In other words, integration is a coordination of functions, not a transubstantiation of identities. Assimilation, by contrast, is a smoothing out of difference, a hegemonic homogenization in which, as Young says, "the privileged groups implicitly define the standards according to which all will be measured", a process that perpetuates the disadvantages of those seeking, or expected, to be assimilated. [35] Young adds that the assimilationist ideal presupposes "humanity in general" and consequently is part of the "humanist" ideal. But this is so only if 'humanism' designates a universalistic onto-axiological standpoint. My own use of 'humanistic' assumes none of this and is designed simply to refer to certain humane values.

Difference can be constructive as well as destructive. [36] It is difficult to know which alternative has been more salient historically. Of course, the presence of negatively consequential difference implies neither that positive difference is diminished in value not that differences, in general, should be transcended. A major problem is to spell out criteria that will make it possible to determine which kinds of difference are relevant and positive for the improvement of democratic practice. On a conventional (usually liberal) pluralist model of democracy, the kinds of difference that are highlighted are those of interest and opinion, as they bear upon possible action in the public political sphere. Here is found the familiar phenomenon of the plurality of contending "interest groups", which seek to use, or at least influence, public power for their own benefit and whose competing interests the (typically non-neutral) state is supposed to accommodate in one way or another. However, as I understand it, the politics of difference is something other than the competitive pluralism of adversary democracy. Difference groups will surely want to defend and pursue their own interests at various levels. Yet, I think that there are several features which can distinguish sociocultural difference groups from the traditional type of interest group. [37]

First, a difference group normally wants to maintain its integrity, cohesion and continuity, whatever its political prospects, whereas an interest group functions largely as a provisional collocation of individuals associated for tactical political purposes. One way to stress the contrast is to say that a difference group professes to have a distinct "identity" that constitutes its members distinctively.

Second, a difference group can make a contribution to the ongoing democratization of social life in general, whereas an interest group – unless it is part of the power elite – usually exerts an influence only on political activity, and that intermittently and qualifiedly. Third, following the argument of Young, an especially relevant difference evinced by some groups is that they are oppressed or disadvantaged, whereas an interest group can probably claim only to be disregarded or marginalized. According to Young, group representation in the public arena should not apply to interest groups or to "ideological" groups bound solely by shared political beliefs but should apply to social groups, that is, to collectives of people "who have affinity with one another because of a set of practices or way of life".[38] There will, of course, be substantial, sometimes intemperate, disagreement about which groups are "oppressed" of "disadvantaged". My own suggestion is that these terms should be understood with reference to socially and politically structured situations and processes that subject groups so designated to anti-humanisitc consequences, wherein they are systematically denied, or deprived of, capacities that enable meaningful participation in the life of society as a democratized practice. This by no means calls either for a self-righteous (often arrogant) condescension on the part of more powerful groups in society or for any kind of diffidence or abasement on the part of the less powerful. In particular, the oppressed and disadvantaged have no obligation to forgive and forget. What is needed is not harmony, which is frequently superficial and one-sided in its expectations, but an emancipatory cooperation which, by the way, is not a sign of weakness.

Some difference may be, for all practical purposes, insignificant with respect to the democratization of society. A rather more complex and disputable issue has to do with what types of difference are pernicious and unworthy of valorization. Not everyone is above reproach. Sometimes even oppressed or disadvantaged groups will oppress (or repress) their own individual members for the sake of operational unity and solidarity. Phillips pointedly remarks that, not infrequently, groups or movements that have proffered pertinent critiques of universalizing, difference-ignoring essentialism have, at the same time, established their own essentialisms that define identity in a dogmatic, conformist manner and that are used to "discipline" the attitudes and conduct of members of the group. [39] Moreover, she states that subordinated and excluded groups should be expected to deal honestly with their own biases, to eschew an exclusionary or separatist politics and to avoid that kind of "communication" that is stifled by the "deafness of resentment".[40] Her concern is not that oppressed or marginalized groups should adjust themselves to the partialities and prejudices of groups with more power. Instead, "the ultimate goal remains the forging of common cause across the boundaries of difference", in order to work collaboratively for progressive change. [41] Concurring with this, I will add two comments: first, a lack of operational, "experimental" solidarity among such groups tends to leave the status quo intact by default and is therefore objectively conservative; second, even if this or that group cannot wholly understand where another group is "coming from", at least it can agree with the other where they hope to be "going" together.

Externally, some oppressed groups may (seek to) oppress other oppressed groups. The politics of difference, customarily conjoined with "identity politics", establishes the valued identity of a group in terms, as much as anything, of its difference from other groups. This can lead to the embodiment of difference in ways that are imperiously separatist, programmatically antagonistic and narrowly exclusivistic. [42] Whatever the difference that difference makes for those who are different, its relevance for democracy lies in at least three considerations. Democracy acknowledges and welcomes difference that is consistent with humanistic values, not merely for the sake of the richness of social life but also for the creative inputs that difference can provide. Further, as a practice of empowerment, democracy seeks to overcome, not difference itself, but the social disablement and disadvantage that attend certain kinds of difference. Moreover, as a cooperative activity, democracy attempts to show the possibility and the importance of working together non-hegemonically, in order to promote, perhaps in different ways, the realization of commonly beneficial tasks and aims.

As "difference" is philosophically and politically problematic, so is its theoretical counterpart, "identity". Dialectically interrelated, identity is exhibited concretely in difference, while difference is a substantive marker of identity. In the remainder of this chapter, I will adduce some remarks about identity and offer a few of my own, including comments bearing upon democracy and identity.

To begin with, what category of entity is it whose identity is of concern? Individuals have identities, as do assorted groupings including the nation-state. Much of the discussion and debate today about identity has to do with collections of individuals rather than with discrete individuals or the nation-state itself. This is so, because of the urgency of the question regarding the role of, and the response to, groups within the latter. At the same time, the phenomenology of personal identity may well shed light upon the nature of the identity of groups; and the dynamics of national identity have many analogies to that of social group identity.

It has become something of a commonplace to assert that identity is "constituted" in one way or another. Two questions (among others) immediately present themselves: what does 'constitute' mean, and how (that is, on the basis of what) does this constituting take place. I must confess that I sometimes experience a sort of conceptual vertigo when faced with the apparently bottomless reservoir of meanings that can be associated with 'constitute'. For present purposes, I will take it to signify that what is constituted is produced, determined, constructed and defined in certain of its important (perhaps most important) features by that which does the constituting. Thus, to say that identity is constituted is to claim that its existence and nature depend more or less definitively upon that which is constitutive. A further complication enters into the picture here. In one sense, identity is that by virtue of which one can be identified or picked out, say, within an ambient context. For example, one might be identified as the person standing next to the window or the person who has been assigned seat 12B on the airplane. These "identities" are typically transient, disposable and, for that matter, can apply to inanimate objects. By contrast, the type of identity considered and contested in cultural (and other) politics is self-consciously affirmed and valorized by those who embrace it as a point of reference and orientation in their understanding of themselves. Others may not comprehend this identity or may, as history amply testifies, impute an identity that is demeaning and dehumanizing. These situations remind of the (perhaps unwanted) indistinctness about difference or of the malignant disparagement of it.

One way to sort out the etiology of (group) identity is to distinguish, as Gould does, between ascriptive identity and that which is voluntarily acquired. Identity, in the former sense, is "constituted", but not because of one's own deliberate choice, whereas, in the latter sense, identity is shaped largely by one's chosen affiliations. [43] Young accords primacy to the second category of identity, arguing that group identity is defined not in terms of "a set of fixed attributes that clearly mark who belongs and who doesn't" but in terms of "a social process of interaction and differentiation in which some people come to have a particular affinity ... for others", which does not presuppose any common human nature and which may well shift over time. [44] To the objection that, for example, racial and gender identities are based upon "fixed attributes", one could reply by making use of Gould's argument that ascribed identities associated with race and gender are not simply a function of skin color or sex, since "what constitutes a relevant difference in social and political terms with regard to race and gender is ... what has been made of these by social and historical construal, largely by discrimination and oppression".[45] This fact about ascriptively constituted identities is especially important for democratization across difference.

With regard to voluntarily acquired identities, affinities prompt and reinforce the association of individuals, who come to identify with each other; but association, as such, does not necessarily engender affinity identification. Indeed, associated individuals may be, apart from calculations of prudence and benefit, largely indifferent to one another. [46] The identity of a group can be ascribed from without or from within. It is sometimes the case that "our identities are defined in relation to how others identify us". [47] One hopes that this circumstance is seldom as starkly demoralizing as that portrayed in Sartre's No Exit. However, the external ascription of (group) identity can pose serious problems for democratic justice and equality, when such ascription is malevolently prejudicial or callously dominating in intent – and even when, in spite of the best intentions, it is either gravely misinformed or thoughtlessly paternalistic.

As for the immanent ascription of (group) identity, the problems, though different, are no less troublesome. Perhaps the main issue is whether there exists an inscribed identity that is "essential", such that social group differences "are fixed essences given once and for all, with traits that are homogeneously distributed among all the group members". [48] Besides questions about the prevalence and genesis of a difference (for example, women, by comparison to men, are said to be more caring and nurturing), there are at least two kinds of misgivings. To take an example, appeal by women to essentialist notions of gender can reinforce existing stereotypes and confine women within existing gender divisions. [49] Perhaps the privatization of gender essence could be obviated. A more valuable development, with regard to democratization and its conditions, would be the socialization of both women and men into the mentality and practice of care. A second, rather more theoretical problem is that group essentialism reflects the same logic of abstract universality that the emphasis on group difference aims to overcome. [50] The erasure of difference can prejudicially affect not only groups as a whole but also individuals within groups. From the standpoint of democracy, individual differences are crucial with respect to the equal satisfaction of human needs, while group differences are pivotal with respect to the interplay of power relations. Correspondingly, both individual and group identities must be taken into account. Phillips, meanwhile, extends a critical word of caution. The engagement of differences with each other can yield, ideally, a perhaps productive politics of "mutual challenge and disruption". Yet, democracy conceived as a contestation of identities, she claims, not only is removed from actual political practice today but also tends to generate unproductive antagonism and resentment.[51] While this might well characterize some "identity" groups, the politics of adversary contest between "interest" groups is more likely to do so. Indeed, insofar as adversary democracy is the paradigm for the liberal democratic nation-state, groups may not so much make a contribution to the common cause as try to obtain as much of the common power as they can. If, at the level of the nation-state, it were possible, to some degree, to move beyond the structures and processes of adversary democracy to a more cooperative model, then, to that degree, non-oppressive identities and differences would serve both to fructify the shared deployment of common tasks and to give specific focus and measure to the empowerment of individuals (and groups) as the core of democratic practice.

Fraser advances a more comprehensive and, in my opinion, substantive critique. As she sees it, neither anti-essentialism (which views all identities as repressive and all differences as exclusionary) nor multiculturalism (which tends to regard all identities and differences as worthy of recognition and affirmation) "provides a basis for distinguishing democratic from anti-democratic identity claims, just from unjust differences".[52] Anti-essentialism cannot adequately distinguish emancipatory identity claims from oppressive ones, nor benign differences from pernicious ones. In addition, it cannot specify clearly which identity claims support inequality and domination or which differences are compatible with democracy. [53] The pluralist version of multiculturalism deals with difference uncritically, ignoring its relation to inequality. Moreover, "it treats difference as pertaining exclusively to culture. The result is to divorce questions of difference from material inequality, power differentials among groups, and systemic relations of dominance and subordination", all of which obscures its connections with democracy.[54] Both anti-essentialism and multiculturalism "restrict themselves to the plane of culture, which they treat in abstraction from social relations and social structures, including political economy". [55]

The inadequacy of interpretation occasioned by downplaying or disregarding these social relations and structures of power, in particular those integral to the pervasive hegemony of capitalism in liberal democratic society, is substantively illuminated by Wood in her Democracy Against Capitalism. Thus, she points out that the various spheres of difference and identity in civil society come "within the determinative force of capitalism, its system of social property relations, its expansionary imperatives, its drive for accumulation, its commodification of all social life, its creation of the market as a necessity, a compulsive mechanism of competition and self-sustaining 'growth', and so on".[56] This is not to "privilege" class status and its relations by derogating from other types of difference and identity. Rather, it is to guard against the situation in which "the totalizing logic and the coercive power of capitalism become invisible, when the whole social system of capitalism is reduced to one set of institutions and relations among many others".[57] Moreover, it is to reject the view, whether explicit or implicit, that politics should be based on diversity and difference other than that defined by class. [58]

Although possessing its own imperious dynamic, class is not, as such, more constitutive than gender, ethnicity, race, cultural orientation, and so on. In addition, like those, it has sometimes accommodated itself to the denigration or exploitation of other identities: persons of different genders, ethnic groups, races, cultural identities, etc., have been complicit in, and benefited from, economic domination, coercion and exploitation characteristic of capitalism, just as both capitalists and workers (including socialists and communists) have been, for example, sexists, racists and cultural chauvinists.

The (non-exclusive) emphasis upon class is not some sort of reductionist socioeconomic determinism. Instead, it is a recognition of the depth and extent of the dominative social relations of capitalism, of the degree to which they determine "the allocation of labour, leisure, resources, patterns of production, consumption and the disposition of time".[59] Furthermore, it calls attention to certain asymmetries between class identity and other identities. On the one hand, antagonisms within and between sexes, races and ethnicities can, in principle and to a discernible degree in practice, be defused; but the objective antagonism between "capital" and "labor" cannot, under capitalist conditions, be overcome. On the other hand, eliminating class inequality requires the elimination of classes; but eliminating gendered, racial or ethnic inequality does not presuppose, per impossibile, the elimination of sex, race or ethnicity. Relevant here, as Wood stresses, is the fact that capitalism can -- as history shows -- adjust to the relative elimination of extra-economic oppressions, for example, of gender and race, but not to the elimination of economic, that is, class, oppression. [60] Indeed, capitalism "is uniquely indifferent to the [non-class] social identities of the people it exploits". [61]

If democracy involves the empowerment of human beings, their "identities" and placement in society must be taken into account. This means that a "postmodern" politics (perhaps a non-politics) of culture should not obscure the salience of class politics. As well, it means that the politics of (non-class) group differences, whether based upon gender, race, ethnicity or something else, should be thoughtfully integrated with a class politics. This is a daunting task, never yet accomplished to an appreciable degree in human history. Yet, its promotion is indispensable if democratization is to advance significantly.

Two further reflections are, I think, not inappropriate. In the first place, following up on the concern expressed by Jean Cohen about the "dismantling" of communication across difference, I wish to re-emphasize the need for some understanding between those whose identities are different. I believe that, even if

107

shared perspectives, values, predilections and ways of life between (non-oppressive) groups are not assumed, understanding adequate for the development of democratic practice is possible. [62] For example, it is possible to understand that individuals (or groups) are oppressed, to understand what individuals (or groups) need and whether these needs have been significantly satisfied, to understand whether individuals have empowering capacities, and to understand when, and to what extent, individuals and groups are cooperating. In the second place, some non-ascriptive identities (quite important to those who have them) can be based upon affinities across space and time, that is, upon close identification with others with whom one only occasionally interacts in any proximate manner. This makes for a rather differently textured "group" identity, which is not less intimate and solidary for all that. Furthermore, this kind of identity has implications for obligation and loyalty, topics that will be considered in a subsequent chapter. [63]

NOTES

1. Rethinking Democracy, p. 60. See also her "Diversity", p. 180. This viewpoint is, in effect, seconded by Young in her statement that justice should be concerned with "provision of the means to develop and exercise capacities" [Justice, p. 3].

2. Gould, appropriately, criticizes Rawls because he "limits the application of the principle of justice in the economic realm only to distribution and not to production" [Rethinking Democracy, p. 137]. This is a deficiency of liberal theories of justice, in general. If justice promotes democracy and if democracy is the empowering practice of positive freedom and if this practice presupposes enabling means and resources as components of individual capacities, then justice in the economy requires democratic control over both production and distribution. Moreover, the practice of positive freedom cannot take place under exploitative and oppressive social conditions; and Young is right when she asserts that "instead of focusing on distribution, a conception of justice should begin with the concepts of domination and oppression" [Justice, p. 3], since the equal practice of positive freedom cannot occur in the context of socially disabling inequities of productive power.

3. On the importance of the distinction between "having" (consuming) and "doing", see Macpherson, Democratic Theory, pp. 51-52, also Young, Justice, p. 25.

4. I believe that Gould is making the same kind of point when she says that "justice requires not the same conditions for each one but rather equivalent conditions determined by differentiated needs", that is, by relevant differences; hence, "this principle builds differentiation into the basic requirement of just treatment" ["Diversity", p. 180].

5. See Political Liberalism, p. 79. Joshua Cohen deploys a very similar rendering of citizen equality in "Procedure", p. 96.

6. Rawls, ibid., p. 19.

7. Ibid., p. 137.

8. Ibid., p. 158.

9. I agree with Richard Hare when he says that Rawls "relies much too much on his own intuitions which are open to question", that the development of substantive principles of justice "is simply not to be settled by appeal to intuitions", and that "Intuitions prove nothing; general consensus proves nothing." ["Justice and Equality", in Justice, ed. James P. Sterba. Belmont, CA: Wadsworth, 1999, pp. 169-171].

10. Political Liberalism, xx.

11. See The Sexual Contract. Stanford: Stanford University Press, 1988, passim.

12. Ibid., p. 167.

13. Ibid., p. 187.

14. See ibid., p. 43.

15. See Political Liberalism, p. 25.

16. Yet the parties do know (as he said in A Theory, p. 137) "the general facts about human society"; and one of these putative facts, about which there is an alleged consensus, is that "our" society condemns the oppression of women [see endnote 79 for Chapter Eight]. Many would be skeptical regarding this "fact".

17. See ibid, p. 24.

18. Ibid., p. 28.

19. Przeworski has voiced similar reservations about social contract theories generally [see Democracy, p. 39].

20. Rawls contends that the worth of political liberties must be approximately equal "in the sense that everyone has a fair opportunity to hold public office and to influence the outcome of political decisions" [Political Liberalism, p. 327]. I must confess that comments like these are, to me, exasperating, for this kind of "fair opportunity" is formal, abstract and not germane to the conditions of real life. If the comments express some sort of regulative idea or ideal, they yet fail to provide any practically intelligible guidance. Perhaps anticipating this type of criticism, Rawls concedes that his conception of political justice is abstract "in the same way that the conception of a perfectly competitive market, or of general economic equilibrium, is abstract" [ibid., p. 154]. The formidable problem here is not only whether these idealized structures are too remote from what is empirically possible to serve as usable guidelines but also whether they are theoretically coherent.

21. Justice, pp. 158 & 184.

22. Ibid., pp. 196-197.

23. See "Toward a Deliberative Model of Democratic Legitimacy", in Benhabib, Democracy,

p. 83.

24. See Democracy, p. 49.

25. See "Gender Equity", pp. 221 & 241.

26. In my view, "good" is philosophically antecedent to "right". The main reason for my saying this -- adverted to earlier -- is that the rightness of a rule or prescription is defined by the purpose it is designed to promote; and a purpose makes sense in terms of the valued end(s) to which it is directed. 'Right' validates an action as correct, that is, as correctly conforming to a rule, whereas 'good' valorizes consequences; but both kinds of normative sanction are relative and contextual. Further, the connection between 'right' and 'ought' is conceptual or semantic; and there is, as such, no necessary moral aspect to this connection. My understanding of terms such as 'right' and 'good' is shaped by a naturalistic standpoint, according to which their moral and non-moral uses are, at bottom, homologous.

27. In attributing priority to good over right and in emphasizing the central role of commitment, as compared to (formally prescribed) obligation, I also consider an ethics of care and responsibility to be, in general, normatively superior to an ethics of justice grounded in right. The latter is, of

110

course, significant and indispensable, not least as a means helping to implement the former.

28. Macpherson offers the important observation that any relative equalization of access to what he calls "developmental power" adds more to those with less developed power that it might subtract from those with highly developed power [see Democratic Theory, p. 75]. In other words, there is a diminished marginal utility, beyond some point, for those with already substantial powers and with capabilities of accumulating yet more. This situation is analogous to that wherein a small accrual of utilities for some may be of greater personal value than a large increase for others, and any losses for the former may be more momentous than larger losses for the latter. These examples suggest caution about applying overly standardized interpersonal comparisons.

29. See After the Revolution?, Revised Edition. New Haven: Yale University Press, 1990, p. 93.

30. See The Truly Disadvantaged, p. 146. A "right" to attempt, whatever the powers and resources at one's disposal, seems somewhat like a "right" to pursue, for example, happiness, even under the direst of circumstances.

31. Ibid., p. 117. While this is more true than many people would care to admit, it omits reference to the role of gender in establishing social disadvantage.

32. See Barbara Epstein, "Radical Democracy and Cultural Politics", in Radical Democracy, ed. David Trend. New York: Routledge, 1996, pp. 128 & 129.

33. See Democracy, pp. 4 & 131.

34. Chantal Mouffe highlights this issue, adding that we should "celebrate and enhance" difference, except for differences "constructed as relations of subordination" ["Democracy, Power, and the 'Political'", in Benhabib, Democracy, pp. 246 & 247].

35. See Justice, p. 164. Phillips concurs when she states that "A politics that tries to transcend (read ignore) difference is one that confirms the inequalities that exist." [Democracy, pp. 43 & 94].

36. Indeed, Young maintains that "oppressed groups have distinct cultures, experiences, and perspectives on social life with humanly positive meaning, some of which may even be superior to the culture and perspectives of mainstream society" [Justice, p. 166]. Mainstream society venerates its own resistance to oppression in the past but is frequently myopic when it comes to discerning the oppression it tolerates or sanctions in the present. Elsewhere, Young remarks that "differences of social position and identity perspective function as a resource for public reason rather than as divisions that public reason transcends" ["Communication and the Other: Beyond Deliberative Democracy", in Benhabib, Democracy, p. 127].

37. However definite the distinction might be, Phillips furnishes an important qualification when she declares that mechanisms for actually representing group difference "often look like the old interest group politics dressed up in more radical guise" [Democracy, p. 117]. A similar point is made by Partridge in Consent, p. 147. For Wood, an unfortunate element of this similarity is that both kinds of groups tend to ignore the systemic power and totalizing social presence of capitalism [see Democracy, p. 260].

38. See Justice, pp. 186 & 187. She also believes that oppressed groups, in order to function effectively, need separate organizations that exclude others [ibid., p. 167]. As a tactical policy that makes for clarity of purpose, concentration of effort and maximum utilization of resources, it is no doubt well advised -- so long as, internally, relations of domination and subordination are avoided and, externally, coalitions with other groups are not routinely excluded.

39. See "Dealing with Difference", pp. 144-145.

111

40. See Democracy, pp. 19 & 160.

41. Ibid., pp. 150 & 161. According to Partridge, there is a need for participation in political and social movements -- not just organized associations -- where wider ideological issues can be raised, discussed and acted on [see Consent, p. 137].

42. See Jean Cohen, "Democracy", p. 188. Cohen perceptively calls attention to another problem with which the politics of difference is occasionally involved, namely, a tendency to dismantle "the language and conceptual resources indispensable for confronting the authoritarian assertions of difference so prevalent today" [ibid.] I consider this to be an extremely important observation. It is doubtlessly the case that uses of language and modes of reasoning are informed, differentially, by those who employ them. Thus, it is often hard to understand just what a person means in discourse, to follow a line of reasoning or to get the point of what is being said. All of this is, of course, endemic to communication. Still, we are able generally to understand that we do not understand, as well as to locate the obscurities of verbal expression and cognitive transition. In response to these problems, we can try to improve our dialogue with others. If identities -- not just those of groups but also of individuals -- are inexorably opaque and recalcitrant to clarification, then it seems that we must all resign ourselves to a rather sterile "egocentric predicament".

43. See "Diversity", p. 182. This distinction recalls that made by Friedman between a "found" community and a "chosen" community.

44. See Justice, p. 172.

45. See "Diversity", p. 183.

46. Young is probably correct, then, at least with respect to the nation-state, when she says that "Politics must be conceived as a relationship of strangers who do not understand one another in a subjective and immediate sense, relating across time and distance" [Justice, p. 234].

47. Ibid., p. 46.

48. Gould, "Diversity", p. 182.

49. See Nancy Fraser, "Gender Equity and the Welfare State: A Postindustrial Thought Experiment", in Benhabib, Democracy, p. 226.

50. See Gould, "Diversity", p. 182.

51. See Phillips, "Dealing with Difference", p. 144. Elsewhere, she identifies certain problems related to the political representation of identity-groups: "the difficulties of establishing which group is most pertinent to anyone's political identity, the dangers of freezing identities in a way that blocks wider solidarities, and the almost impossible tasks of making group 'representatives' accountable to 'their' group" [Democracy, p. 14].

52. See "Equality, Difference, and Radical Democracy", in Trend, Radical Democracy, p. 203.

53. Ibid., p. 205.

54. Ibid., p. 206.

55. Ibid., p. 207. Epstein claims that the object of radical cultural politics "is to take control of discourse" ["Radical Democracy", p. 135]. However, the control of discourse occurring primarily among like-minded intellectuals is one thing, but the control of discourse in society at large is another.

56. Democracy, p. 246. The commodification of social life comprises the commodification of cultural identities, which can be marketed, both actually and vicariously, in a variety of media.

57. Ibid., p. 245.

58. Ibid., p. 257.

59. Ibid., p. 263.

60. Ibid., pp. 269-270.

61. Ibid., p. 266.

62. At least from the standpoint of a behaviorist theory of meaning, a modestly workable degree of communication and comprehension can probably be achieved. Admittedly, this will not enable outsiders to understand, and talk insightfully about, the deeper, more nuanced significance of particular identities and differences, an understanding characteristically based upon "knowledge by acquaintance". This is a limitation also experienced by anyone who learns to use a foreign language in a somewhat mechanical manner but who, not having been immersed in the culture and habits of those for whom it is their native language, is not quite able to negotiate subtler uses that are colloquial and idiomatic.

63. I have examined, in another place, this kind of affinity, together with associated concepts, in a discussion of "rootless cosmopolitanism".

CHAPTER 8

MODELS OF DEMOCRATIC ACTIVITY

Presupposing the general interpretation of democracy as the communal development and exercise in multiple contexts of positive freedom (empowerment), aligned with humanistic values, I now wish to examine and evaluate several paradigms of democratic activity, to wit, the unitary, the adversary, the deliberative and what I will designate as the cooperative. In view of the magnitude and demands of a thorough treatment here, I must limit my exposition and commentary to what, for me, are manageable proportions. Nevertheless, I hope to show why I endorse a cooperative model.

I

In her illuminating discussion of different models of democratic activity, Mansbridge differentiates between unitary democracy and adversary democracy in the following manner:

> Unitary democracies are like friendships. They assume a
> high degree of common interest. They are distinguished by
> consensus, face-to-face assembly, and an emphasis on a
> rough equality of respect among the members. Adversary
> democracies, on the other hand, are compatible with
> large-scale politics in which the members do not know or
> care for one another. They assume conflicting interests.
> They are distinguished by majority rule ... and an emphasis
> on the equal protection of the members' interests rather
> than on equal respect. [1]

Unitary democracy, which I will scrutinize first, thus invokes deeply shared interests and values, as well as the kind of commonality and reciprocity that exists in a fundamentally homogeneous community. Further, it aspires to engender consensual decision-making based upon regular, inclusive, direct contacts, as contrasted to that based upon majoritarian influence mediated through representation.

Functionally, unitary democracy is akin to (direct) participatory democracy with its orientation on minimally mediated participation by equally authorized participants in the making and implementation of decisions, all of this against a background of similar interests, values, aims and, quite possibly, worldviews. Substantively, unitary democracy is more or less reflected in – to use an earlier idiom, now resurrected – republicanism, as well as in contemporary communitarianism. Insofar as both republicanism and communitarianism are judged to be properly applicable to national society, the more unmediated and directly participatory aspects of unitary democracy recede and unitariness becomes, instead, an inspirational and regulative principle, guiding the emotional and practical orientation of republicans on country and communitarians on national community.

Involving more than a mediating or equilibrating function, republicanism purports to express the ethical life of society, such that "in addition to the hierarchical regulations of the state and the decentralized regulations of the market ... solidarity and the orientation to the common good appear as a third source of social integration", a source considered genetically and normatively prior to the other two. [2] On the republican view, citizens are guaranteed "the possibility of participation in a common praxis", where they can become "politically autonomous authors of a community of free and equal persons". [3]

For their part, communitarians avow that communal attachments serve as a foundation for personal identity and, in addition, bestow meaning upon one's life.[4] Furthermore, communitarians typically believe that the most debilitating social malaise today is a loss of (unitary) community in multiple spheres, leading, on the one hand, to "loneliness, divorce, deracination, political apathy" and, on the other, to individuals who are "seriously disturbed" and who experience acute disorientation and "damaged human personhood". [5] Since, say communitarians, one's very identity is constituted by the communities of which one is a member, particularly by communities of tradition and "memory", weakening or ignoring these communities places one's personal wholeness in jeopardy, thereby fostering atomized, callous individualism and causing individuals themselves, in the words of Amitai Etzioni, "to lose competence, the capacity to reason, and self-identity".[6] Add to this that communitarianism normally involves a notion of equality understood in terms of equally shared opportunities and responsibilities situated within a unitary community, together with an idea of justice as that which is prescribed and/or deserved on the basis of the community's historically evolved conception of the good, and it seems that any "empowerment" is derivative and parasitic and that the contours of "participation" are sharply demarcated by the quest for community virtue. Here, the social self becomes the substantially socialized self, and the creative impulse in democracy is missing.

Although a unitarily constituted community may be more or less civil and tolerant in its external deportment, it can, at the same time, allow, even enjoin, forms of domination and/or conformism internally. Of course, many members of this kind of community may well prefer "traditional" values of stability, security and comfort furnished by this community to any personal status of existential "exile". Others, though, may not care for the relations of subordination to which they are subjected. Communitarians place much value and hope in a national community, a community not likely to exist, however, in the proximately democratic circumstances of the differentiated, multicultural, immanently adversarial nation-state. Ironically, and tragically, such a national community can be embodied rather thoroughly in distinctly undemocratic environments.[7] Even when a projected or postulated unitary national community is willing (at least nominally) to valorize all insiders and to incorporate some outsiders, it may insist that the latter become socially and morally assimilated (that is, homogenized) in accordance with traditional norms. In this context, it is instructive to note that communitarians frequently claim that ideals and policies promoting – or even condoning – diversity and difference threaten to exacerbate social divisions and tensions. [8]

Much of the outlook of communitarianism is defined, of course, by an explicit contrast to its *bête-noire*, liberalism, often with respect to the latter's putative conception of the self. Friedman describes this conception nicely:

> Abstract individualism considers individual human beings as social atoms, abstracted from their social contexts, and disregards the role of social relationships and human community in constituting the very identity and nature of individual human beings. Sometimes the individuals of abstract individualism are posited as rationally self-interested utility maximizers. Sometimes, also, they are theorized to form communities based fundamentally on competition and conflict among persons vying for scarce resources, communities which represent no deeper social bond than that of instrumental relations based on calculated self-interest. [9]

For communitarians, the unitariness of genuine community (and of related democratic participation by those who are equally members of the given community) is incompatible with atomistic or voluntaristic conceptions of the self: the former conception affirming that individuals are "self-sufficient", the latter that they constitute themselves as they prefer, independently of given attachments. [10] In opposition to communitarian misrepresentation or misapplication of the notion of the self, Friedman relevantly and perspicuously delineates a conception of the "social self", which "fundamentally acknowledges the role of social relationships and human community in constituting both self-identity and the nature and meaning of the particulars of individual lives". [11]

The intimately participatory quality envisioned by unitary democracy fits well with the equality of status valorized therein. Yet, equality of status does not necessarily, and sometimes does not easily, translate into unified outcomes. Although unitary democracy functions better, on the whole, in relatively small contexts with their more likely coincidence of views, values and expectations, even here division and conflict can manifest themselves. Moreover, the nisus toward a desired consensus can impede the practical resolution of issues and disagreements.[12] Small groupings may be closely integrated sociologically, without being homogeneous or harmonious psychologically. Any decisional consensus that is attained may be, predominantly, reproduction of an already existing consensus that consensus is necessary. If consensus becomes an overriding moral, not simply practical, imperative, then honest scruples and objections may be suppressed by participants for the sake of the "common good".

The intentions behind unitary democracy are often estimable. Dialogue, cooperation, mutual trust and respect, etc., are surely not to be despised. However, apart from its impracticality for large-scale contexts, such as the nation-state, unitary democracy can be disposed to be somewhat monolithic in its presuppositions and assimilationist in its objectives, both of which distract from appropriate, positive difference. [13] Unitary democracy has its place; but it must guard against chauvinism, disdain for alterity, and the subtle influence of conformism.

As remarked above, a substantive reflection of unitary democracy in the specific context of the nation-state is believed by some to reside in (civic) republicanism. Whatever the necessary adjustments and innovations required because of the scale and complexity of this polity, one factor remains central: the democratic process involves an ethical-political discourse situated within the framework of "a culturally established background consensus shared by the citizenry".[14] For small groupings, such as marriage, a continually re-enacted unity, fluid and dynamic, supports the possibility of genuine community, expressing similar values, common concerns and shared tasks, all democratically coordinated. But the multidimensional pluralism and disjointedness of the nation-state disrupt any ethical circumscription of political discourse, where politics would become, at its core, "a hermeneutical process of self-explication of a shared form of life or collective identity" and democratic will-formation would have the solemn function of constituting society as an actively integrated political community. [15]

The political society of the nation-state is the public domain in which civic republicanism wants to revitalize citizenship as "common membership of a shared community, where we acknowledge others as being of equal account".[16] Yet, I repeat, national society cannot be a genuine community, consistently motivated by all-round care and mutual concern, willingly seeking the humanistic empowerment of all members. In fact, to a significant extent, the "unity" of a national society merely expresses "the facticity of people being thrown together, finding themselves in geographical proximity and economic interdependence such that activities and pursuits of some affect the ability of others to conduct their activities".[17] Under these circumstances, collective tasks, based upon common issues, problems and interests, will emerge and more or less suitable mechanisms for addressing them will be formulated. Nevertheless, this is a "sharing" that is exigent and pragmatic, not indicative of anything deeper (except in imagination or aspiration). It reflects the need to "take care of business". Part of this political enterprise will be a sharing of obligations. Whether there is also a generalized sharing of loyalties (to each other, to a sacralized national identity, or to something else) is another, rather more ambiguous matter.[18] Later, I will offer some observations on the difference between obligation and loyalty.

Republicanism, it is argued, reinforces the invidious conventional distinction between public and private spheres. In the public sphere, one should be a good citizen, participating conscientiously in the political life of society, thereby not only facilitating the elevation of politics beyond crass self-interest and cynical manipulation but also deriving substantial personal enrichment and meaning in life. Apparently, almost anyone can have a "career", so to speak, in civic activity.

As "public-spirited" as all of this may be, the bifurcation of the public and the private, as discussed earlier, is not without problems. On the one hand, the paradigm of the citizen may valorize specific characteristics associated primarily, or even exclusively, with certain, usually privileged groups. Thus, for republicanism, the concept of a citizen "abstracts from differences between men and women", as well as from group differences in general. [19] Of course, it might be argued that the citizen is a purely "legal" entity, transcending gender, and other, differences. Yet, apart from the consideration, insisted upon by many feminists, that gender bias infiltrates presumably neutral legal categories, the concrete expectations and appraisals of the civic activity of citizens are frequently skewed according to gender. Even if "manly" attitudes and semi-martial values would represent an outdated caricature, republicanism is nonetheless more likely to emphasize, for example, duty rather than care. On the other hand, privileging of the public, national sphere as the pre-eminent focus of concern may be understandable, especially in light of the sorry state of affairs often prevailing in the modern, "advanced" state. Yet, with this prioritizing focus, republicanism ignores the equally compelling need to democratize the forms of everyday life, including the domestic realm.[20] In addition, republicanism overlooks the point that democracy is not, as such, embodied in the procedural activities of the national republic but in the kinds of empowered human practice (positive freedom) for which these activities can serve as a partial means.

If, so it seems, republicans want to establish the national polity as a civic community, communitarians want to model the nation-state according to salient features that they consider of great value in the non-political communities of "civil society". Neither aim is really feasible. Whereas a unitary model of democracy may succeed in some small-scale contexts, its success presupposes an appreciable congruence of interests, an adjustable concordance of preferences, and a solidarity of mutuality and sharing that do not obtain at the level of the nation-state and, for that matter, are not tenable for all small groupings, in some of which, on occasion, intimacy and homogeneity can actually engender or aggravate conflicts. Furthermore, anything purporting to be a substantive national consensus may well be either uniformity imposed "from above" or conformity induced "from below".

II

In view of the impracticality of unitary democracy for the nation-state, it is customary to recommend an adversary (competitive) model of democracy either as sober *Realpolitik* or as a pragmatic means for the relatively balanced accommodation of irreducibly plural and competing interests. This, to some extent, it may do. In the process, however, some categories of competitors tend to dominate the field not only because they possess continuing resources of superior power but also because they themselves define the terms of the competition. [21] In any case, adversary democracy does not require, nor does it foster, community and consensus, for consent (real or hypothetical) of the governed members of society is deemed sufficient. In adjudicating and, at least provisionally, resolving the competing claims and conflicts of a contentiously pluralistic society, adversary democracy aims both to secure an efficacious degree of social equilibrium and to contain the claims and conflicts within acceptable institutional and legal parameters.

In this context, the social pluralism of interests and objectives, often embodied in interest and difference groups, may be reflected as well in the pluralism of political parties that compete for influence and power. [22] There are, however, at least two related limitations to this possible transformation: first, only some interest and difference groups manage to establish a presence in political parties, many of which themselves have only a minor voice in the processes of the national polity; and, second, the most effective political parties are those that represent powerful social and economic interests, thereby rendering any attention by those parties to the needs and interests of oppressed or excluded groups largely

25

121

a form of political "charity" or timely electoral calculation. [23]

The first of these limitations is noted by Partridge in his comment that "a stable and highly organized party system tends to channel and constrict to some degree the tendencies of opinion and demand that can exert influence on policy and action", thereby restricting the effectiveness of citizen interests and issues to what the parties are disposed to consider and support. [24] Political pluralism, as manifested in the existence of multiple political parties, may well be conjoined, then, with an ideological pluralism that is active and visible but not influential. This situation often obtains insofar as "'convergence' in the thinking and policies of the major political parties and the formation of an unusually high level of social consensus do have effects that inhibit and stultify the responsiveness of a system to all the forces active within it". [25] Major political parties thus both reflect the competitive aspects of adversary democracy and, at the same time, help to contain any adversarial tendencies of a political kind within acceptable bounds demarcated by a relatively stable social consensus; that is, political dissensus is circumscribed by social consensus.

Whether political parties or social interest groups are focused upon, adversary democracy is believed by many to be the most reasonable and effective model pertaining to modern national society. Mansbridge sees adversary democracy as having roots in "the rise of mercantilism and the spread of market relations in the seventeenth century", a provenance not surprising in view of the fact that the "theory of adversary democracy is remarkably similar to modern laissez-faire economics". [26] Both manifest a competitive pluralism, replete with similar justificatory principles (read "myths"). What sells well, respectively, in the free enterprise system and in the adversarial political system is thereby certified as better. [27] Economically, supply is supposed to be coordinated somehow with demand, as, politically, policy is supposed to be responsive to the preferences, interests or needs of citizens. However, it matters much whether those consumers with "demands" are rich or poor, as it makes a considerable difference whether the interests, etc., expressed are those of powerful groups or not. Another analogy is found in respective claims that failure in economic competition, as with failure in political competition, need not rule out future success. In principle, this may be so; in practice, the analogy weakens. The best hope for an economically weak or unsuccessful competitor is to be bought out, in one way or another, by some strong competitor. For a politically weak or unsuccessful competitor, the prospects are minimal unless the weak competitor "sells out" to a strong one or unless the unsuccessful competitor is only a temporary loser in the contest of the (typically few) major political parties.

Besides the presumed instrumental value of adversary democracy as a means for mitigating and arbitrating conflicts at the national level and thereby helping to maintain social equilibrium and the possibility of relatively consistent national policy, other considerations may be adduced on behalf of this model. In the first place, if it is accepted that conflict, disagreement, contestation, even antagonism, are ineradicable features of a pluralistic national society, the conclusion may be drawn that it is prudent to institutionalize mechanisms for rationally managing this competitive pluralism. [28] In the second place, some may be enamored with the principle (questionable, but apparently idealized by proponents of deliberative democracy) that rational decisions, or at least reasonable intersubjective agreements, can issue reliably from a thoughtful, egalitarian contestation of ideas and beliefs. Thirdly, and rather differently, it may be said that the adversarial interplay of views does not so much conduce to reasoned, validated agreement as that it brings out fairly clearly which standpoints have the strongest political/social forces behind them and which, therefore, require the most attention, practically speaking. Finally, since not every contending individual or group can enjoy continual support for its preferences or interests, "losers" can be not only consoled by the hope that they will fare better on a later date (a putative inference from the doctrine of "equal opportunity") but also admonished that, since they have had (the opportunity for) their "say", they should be willing to accept unfavorable outcomes validated according to majority rule. Where compromises or bargains, as well as an improbable consensus, elude the adversary approach, majority decision-making presents itself as a plausible and ostensibly fair technique. A number of issues and problems associated with majority rule will be surveyed in a subsequent chapter. For now, it may be sufficient to observe that majority rule, as procedure, can be in uneasy relationship to the value of substantive outcomes. Moreover, since, in general, outcomes themselves under adversary democracy are uncertain, there cannot be, as Przeworski points out, "prior commitments to equality, justice, welfare, or whatever". [29] To be sure, there can be a formal endorsement of these factors, as well as a perhaps sincere attempt, here and there, to implement them with some degree of generality; but without their institutionalization in structural social features, legal mandates (such as those of enforceable human rights) and consistent public policy, they will always be at risk.

That a large, deeply pluralistic society is inevitably competitive and fractious may well dictate that something like adversary democracy is called for; and the latter can be, with patience and good intentions, a fairly tolerable form of governance. However, it surely overstates the matter to say that the give and take of adversary democracy leads to an "integration" of views, such that "the views of all are reflected to an important extent in the outcome". [30] In addition, although a well-tooled adversary democracy can often diminish conflict and antagonism by means of constructive engagement between disputants, the point, among others, of democracy is to minimize prejudicial disparities of power and the presence of domination and exploitation. Related to this is the fact that, under adversary democracy, augmenting one's power in comparison to others is frequently achieved by getting power over them. [31] Dahl demurs at "theories of domination", asserting that "they give little weight to the importance of organized competition as an instrument by which nonelites may influence the conduct of political elites".[32] Yet, the modalities by which nonelites can influence elites are rather limited. To cite elections is only partially relevant; for elections can create or activate, as well as legitimate, elites, giving rise to what has been called "democracy by proxy". [33] Even more questionably, Dahl alleges that monopoly domination is not possible either in business or in politics, so long as, respectively, new firms or parties can enter the competition. [34] It may be that the exclusive domination of a single business or political party is not possible; but this does not preclude the collective domination of monopolizing businesses or monopolizing parties which, in effect, competitively parcel out economic or political space among themselves.

It cannot be gainsaid that, by and large, adversary democracy can "work" at the level of the nation-state. So long as not too much is expected – in spite of too much that is claimed – adversary democracy (strictly speaking, in my opinion, an oxymoron) is tolerable, though by no means beneficial, for most people. Electoral procedures and majority rule can usually generate consent, even if not always informed. Social contract thinking and game-theoretical calculation can be brought into play to render adversary democracy less unruly. The elusiveness of genuinely mutual cooperation can be obviated by emphasizing, instead, pragmatically effective coordination of efforts, however differential their requirements or their benefits.

It may be that some, possibly many, have a compelling emotional or ideological need to designate the adversarial politics of the nation-state as "democracy". For my part, I prefer, making use of the concept of democracy as the empowering practice of positive freedom oriented on humanistic values, to acknowledge this concept's restricted applicability to the nation-state and to look for the possibilities of its fuller embodiment elsewhere.

III

An increasingly influential conception of democracy is expressed in the deliberative (discourse) model associated, above all, with Jürgen Habermas. In this section, I do not attempt to provide a comprehensive overview of Habermas's thinking or to examine the details of his discourse theory. Rather, I am concerned to see how his version of deliberative democracy constitutes an alternative to unitary democracy and to adversary democracy and how it might be subjected to critique.

Characterized succinctly, deliberative democracy supposes that individuals participate as rational beings in a deliberative process about publicly relevant issues, where the process emphasizes giving cogent reasons leading to an ideally consensual agreement. [35] More specifically, the deliberative procedure involves reasoned argumentation, inclusiveness of participation, a discussion not bound by pre-existing norms or requirements, and the equal opportunity of participants to contribute to deliberation that is settled by the "better argument". Deliberation is ongoing; but if a decision is needed and consensus is not forthcoming, then majority rule is invoked. Moreover, deliberations take into account the unequal distribution of resources that undermines the equality of deliberation. Any common good is not assumed prior to deliberation but is decided by it. [36] Democracy, it is stressed, is essentially related to the customary political sphere: "the central element of the democratic process resides in the procedure of deliberative politics", which "consists in a network of discourses and bargaining processes". [37]

Both discourses and bargaining – the latter amounting to a shift from communicative action to strategic action – "can develop their problem-solving force only insofar as the problems at hand are sensitively perceived, adequately described, and productively answered in the light of a reflexive, posttraditional transmission of culture". [38] In addition, the "communicative reason" that is supposed to be employed in the discourses of deliberative politics must, ideally, "ascribe identical meanings to expressions, connect utterances with context-transcending validity claims, and assume that addressees are accountable, that is, autonomous and sincere with both themselves and others". [39] The occasions for communicative, deliberative action often develop from the private dimensions of the lifeworld of individuals who interact in the processes of informal opinion-formation. These interactions take place in a civil society, demarcated from both the state and the economy, that "is composed of those more or less spontaneously emergent associations, organizations, and movements that, attuned to how societal problems resonate in the private life spheres, distill and transmit such reactions in amplified form to the public sphere". [40] The public sphere itself, an intermediary structure between the political system and the private sectors of the lifeworld (together with the more intersubjective dimensions of the related civil society), is "a network for communicating information and points of view" in "the social space generated in communicative action". [41] This communicative network transmits its results to the political system by means of institutionalized procedures, for "political influence based on public opinion can be transformed into political power" only in this way. [42] Within the framework of flows of communication between citizens and the state, legally institutionalized "will-formation depends on supplies coming from the informal contexts of communication found in the public sphere, in civil society, and in spheres of private life". [43]

Although the deliberative (discourse) theory of democracy corresponds to the image of a "decentered" society, in which the political system is simply one action system among others, it is yet the case, for Habermas, that deliberative democracy is not a model for social institutions in general but only for the political system. [44] Cognate with this is his position that "the democratic principle is applied only to norms that display the formal properties of legal norms"; therefore, "In assuming a legal shape, the discourse principle is transformed into a principle of democracy." [45]

Habermas's conversance with a variety of positions and arguments, his disciplined attention to detail, his painstaking analyses and his appreciation of the relevance of "empiricist" standpoints all testify to a realistic and informed approach to democracy and its problems. In spite of a number of problems internal to his own point of view – problems that he acknowledges and which I will include in a listing of objections to his deliberative model of democracy – he maintains that, with respect to that model, there is no "opposition" between the ideal and the real, for the model's normative content "is partially inscribed in the social facticity of observable political processes", such that it is possible to "identify particles and fragments of an 'existing reason' already incorporated in political practices, however distorted these may be".[46] On the other hand, he characterizes the idealized "communication community", in which, purportedly, this reason plays a role, as a "methodological fiction" that enables one to identify deviations from communicative action [in the real world?]. [47]

In my judgment, I believe "deviations" would be considerable. In the first place, I think it unlikely that "communicative reason" could pervasively ascribe identical meanings, rely upon validity-claims uniformly transcending context, or count upon "addressees" being consistently accountable. The category of "identical meanings", while capacious, is not congenial to the kinds of ambiguous and/or vague locutions endemic to the expression of social and political ideas. Appeal to "ordinary language" does not eliminate the problem, since understanding depends very much upon the kind of "language-game" that is in operation. To "ascribe", concessively, identical meanings to expressions is not necessarily to understand the uses of those expressions in an identical manner. Taking a somewhat pedestrian example, 'democracy' might be uniformly defined as 'rule by the people'; but the vagueness and the ambiguity of the definiens mean that it is most improbable that the definiendum will be construed in an identical sense by those deliberating about democracy.[48] Instead, one will have to follow

128

the precept to look not for the meaning but for the use. It should also be recognized both that one can understand meanings considered incorrect and also that mutual understanding can provoke or aggravate disagreement as well as resolve it.

Along with types of possibly insuperable open-endedness in the semantics of language-use, problems of "pragmatics" (alternatively, "illocutionary" or "perlocutionary" acts) in the use of language occur as well. Young has accentuated a number of these in her critique of deliberative democracy. For example, she states that "most theorists of deliberative democracy assume a culturally biased conception of discussion that tends to silence or devalue some people or groups". [49] Thus, even if (contrary to probable fact) those participating in the communicative action of deliberation equally had a voice in spite of economic dependence and political domination, their voices would not be equally heard, due to their particular ways of speaking and other cultural differences. [50] Young argues that the deliberative model involves an agonistic, competitive form of argumentation, which privileges communication that is formal, general, "logical", dispassionate and non-figurative. According to her, these typically "masculine" speaking styles discountenance the use of gestures, expressions of emotion and figurative language.[51] I must say, however, that (masculine) oppressors have often utilized the latter techniques to communicate their dominative interests and hegemonic intentions. In general, rhetoric in support of reasons is one thing; rhetoric in place of reasons is another.

Additionally, though maybe I miss his point, Habermas's use of 'validity' is vague. To use 'validity' in some sense other than that in which it designates a formal property of inferences is to employ 'validity' in a sense perhaps tantamount to something like 'justifiability'. Yet, such a use of 'validity' will be context-dependent with regard to the criteria of validity, that is, claims will be valid where and insofar as they are validated according to criteria agreed upon in some context. As reasoning and its rules are context-dependent, so is "reason" itself.

Continuing, how can the "inclusiveness' of participation be ensured? No doubt, most people participate, in one way or another, at some level or another, in some form of deliberation (at least in that individualized form that is a necessary constituent of what is conventionally called "free will"). But much, even collective, deliberation fails to go very far in the "communication flows" leading into the public sphere and, possibly, into the administrative activity of the state. Furthermore, not all who are affected by norms, regulations, etc., are <u>able</u>, for one reason or another, to participate in affirming their legitimacy. Another difficulty lies in Habermas's reference to "the genuinely normative sense of the intuitive understanding of democracy". [52] Is 'intuitive' being used here in the sense of unmediated awareness, in the Rawlsian sense of "considered convictions" and "fundamental ideas we seem to share", in the sense of what is simply taken for granted, or what? Is there irony in the fact that a deliberative theory relying crucially and systematically upon <u>reasons</u> must nonetheless appeal to an <u>intuitive</u> understanding , which, it appears, cannot itself rely upon reasons?

On the subject of reasons, several matters call for clarification. First, what reason is there for taking reasons into account? If agreement (assent) is what is wanted, then there are various ways whereby this can be produced. Of course, theorists of deliberative democracy are understandably concerned with <u>how</u> agreement is reached. The presenting and exchanging of reasons (to which everyone involved could, in principle, assent) is vital. However, I suggest, reasons are not inherently persuasive or compelling: one must be <u>disposed</u> (or motivated) to take reasons, in general, and certain kinds of reasons, in particular, into account. Doubtlessly, "reasons" can be given to help instill or sustain this disposition. If so, the reasons will surely be consequentialist. It may be argued, as it often is, that reasons (or reasoning) deal with justification rather than motivation. To this it may be queried: why, that is, what reason is there to, <u>care</u> about justification? In other words, how justify the relevance of justification? I imagine that, at this point, I might be faulted for lapsing into a "performative"

130

contradiction. Be that as it may, it seems that a <u>normative</u> mandate for the magisterial role of reasons needs some reason(s). Second, a significant purpose (reason?) for giving reasons is not necessarily to try to persuade or convince someone else but to clarify and explain one's own position to the other. There may be no expectation that any agreement can be reached. Yet, it may be worthwhile for participants to understand better where, specifically, any disagreement lies and why it cannot be overcome. Third, deliberation, in the sense envisioned, may well play, in fact, only a limited role in nominally democratic processes. Thus, Przeworski alleges that "modern representative democracy generates outcomes that are predominantly a product of negotiations among leaders of political forces rather than of a universal deliberative process." [53]

Further, how is agreement reached that the reasons given on behalf of some position are compelling and, antecedently, that the reasons are even relevant to the topic being considered? In other words, how determine or show that the reasons being advanced are "good" reasons, in the dual sense of pertinence and persuasiveness? [54] Joshua Cohen argues that a reason is not a "sufficient" reason, if it justifies a law or policy that would preclude a person's compliance with her or his religious obligations, since these reflect "the special role of religious convictions from the point of view of the person who has them". [55] On this theme, I submit that personal loyalties and (secular) moral convictions can be just as "special" as any religious convictions. Incidentally, I am convinced that people will sometimes accept a bad reason as if it were a good reason. What I am less sure about, however – although I think it is possible – is whether people can accept a good reason for the wrong reasons. Finally, in this context, it seems to me that the Habermasian force of the better argument would frequently be, in fact, the "better" <u>force</u> of an argument.

Other types of criticism of Habermas's deliberative model of democracy have been put forward. In <u>Justice and the Politics of Difference</u>, Young develops a substantial set of overlapping criticisms of deliberative democracy's

131

valorization of impartiality. According to her, the ideal of impartiality tends to foster cultural imperialism by allowing the experiences and the perspectives of privileged groups to appear as universal. Also, "the ideal of impartiality ... expresses a logic of identity that seeks to reduce differences to unity". Further, while supporting the deceptive idea of a "neutral" state and legitimizing both bureaucratic authority and hierarchical decision-making, official impartiality "reinforces oppression by hypostatizing the point of view of privileged groups into a universal position". Lastly, the "situated assumptions and commitments that derive from particular histories, experiences, and affiliations" of individuals render impartial deliberation by them impossible. [56] Some would undoubtedly judge these strictures on impartiality to be misdirected or overdrawn. For example, Benhabib says an impartial standpoint entails that processes of collective deliberation be "conducted rationally and fairly among free and equal individuals". [57] In a rather different vein, Rawls announces that impartiality "is altruistic (being moved by the general good)".[58] If Benhabib means by 'impartiality' consistent reasoning, then her statement is unobjectionable. However, if it implies that premises, postulates and auxiliary assumptions are 'impartial', then it is misguided; for, whereas "impartiality" in the former sense is operationally value-free, in the latter sense it is not and very often incorporates unrecognized or unacknowledged biases, interests and motivations. This eqivocality in 'impartial' is reminiscent of a similar one in 'rational', where it can signify either inferential consistency or else an outlook that satisfies certain normative criteria. [59] Perhaps, however, the concept of impartiality, as used by Benhabib, relates primarily to how people are (to be) taken into account. Individuals, as participants, are properly taken (incorporated), equally, into a process of collective deliberation. Yet, this does not mean or entail that what they contribute therein (their reasons and proposals) should be equally taken into account.

As to Rawls, his quoted use of 'impartiality' is, I believe, tendentious and misleading and, in any case, not really germane to the problematic of deliberative democracy. More relevant is his statement that "our exercise of political power is proper only when we sincerely believe that the reasons we offer for our political action may reasonably be accepted by other citizens as a justification of those actions". [60] The kinds of reasons that are capable of being justificatory are, in general, set out by "public reason", which "does not, as such, determine or settle particular questions of law or policy. Rather, it specifies the public reasons in terms of which such questions are to be politically decided." [61] Whether public reason does, indeed, have this type and degree of regulative influence over institutionalized political decision-making is open to serious question. Habermas more realistically acknowledges the existence of "inertial" obstacles to the influence of (reasoned) public deliberation and communication upon the political system. At one point, he remarks that civil society "can have at most an indirect effect on the self-transformation of the political system"; at another, he stresses that insofar as the public sphere is "infiltrated by administrative and social power and dominated by the mass media ... one will be rather cautious in estimating the chances of civil society having an influence on the political system". [62] If Habermas is right on this point – as I believe he is – then it is difficult to see how the diversified concatenation of reasons (and reasonings) that exists in the public sphere of opinion-formation can be regulative or authoritative for deliberations leading to will-formation in the institutionalized political system. The problematic relationship between public thinking and (politically) administrative decision-making is, in the view of Habermas, also discernible with regard to the issue of legitimacy. He mentions that, according to the discourse theory of democracy, "binding decisions, to be legitimate, must be steered by communication flows that start at the periphery and pass through the sluices of democratic and constitutional procedures situated at the entrance to the parliamentary complex or the courts". He adds, however, that existing democracies "cannot satisfy such strong conditions".[63] It seems to me that this is a considerably less confident and peremptory appeal to "public reason" than is found with Rawls.

Another kind of criticism of Habermas's deliberative democratic model is urged by Mansbridge concerning the need and justification for coercion. She avers that theorists of deliberative democracy have ignored the need for coercion in democratic contexts, failing to pay sufficient attention to the fact that, on some issues, deliberation, however reasonable and thoroughgoing, will not generate agreement. [64] Among such theorists she includes Habermas, who is said to "extol the role of democratic deliberation in discovering, creating, and maintaining commonality", an aim often unattainable and requiring, by contrast, some sort of compromise backed by coercion. [65] Against Habermas, she maintains that coercion-free deliberation is not likely, due, in part, to "illusionary" convictions that are "produced by the capacity of some to keep others from perceiving their interests". [66]

Mansbridge's criticism of Habermas is, I think, misdirected. Habermas, in fact, devotes a fair amount of attention to the issue of coercion. On several occasions, he refers to coercion as a feature of legal systems, which is compatible with his view, noted above, that deliberative democracy is not a model for social institutions in general but only for the legally institutionalized political system. In addition, it has been mentioned previously that he recognizes the role of bargaining, compromise and majority rule when a consensual agreement cannot be reached. I do not think he has any illusions about the uniform success of deliberative democracy in practice. My own complaint here is that the conception of democracy should not be restricted to the "political system".

Remarking that coercion relates to the tension between facticity and validity and, in particular, to that between the positivity and the legitimacy of law, [67] Habermas also concerns himself with the issue of the legitimacy of coercion, which he deems proper insofar as the legitimacy of law, on whose behalf coercion is exercised, is duly established. [68] If consistent satisfaction of a normative legitimacy criterion is only ideal, then one may question why citizens ought to comply with putatively legitimated laws. Here, a "tension" between justification and motivation also appears. Ought one to obey a rule simply because it is right, that is, rightly legitimated or, rather, because it is in one's prudent interest to do so – or both? Mansbridge contends that a willingness to accept some coercion as legitimate "derives largely from a conventional and unreflective consensus rooted in the internalization of social and cultural traditions". [69] Habermas is no less down-to-earth: he states that the coercive character of law does not require "addressees" to comply only on the basis of the communicatively informed acceptance of a legitimacy claim, but to comply, if necessary, on the basis of utility calculations. [70]

Having recognized the need for coercion in democratic societies, Mansbridge yet emphasizes the importance of constraining it. To do this, she recommends "informal deliberative enclaves of resistance", "deliberative arenas" and "subaltern counterpublics". [71] On his side, Habermas seems to have a positive attitude toward civil disobedience, when it is a protest against rules or decisions that are believed to be "illegitimate in the light of valid constitutional principles". [72] I must prorogue any discussion of consent and dissent until later. For the moment, I will merely raise a dual question for future reference: can one willingly consent to what one does not consider legitimate and can one knowingly refuse to consent to what one does consider legitimate?

IV

Unitary democracy expects too much, adversary democracy expects too little, and deliberative democracy expects what is not feasible – at least in large social contexts such as the nation-state. Different from any of these is a model of democracy founded, in particular, upon cooperation, a model that can be uniquely consonant with the conception of democracy as the empowering practice of positive freedom. In cooperative endeavor, various individuals or groups with more or less divergent interests and values, yet common needs and common concerns, agree upon and adhere to modes of activity, for some period and in one or more instances, that subserve tasks or ends recognized collectively to be worthwhile individually. Cooperation, minimally, requires no consensus other than the agreement to cooperate, comprising agreement about the ends of, and means for, cooperation. Although, strictly speaking, only this limited consensus is assumed, cooperation itself is an operational form of consensus in practice. Such minimalistically consensual cooperation can take place in the absence of friendship, benevolence, compassion or anything of the sort. The only shared value explicitly presupposed is a belief in the value of cooperation. Individuals or groups cooperate when, acknowledging relations of mutual dependence and realizing the augmented potential of collaborative action, they consciously and deliberately work together – in the process eschewing patterns of exploitation and domination (otherwise, cooperative efforts will be counterproductive and "democracy" cannot attain the level of mutual empowerment) – so as to produce results that are expected to be of appreciable benefit for everyone concerned.

Social cooperation, involving mutual agreement, trust, reciprocity and fairness, is sufficient for the purposes of a quasi-democratic type of decision-making, problem resolution, and so on. However, for the purposes of democracy as the empowering practice of positive freedom, something more is required, namely, specifically communal cooperation involving, in addition to the preceding factors, solidarity, caring and communality (*Gemeinschaftlichkeit*). Communally cooperative democratic practice can probably exist only in relatively small-scale contexts. In the context of the nation-state, by contrast, with its complexity and factionalism, a socially cooperative type of democracy can, at most, obtain if cooperation is sustained by commitment to genuinely representational mechanisms, by abjuring exploitative and oppressive structures, by minimizing hierarchy and bureaucracy, and by institutionalizing a measure of support for conditions of empowerment by means of enforceable human rights.

Although social cooperation may be reasonably effective for purposes such as resolving conflicts, overcoming impasses, making decisions and implementing certain kinds of tasks – as well as, at the level of the nation-state, possibly endorsing (but not necessarily ensuring) empowerment by institutionalizing appropriate human rights – democracy, as the empowered practice of positive freedom, needs the environment of communal cooperation. Communal cooperation is not simply a strategic technique for producing desirable outcomes but an activity that is itself an embodiment of positive freedom. A communal type of cooperation exists only in the context of community. Hence, this type of cooperation is not manifested at the level of the nation-state, since it cannot be constituted as a genuine community, regardless of the seeming fancies of communitarians. Indeed, the only kind of "community" on this scale would be a pseudo-community based on, and energized by, nationalistic chauvinism, quite possibly of malignant proportions.

Young asserts that "The ideal of community expresses a desire for social wholeness, symmetry, a security and solid identity." [73] This may be the ideal for communitarians or social chauvinists, for example; but it is not a norm for either social or communal cooperation. Moreover, it is not, for that matter, necessary for either type of cooperation. Social cooperation, elements of which have been identified above, requires neither mutual liking nor respect (although trust is necessary), nor does it need uniformity or shared identities. It does, however, require a recognition of mutual relatedness and of similar needs, problems and tasks, together with an awareness that successful outcomes are contingent upon, and facilitated by, potentialities inherent in the conditions of social cooperation. [74] Cooperative democracy, exemplified most adequately in conditions of distinctively communal cooperation, involves more than mutuality, trust, reciprocity and fairness, all of which can exist even between antagonists. [75] Communal cooperation evinces both ties of loyalty and care that go beyond what is merely instrumental and, as well, a profound and principled recognition of interdependence and of the synergistic efficacy of non-exploitatively shared endeavor comprising, at the same time, a mutually acceptable division of labor. In this context, democratic cooperation is a continuing, ever unfinished project of building forms of partnership and collaboration, so that human beings might have greater communal control over their lives in accordance with humanistic ends.

Cooperation is, or is expected to be, a "positive-sum game". To characterize cooperation this way is to acknowledge that it can be substantiated empirically, whether or not it is "justified" normatively. To be sure, a cooperative model of democracy essentially incorporates "existential" commitment and non-instrumental valuation. Nevertheless, it is important to recognize that the appeal to it does not depend solely upon the persuasiveness of moral exhortation but can be backed up by citing its utility and efficacy even in extra-democratic contexts.

Thus, a rudimentary form of cooperation, modeled and tested in a computer tournament based upon an iterated Prisoner's Dilemma game, has been shown to be effective. [76] This game-theoretical species of cooperation requires no intentional, foresightful choice. Indeed, it is said, the durability of reciprocity over repeated interactions, complemented by "trial-and-error learning about possibilities for mutual rewards", provides a more reliable foundation for cooperation as such than do moral or emotional alignments embodying factors like respectful trustfulness.[77] Besides game-theoretical calculation, something like cooperation can exist as mutually beneficial coordination even among non-human organisms, where such coordination, though obviously not consciously or deliberately selected, nonetheless has distinct survival value.[78] Democratic cooperation among communally minded humans clearly involves much more than these partially developed or primarily strategic forms of coordination and cooperation. Yet, they show that certain kinds of mutual interdependence and interaction are objectively productive and, further, suggest that a specifically conscientious and committed kind of cooperation, focused on empowerment in accordance with humanistic values and sustained by confidence in the efficaciousness of equitably shared activity, should be even more so. Incidentally, the reference to "humanistic values" is required, in view of the fact that people may cooperate for the sake of deleterious purposes and baneful ends, hence for goals that are incompatible with democratic practice.

In addition, human relationships operative under a cooperative model of democracy are not the same as those stipulated for a "social contract", even for a Rawlsian version that stresses social cooperation. In the first place, democratic cooperation is more, indeed other, than social, contractual, strategic transactions about positions, prerogatives and outcomes, involving particular attention to political legitimation, abstract justice and "reasonable" political arrangements. Instead, it is motivated by a communal concern for the humanistic empowerment of individuals in mutually supportive environments of solidarity and care. Second, democratic cooperation, at its best, is endogenously self-enforcing (or, rather, reinforcing), by contrast to more traditional models of social contract, which presuppose exogenous enforcement. For Rawls, to be sure, political cooperation is vindicated by its success in supporting and expressing an "overlapping consensus". As Rawls puts the matter: "Gradually, as the success of political cooperation continues, citizens gain increasing trust and confidence in one another. This is all we need to say in reply to the objection that the idea of overlapping consensus is utopian." [79] Cooperation in the "original position" is methodologically enforced by the constraints of the "veil of ignorance"; but, if Habermas is right, cooperation in Rawls's derivative society is primarily valorized because it preserves political stability. [80] Contrary to the imputations or expectations of Rawls, it is likely that consensual cooperation in extant democracies is, in fact, basically a modus vivendi, wherein compromises are "compelled by circumstances". Third, the rationale for some forms of social contract is to manage, where necessary to mitigate, competitive, adversarial human relationships. In this competitive context, game-theoretical strategic cooperation comes into play, involving calculated bargains and compromises, since, in n-person games, participants "must form coalitions with others and consider what inducements they must offer and accept". [81] This species of quasi-cooperation is suitable for adversary democracy. However, for (communally) cooperative democracy, it is inadequate and misplaced, since, to draw upon Friedman's discussion of the social self, in cooperative democracy "Conflict and competition are no longer considered to be the basic human relationships; instead they are being replaced by alternative visions of the foundation of human society derived from nurturance, caring attachment and mutual interestedness." [82] Contractual cooperation is an accommodationist strategy giving priority to negative freedom, whereas democratic cooperation is an enhancement policy and practice giving priority to positive freedom.

Participants in the practice of cooperative democracy are linked by mutual loyalty and trust – thus solidarity – by commitment and care, and by a life that involves various common elements. It need not at all include any shared "comprehensive doctrine". [83] Cooperative democratic practice is guided by commonly acceptable principles and priorities, by ends and means mutually agreed upon to a practicable degree, and by compatible values (whether or not common); but it is sustained more by loyalty to, and concern for, persons than by obligation to (abstract) principles. As acknowledged earlier on, the motivating factor of communality is most unlikely to exist at the level of the nation-state. It is there that social (not communal) cooperation, perhaps of a socially contractual nature, may be manifested. [84]

For Rawls, the original position specifies "the terms of social cooperation in the case of the basic structure of society". [85] Participants in the original position are postulated as "reasonable", and any inclination they might have to be otherwise is blocked by the methodological constraints of the veil of ignorance. Hence, it is only natural that they will cooperate therein. However, for those in actually existing society who, presumably, will institutionalize the social contract's principles of justice, the situation may well be different. Real individuals cannot be posited as reasonable, though they may be expected to be reasonable – which may or may not be a reasonable expectation. If they are reasonable, they are willing "to propose fair terms of cooperation and to abide by them provided others do". [86] From Rawls's standpoint, reasonable individuals can be expected to cooperate fairly, since being reasonable, by definition, involves having the capacity for a sense of justice. [87] Yet, social cooperation according to rules/principles (of justice) is not the same as communal cooperation for the sake of the good of mutual humanistic empowerment. Social cooperation, oriented on justice, is doubtlessly adequate for the political purposes and exigencies of the nation-state (which is the context upon which Rawls focuses); but communal cooperation, oriented on the democratic practice of positive freedom, presupposes a different kind of interpersonally "political" relationship, one in which individuals are fair to others because they care about them – and not always impartially at that. Once again, in my view, the type of polity possible in the nation-state, founded on social cooperation, is, at best, quasi-democracy. A more genuine type of democracy, based upon communal cooperation, can only be situated elsewhere.

Apart from the question whether social cooperation would be as viable and dependable in existing society as in the original position, a further problem, according to Habermas, is how, if the cooperatively decided principles of the original position remain intact, their specific implementation in constitutional essentials, basic law, etc., can be subject to constructive modification required by new experience, reconsidered convictions, and so on. As stated by Habermas: in the just society constituted on the basis of the original position, citizens "find themselves subject to principles and norms that have been anticipated in theory and have already become institutionalized beyond their control", a situation that prevents the assimilation of fundamental new insights. That is, since the act of founding a democratic constitution cannot be repeated "under the institutional conditions of an already constituted just society", the process of necessary revision is not open, regardless of "shifting historical circumstances".[88] In a constitutional democracy, favored by Rawls, revision of the constitution may be effected through amendment; but this would not be the same as (substantive) revision or amendment of the basic principles of the "conjecture" stipulated for the original position that constitutes the social contract.

A cooperative model of democracy, as I conceive it, is intended not just to resolve problems but to amplify possibilities, not just to arbitrate conflicts but to engender mutually supportive endeavors, not just to establish what is fair but to promote what is humanistically fruitful, not just to keep the supervisory and hierarchical political power of governments within acceptable boundaries but to steer non-dominative "political" power in interpersonal relationships into constructive forms, not just to organize the selection of rulers but to facilitate the communal combination of social partners, not just to delegate (legitimated) power to others to act on one's behalf but to develop oneself as an empowered human being.

The practice of liberatory positive freedom by inherently social individuals presupposes cooperation as both means and end, that is, not only as an instrumentality for furthering empowerment but also as a mode of meaningfully empowered existence. In other words, cooperation, especially that which is communal, both enhances and expresses humanized existence. Democracy, then, is a project for promoting this kind of existence in multiple areas of human life.

It is to be hoped that the motivations and mechanisms of social cooperation, based upon forms of contractual concord that are reliable and enduring, might be extended as widely as possible, even beyond the bounds of the nation-state. Whether this is possible to an appreciable extent is, to say the least, uncertain; and whether there can be, at the level of the nation-state, anything more than a socially cooperative type of quasi-democracy is unlikely. But even if democracy is instantiated in less than global or national forms of life (for example, in those of marriage, work organization or other social groups and associations), this is no mean achievement; for therein democracy can function both to empower and enhance one's lifeworld with others and to remind us pointedly how much is yet to be done to democratize other spheres of the state and civil society.

143

NOTES

1. Beyond Adversary Democracy, x.

2. Jürgen Habermas, "Three Normative Models of Democracy", in Benhabib, Democracy, p. 21.

3. Ibid., p. 22. Looking at the matter differently, though, Young contends that republicanism is committed "to a unified public that in practice tends to exclude or silence some groups" [Justice, p. 183].

4. See Daniel Bell, Communitarianism and Its Critics. Oxford: Clarendon Press, 1995, pp. 4 & 8.

5. Ibid., pp. 11 & 100.

6. "Old Chestnuts and New Spurs", in New Communitarian Thinking, ed. Amitai Etzioni. Charlottesville: University Press of Virginia, 1995, p.22.

7. See the enlightening and sobering work by Peter Fritzsche, Germans into Nazis. Cambridge: Harvard University Press, 1998.

8. See Thomas A. Spragens, "Communitarian Liberalism", in Etzioni, New Communitarian Thinking, p. 49.

9. "Feminism", p. 275. Perhaps it might be said that communitarians consider interpersonal relationships of the members of a community to be ontologically "internal" (rather than "external"). It is as if a member's self is synthesized by the community from its particular values, understandings, traditions, and so on. At the risk of possibly great oversimplification, I will suggest that communitarians stress who we are, whereas liberals put the emphasis on what we are. Communitarians confound this distinction , as Jean Cohen notes, by conflating the "legal" person with the "natural" person, where legal personhood "presupposes no particular conception of the natural individual or of the self" ["Democracy", p. 198]. Instead, the legal person (or self) belongs to a "conferred" category [ibid., p. 213]. A similar point is made by Rawls when he states that, in the liberal theory of justice, the philosophical conception of the person as a moral agent is replaced by the political conception of the citizen (as free and equal) [see Political Liberalism, xlv; see also "Reply to Habermas", Journal of Philosophy, XCII, No. 3, March 1995, pp. 138 & 150]. However, "identity" theorists are likely to criticize Rawls for ignoring the fact that even legally identified citizens are often constituted, in practice, by the identities they derive from identity-bestowing cultural groups or categories.

10. The labeling of these two conceptions comes from Jean Cohen's critique of communitarian resistance to privacy rights [see "Democracy", p. 196]. Incidentally, reflection should make plain both that individuals are not, and cannot be, "self-sufficient" and that (non-voluntary) involvements are not the same as (primarily voluntary) attachments. To say, as communitarians are disposed to do, that our attachments flow from our embeddedness in the contexts in which we find ourselves is to ascribe overdetermination and gratuitous closure to these contexts. Phillips rightly affirms that the relevant issue is "not whether we can imagine a self without attachments,

but whether it is possible to detach ourselves from particular values or practices or goals" [Democracy, pp. 61-62]. By so doing, we evince an ability and a willingness for critical reflection on ourselves, on our attachments and on the possibilities for restructuring social relations.

11. "Feminism", p. 276. In contrast to communitarianism, this conception does not define the (individual) self in terms of an identity it shares with others, but in terms of interrelationships and interactions with others. An individual, inherently a social individual, is, so to speak, "constituted" by these interconnections; but this does not mean that the individuality of an individual is altogether so constituted. The social self need not be, without remainder, simply a socialized self.

12. Mansbridge maintains that "The greatest problem confronting a unitary democracy is its inability to resolve conflicts through bargaining." [Beyond Adversary Democracy, p. 265] Further problems for direct, participatory democracy (especially in contexts of larger scale) have been cited by Phillips: the subtle pressures for consensus and the difficulty in obtaining enough (released) time for active participation, particularly by women [see Democracy, pp. 109-111]. In general, "The higher the demands placed on participation, the more inevitable that it will be unevenly spread around; the more active the democratic engagement, the more likely it is to be carried by only a few" -- who tend to be self-selecting [ibid., p. 112]. Partridge, for his part, singles out certain limitations of popular political participation: many, probably most, people are not members of organizations that carry definite political influence; the power of organizations in which people do or can participate is very unequal; and participation in politically significant organizations is often low and their leadership is frequently elitist [see Consent, p. 65].

13. While much of the substance of the ideal of community assumed by unitary democracy is, indeed, often unduly homogenous, Young is wrong, in my opinion, in rejecting community tout court, alleging that "it expresses a desire for the fusion of subjects with one another which in practice operates to exclude those with whom the group does not identify" [Justice, p. 227]. In the first place, "fusion" has no proper place in the unity with difference of a solidary community; and in the second place, one can, practically speaking, identify, even if one cannot share a "constituted" identity, with those outside one's own community.

14. See Habermas, "Three Normative Models", p. 26.

15. See ibid., pp. 23, 24 & 28.

16. See Phillips, Democracy, p. 84.

17. Young, "Communication", p. 126.

18. Not only ambiguous but controversial. For example, Benjamin Barber, who seems to endorse something like civic republicanism, declares that it is important to take on the "loyalty of American citizenship", which includes recognition of "American exceptionalism", the "global appeal" of America, and America's status as the "last best hope" for all people in the world [see "Constitutional Faith", in Martha Nussbaum et al. For Love of Country. Boston: Beacon Press, 1996, pp. 31-33]. This outlook, in my opinion, goes beyond "civic patriotism" to national chauvinism.

19. See Phillips, Democracy, pp. 78 & 81. She insists that the concept of citizen requires a gendered interpretation [ibid., p. 49].

20. Ibid., p. 80.

21. Success in political (as well as economic) competition is often due not so much to superior skill, insightfulness or technical knowledge, but to the ability to control, in one way or another, the behavior of, or the information available to, competitors. In this regard, such competition is unlike

145

that of a game, such as chess, where the moves of competitors are "autonomous", the rules of the game are impartial, and the respective positions of competitors are transparent.

22. Macpherson notes that "The democratic political system is typically presented ... as a mechanism whose function is to reconcile or balance or hold in adjustment a multitude of diverse and conflicting individual interests. The control mechanism is the party system, which is seen as an entrepreneurial system." [Democratic Theory, p. 187] On this view, democracy is a mechanism for maintaining social equilibrium within the framework of competition between two or more elite groups for the power to govern the whole society and in which voters function as political consumers [see ibid., pp. 78-79].

23. The claim made on behalf of the pluralist model that multiple competing groups constitute dispersed centers of power and that none is consistently dominant is, with regard to political parties, only partially true and, with regard to both classes and "identity" groups, hardly true at all [on the given claim, see Held, Models, p. 187]. The disjunction between political party and social difference group under adversary democracy is addressed in the following observation by Phillips: "Liberal democracy presumes a continuing plurality of opinions and beliefs (as its insistence on multiparty competition confirms), but ... it does not see this plurality as relating to different, and unequal, social groups" [Democracy, p. 115].

24. See Consent, p. 117.

25. Ibid., p. 133. A further factor restricting citizen input is that "Parties tend to select issues which promise the greatest electoral advantage and the least electoral risk." [ibid., pp. 130-131]

26. Beyond Adversary Democracy, pp. 8 & 17.

27. The self-authenticating nature of "quality" commercial products for consumers and of "elite" political rule for citizen-voters is, it seems to me, a case in point. Elitism, then, is a not unexpected concomitant of political pluralism; for success in competition is typically taken to establish the superiority, not merely the preferability, of winners. It is instructive, moreover, that the marketing concept of "brand" has been held to be singularly relevant for defining and advertising not only commercial products but also both personal political identity and national identity. Concerning the latter, the imperious, possibly awesome "brand" that identifies a country can be an important geopolitical factor [see Thomas Frank, One Market Under God. New York: Doubleday, 2000, p. 252].

28. Mouffe says that pluralist democracy must accept "the permanence of conflicts and antagonisms" ["Radical Democracy or Liberal Democracy", in Trend, Radical Democracy, p. 20]. In another place, she argues that democracy should consider conflict and division legitimate, as part of its purpose to "celebrate and enhance" difference [see Democracy", p. 246]. In fact, she asseverates that domination and violence cannot be eliminated but only "limited and contested" [ibid., p. 248]. As a description, all of this is probably accurate, to a considerable degree, for the nation-state. At the same time, it supports the thesis that the existence of democracy, understood as the humanistic empowerment of human beings, that is, as the practice of positive freedom, is problematic for various social contexts, especially large-scale ones.

29. See Democracy, p. 32. At least, the commitment can be only to purely procedural forms of equality, justice, etc.

146

30. See Holden, Nature, p. 118. Many views, though, are "reflected" by their being tentatively taken into account and then more or less ignored. Holden's perspective reflects a sublime disregard of the fact that the politics of bargaining, negotiation, etc., is most likely to be "a form of politics that will almost inevitably accord a central role to political, bureaucratic or organizational élites and thereby tend to exclude the rank and file from the experience of political involvement" [Partridge, Consent, p. 137].

31. See Macpherson, Democratic Theory, p. 42.

32. See Democracy, p. 275. Nevertheless, domination, as characterized by Domhoff, is a persistent fact of American political life. Domination means "the ability of a class or group to set the terms under which other classes or groups within a social system must operate. By this definition, domination does not mean control on each and every issue, and it does not rest upon government involvement alone. Involvement in government is only the final and most visible aspect of power elite domination, which has its roots in the class structure, the nature of the economy, and the functioning of the policy-planning and opinion-shaping networks." [Who Rules, p. 150]

33. See Robert Redeker, "In Place of Politics: Humanitarianism and War", in Masters of the Universe?, ed. Tariq Ali. London: Verso: 2000, p. 173.

34. See Democracy, pp. 275-277. He believes that, given competition among political elites, the policies of government will perforce be responsive to preferences of the majority of voters. This would be the case only if the status and power of elites actually depended primarily upon (the majority of) voters -- something that I do not find plausible. Indeed, I believe that the converse often obtains, such that many cases of ostensible majority rule are, in fact, exercises in ratification of minority rule by the majority.

35. Although I do not define democracy in terms of a process of decision-making, the latter together with the deliberation that is involved in it are integral to democratic life. More particularly, deliberation is a component of (cognitive) empowerment , an ability that is important for decisional autonomy, that is, for the exercise of "free will", since deliberation is a necessary condition of that exercise.

36. See Habermas, Between Facts and Norms. Cambridge: MIT Press, 1996, pp. 305-306. Both resolution and validation derive from the fact that, on a "discourse-theoretic interpretation ... democratic will-formation draws its legitimating force not from a previous convergence of settled ethical convictions but both from the communicative presuppositions that allow the better arguments to come into play in various forms of deliberation and from the procedures that secure fair bargaining processes" ["Three Normative Models", p. 24]. For Habermas, the "practical reason" at work in deliberative democracy "withdraws from universal human rights, or from the concrete ethical substance of a specific community, into the rules of discourse and forms of argumentation" [ibid., p. 26]. Rawls alleges that Habermas's proceduralist paradigm tacitly incorporates substantive values, for example, regarding outcomes issuing from the public use of reason. This is unavoidable, since "the justice of a procedure always depends ... on the justice of its likely outcomes, or on substantive justice" [see "Reply to Habermas", p. 170]. I concur fully with Rawls here.

37. Habermas, Between Facts and Norms, pp. 296 & 320.

38. Ibid., p. 324.

39. Ibid., p. 4.

40. Ibid., p. 367.

147

41. Ibid., p. 360.

42. Ibid., p. 363. Habermas states that "The public opinion that is worked up via democratic procedures into communicative power cannot 'rule' of itself but can only point the use of administrative power in specific directions" [ibid., p. 300].

43. Ibid., p. 352.

44. Ibid., pp. 301 & 305. Habermas's restriction of deliberative democracy to the political sphere is at odds, for example, with Banhabib's claim that this model of democracy is applicable to "the major institutions of society on the basis of the principle that decisions affecting the well-being of a collectivity can be viewed as the outcome of a procedure of free and reasoned deliberation" ["Toward a Deliberative Model", p. 68].

45. Ibid., pp. 460 & 455.

46. Ibid., p. 287. Benhabib's variant on his "partially inscribed" is her "already implicit" [see "Toward a Deliberative Model", p. 84].

47. Ibid., pp. 322-323. Habermas's depiction of the communication community as a methodological fiction specifying ideal norms is, in my view, more forthright and realistic than Rawls's stance to the effect that, while the "moral psychology" relevant for both a political conception of justice as fairness and for an ideal of citizenship is non-empirical, this "psychology" is not impractical, since human nature is "permissive" and historical experience is "full of surprises" [see Political Liberalism, pp. 86-87]. It should not be forgotten, however, that human nature and human history have "permitted" some very unpleasant "surprises".

48. The matter is complicated by the fact that, from the perspective, say, of a behaviorist theory of meaning, identical meanings of expressions are shown in the sameness of responses by individuals to their use. Although this is a meaningful use of 'identical meanings', it is clearly not what Habermas means by the meaning of 'meaning'.

49. "Communication", p. 120.

50. Ibid., pp. 122-123. Young's criticisms of deliberative democracy perhaps apply less directly to Habermas's orientation, since, as noted earlier, he limits its articulation to the public political system.

51. Ibid., p. 124.

52. See Between Facts and Norms, p. 296.

53. Democracy, p. 13.

54. Jean Cohen states that the relevance of reasons is contextual [see "Democracy", p. 209]. This applies, in her example, to the reasons that one accepts from the standpoint of the decisional autonomy of one's privacy [ibid., p. 202]. Habermas himself seems to grant, qualifiedly, that reasons are contextual, when he declares that "what counts as a 'good reason' manifests itself only in the role it has in an argumentation game, that is, in the contribution it makes according to the rules of the game for deciding the question whether a contested validity claim may be accepted or not" [Between Facts and Norms, p. 227]. This relativity of reasons is allegedly transcended in a rationally motivated consensus [Einverständnis], which "rests on reasons that convince all the parties in the same way", as contrasted with a compromise [Vereinbarung], which "can be accepted by the different parties each for its own different reasons" [ibid., p. 166].

148

55. See "Procedure", p. 103.

56. These criticisms can be found, respectively, at p. 10, p. 97, p. 112 & p. 115. I do not think Young would be reassured by Habermas's comment that if "public discourses that spring from autonomous public spheres ... take shape in the decisions of democratic, politically accountable legislative bodies, then the pluralism of beliefs and interests is not suppressed but unleashed and recognized in revisable majority decisions as well as in compromises" [Between Facts and Norms, p. 186].

57. See "Toward a Deliberative Model", p. 69.

58. Political Liberalism, p. 16.

59. These different connotations of 'rational' are, I think, roughly cognate with the distinction that Rawls makes between (instrumental) rationality, which employs means-ends reasoning, and being "reasonable", namely, demonstrating a "moral sensibility" that emphasizes fairness and reciprocity for the sake of a mutually beneficial society [see ibid., pp. 50-54].

60. Ibid., xlvi.

61. Ibid., liii. Interestingly, Rawls alleges that the content and the method of public reason "are to rest on the plain truths now widely accepted, or available, to citizens generally" [ibid., p. 225]. A question that comes to mind is whether the "truths" are widely accepted because they are "plain" or, rather, whether they are "plain" because they are widely accepted -- or, for that matter, whether they are even widely accepted.

62. Between Facts and Norms, pp. 372 & 379. In view of these reservations prompted by awareness of "inertial" obstacles, it is somewhat perplexing that Habermas also maintains that "a public use of reason and a communicative power ... do not just monitor the exercise of political power in a belated manner but more or less program it as well" ["Three Normative Models", p. 186].

63. Ibid., p. 356. At the risk of appearing somewhat cynical, I will suggest that flows of communication are not infrequently "polluted": from citizens to government, they can be egocentric, confused or irrelevant; from government to citizens, they can be tendentious, disinformative or opaque.

64. See "Using Power/Fighting Power: The Polity", in Benhabib, Democracy, pp. 46 & 47.

65. Ibid., p. 48.

66. Ibid., p. 51.

67. See Between Facts and Norms, pp. 39 & 129.

68. Ibid., p. 447. As I understand Habermas, the legitimacy of law is a special case of the legitimacy of regulations "to which all who are possibly affected could assent as participants in rational discourse" [ibid., p. 458]. This counterfactual criterion clearly exhibits the tension between facticity and validity.

69. See "Using Power", p. 55.

70. See Between Facts and Norms, p. 121.

71. See "Using Power", pp. 47 & 56-58

149

72. See Between Facts and Norms, p. 383.

73. Justice, p. 232.

74. The great instrumental importance of (social) cooperation is emphasized by Sen in On Ethics, p. 85.

75. See Robert Axelrod, The Evolution of Cooperation. New York: Basic Books, 1984, p. 22.

76. See ibid., pp. 40-46, 109-113 & 137. Axelrod observes that "what is best for each person individually leads to mutual defection, whereas everyone would have been better off with mutual cooperation" [p. 9]. See, also, Sen, On Ethics, p. 82. On my view, "defection" does not occur insofar as communal cooperation is genuinely based upon the commitment of those engaged in it.

77. Ibid., p. 282. Interestingly, for competitive zero-sum games, communication is unnecessary [see Morton D. Davis, Game Theory. New York: Basic Books, 1983, p. 92]. Of course, for the positive-sum "game" of cooperative democracy, communication is crucial.

78. On this evolutionarily beneficial "mutualism" among biological organisms, see Douglas H. Boucher (ed.). The Biology of Mutualism. New York: Oxford University Press, 1985; Axelrod, The Evolution, chapter 5; and Davis, Game Theory, pp. 136 & 149.

79. Political Liberalism, p. 168. An overlapping political consensus is, no doubt, feasible. However, in spite of what Rawls says, there is, in "our" society, no consensus reflected in what he cites (incorrectly, in my opinion) as examples of "our considered judgments with their fixed points", namely, condemnation of "the subjection of the working classes, the oppression of women, and the unlimited accumulation of vast fortunes" [see "Reply to Habermas", p. 178]. While an overlapping consensus may not be utopian as such, confidence that these "considered judgments" are existing "fixed points" is so.

80. See "Reconciliation through the Public Use of Reason", Journal of Philosophy, XCII, No. 3, March 1995, p. 128. Further, even "cooperation" may be a gloss on what is really happening. Thus, Partridge suggests that social stability may be due as much or more to consensus among political and administrative elites than to any popular consensus, the latter normally expressing, in fact, hardly more than conventional attitudes and customary behavior [see Consent, p. 54]. He asserts, rather bluntly, that "inertia, indifference, habituation, a relatively unthinking conformity with practices and norms supported by élites and authorities all form part of the social state we call stability" [ibid., p. 121].

81. See Davis, Game Theory, p. 163.

82. "Feminism", p. 276. I prefer a term like 'solidarity' to one like 'nurturance', which strikes me as somewhat too maternalistic/paternalistic.

83. Accordingly, I use 'community' in a sense different from that of Rawls in his Political Liberalism [see, for example, p. 42], as well as from the communitarian use of that term.

84. Rawls states that the nature of the political relation in a (constitutional) democratic regime is one of "civic friendship" [see ibid., li]. If this interpersonal relation is not to be construed merely abstractly, then it can at most be, I submit, "civic friendliness" or "civic civility". Such considerateness, indeed cordiality, is humanly valuable and politically beneficial; yet it can be directed toward people about whom one does not particularly care or with whom one does not "identify".

85. Ibid., p. 26

86. Ibid., p. 54.

87. See ibid., p. 52.

88. See "Reconciliation", p. 128. A similar reservation about social contract theories in general is advanced by Partridge in Consent, p. 20

CHAPTER 9

LEGITIMACY, OBLIGATION AND LOYALTY

I

It has been argued that the forms of politics and government, including institutional and bureaucratic structures, of contemporary nation-states considered democratic are not determined primarily by the goal of realizing democratic values. [1] In addition to the goals these forms do promote of sustaining political stability and continuity, as well as providing for both the "general welfare" of the people and the special interests of certain constituencies therein, they serve to characterize and, evocatively, to legitimize the state as "democratic", even though the state is not significantly involved, as such, in the democratization of human life.

The meaning of political legitimacy, with respect to democracy, and the criteria for democratic legitimation are complex and contested issues. One formulation, often taken to express a necessary condition of democracy, is that "government ought to be founded on the consent of the governed, that only those governments which enjoy the consent of their subjects possess rightful authority and can legitimately demand or expect obedience". [2] Before examining the nature of consent, I want first, however, to inspect the meaning of political legitimacy (as status) and legitimation (as process). Roughly, a structure or institution is legitimate if it is established according to criteria/rules defining legitimacy, and an action or activity is legitimate if it proceeds in conformity with such criteria/rules. These criteria/rules are socially constituted, with a validity that is immanent to the social bodies promulgating them. As non-logical "validity" does not transcend particular contexts, so neither does legitimacy. Some criteria/rules, by virtue of which something is legitimate, are, to be sure, more basic than others; and their prioritization and ranking is concretely exemplified, correspondingly, in the system of laws prevailing in a country. Moreover, any "crisis" of legitimation, it seems to me, is due either to the internal incoherence or inconsistency of those criteria/rules or else to their external failure to be convincing to a sufficient proportion of the citizenry.

Conventionally, authority is viewed as power that is legitimate, in other words, as might that has established itself as having a right to rule. Disregarding preternatural sanctions for democracy as irrelevant, even incongruous -- a metaphysically supernal sanction for authority will no doubt be noticeably undemocratic -- one will find, I think, that, historically, ostensibly democratic forms have usually been originarily instituted by an elite consensus that would be able to appeal only to hypothetical, implicit or ex post facto consent of the governed. For example, socially transformative political revolutions with professedly democratic aims are not made contingent upon prior majority authorization by the people the revolutions are expected to benefit. To a decisive extent, then, legitimacy in such contexts is, factually, self-selecting. Once the foundations of authority are laid down, other social/political forms and processes derive their own legitimacy therefrom.

To consent to something is, at least, to accept it. However, the converse does not necessarily hold, for one may accept something (perhaps resignedly as unavoidable) without (willingly) consenting to it. At the same time, one might argue that acceptance is simply one of the ways in which consent is manifested. Thus, Partridge has set out an instructive taxonomy of types of consent: acquiescence under duress; voluntary agreement based upon manipulation of consciousness; acquiescence arising from "sheer apathy, indifference or habit", with no inclination toward dissent; acceptance of established traditions of conduct as furnishing norms of right behavior; socialization, that is, an internalization of values that prompts identification with major institutions and authorities; deliberately granted permission, going beyond mere approval or support for what is done; and active willing (not just permission) that something be done, that government should implement the "will" of the people. [3] Acknowledging these varied modalities, it remains the case that consent comprises acceptance, an acceptance that is often more affirmative than a "tacit consent" of "passivity or indifference" or "resentful or rebellious acquiescence". [4]

According to Habermas, acceptance is one thing, acceptability is another: the former is descriptive, the latter normative, related to a (non-logical) type of validity. [5] In these senses of terms, legitimacy correlates, as a matter of fact, either with conformity to authorized patterns, procedures or results already existing or else with acceptance (consent) by persons affected. Here, legitimacy is acceptedness, theoretical or practical. It is expressed, in effect, in the sanction of positive law. An implication of this standpoint is that legitimacy is to be categorially distinguished from justice: what is legitimate may not be just, and what is just may not be legitimate, that is, legitimated. Consequently, if consent of the governed somehow legitimizes government, then citizens may well consent to government that is legitimate but unjust. Many people, much or most of the time, probably judge that the actions of their legitimate (duly constituted) government are, by and large, just, in the sense of justified or justifiable. However, this presumption of justifiability, indicating congruence with what is legitimate, is not the same as a definite belief in the justice of what is done -- as attested by frequent complaints that what the (legitimate) "authorities" do is unjust or unfair.

Rawls is even more explicit than Habermas about the distinction between 'legitimate' and 'just'. In the language of the former, "democratic decisions and laws are legitimate, not because they are just but because they are legitimately enacted in accordance with an accepted legitimate democratic procedure"; indeed, "Laws passed by solid majorities are counted legitimate, even though many protest and correctly judge them unjust or otherwise wrong." [6] Rawls considers Habermas's analysis defective because it emphasizes legitimacy rather than justice. [7] For his part, Habermas claims that Rawls's analysis fails to "bridge the chasm between ideal theoretical demands and social facts", to keep in touch with "the harder material of institutions and action systems". [8] Habermas himself, I think, is not above reproach in this matter. If Rawls locates the foundations of justice in the consensus of a <u>hypothetical</u> social contract, Habermas finds them in a consensus about what is rationally acceptable from the standpoint of <u>ideal</u> deliberation. Both perspectives have been criticized in previous chapters; and I have argued earlier that principles of justice are not so much "justified" as affirmed, that is, valorized through commitment.

The distinction between legitimacy and justice, even if not altogether exclusive, is important for several reasons. Analytically, it invites attention to the significant difference between the "is" and the "ought", between the descriptive and the normative. [9] This difference is reflected in the fact (remarked above) that legitimacy and justice can each exist apart from the other, a situation of some moment in that unjust, non-democratic governments can nevertheless possess legitimacy. Related to this is the question whether a dictatorial/authoritarian government could be legitimized by democratic means. If legitimacy is founded upon consent (of the governed) and if "democratic" legitimation obtains through electoral mechanisms, then it seems, paradoxically, that elected dictatorial authority -- especially if subject to a requirement of occasional relegitimization -- might be considered to possess democratic legitimacy. This counterintuitive inference indicates, in my opinion, not that the governed cannot consent to dictatorial governance (they can and have done so historically) [10] but that elections are an insufficient, incomplete means by which to establish legitimacy that is democratic. Even if one concedes that voting in so-called liberal democratic societies somehow contributes to the legitimacy of the political system that makes use of it, as well as the outcomes of the voting itself, endorsement of the system or of the outcomes is not thereby entailed. Participation in voting may well be calculatedly pragmatic, evincing not negligible measures of opportunism or cynicism, frequently merited in view of the virtually "pre-ordained" nature of the choices made available and also the often skewed and objectively inequitable character of the procedures for voting. Furthermore, abstention from voting does not bestow consent by default, because, I believe, it is more often a rationally directed sense of the irrelevancy of voting rather than sheer apathy that is at work here, especially among subordinated and marginalized groups. Not participating may be a type of explicit dissent instead of a type of implicit consent.

As I have argued previously, democracy involves justice, that is, arrangements and processes that are non-exploitative, non-dominative and non-oppressive. For any context where this fails to be the case, power may be legitimate because legitimized, but it is not democratic. Legitimacy is determined by the means that establish it, whereas justice, like democracy, is not independent of the recurring tasks and goals that define it. From this it follows that democratic legitimation is based upon means that are specifically oriented upon democratic tasks and goals.

Before proceeding, I wish to anticipate a point that will be elaborated later in this chapter, namely, that, while one may have a practical or prudential obligation toward what is legitimate, one need not experience or profess loyalty to it. Thus, while one may be loyal to democratic (and humanistic) values and to those individuals with whom one stands in democratic solidarity, one may yet be merely obligated or required to conform to legitimate rules and regulations: in short, obligation toward laws or rules but loyalty to persons.

An additional consideration is that consent need not be a criterion of political or legal obligation. Thus one can be obligated to obey, that is, conform to, (legitimate) laws or rules to which one did not give consent, either because one dissented from them or because one was not in a position to consent, as, for example, when one is a visitor in another country and/or a minor in one's own. Perhaps it might be said that, in these kinds of cases, one implicitly consents to comply with laws or rules to which one has not explicitly consented. Something analogous to this is usually invoked to justify compliance on the part of those who disagree with the outcomes of majority decision-making. The moral of all this may be that "consent of the governed" is rather often really "consent to be governed". Correspondingly, a distinction may be made between "consent to an obligation" and " consent to be obligated". By the latter expression, I mean an acceptance of the fact that legal or moral prescriptions have been, or will be, directed toward persons in situations applying to oneself (and others), an acceptance that may, or may not, issue in one's action in accordance with the prescriptions. Here, one simply recognizes that one is obligated to be obligated. By the former expression, I mean a voluntary commitment to comply with a particular obligation, understood as something of which one approves.

Obedience to authority may take place for different kinds of reasons: if it is passably democratic and just, an authority to which one has consented or would consent, obedience is reasonable; if, however, it does not or would not elicit one's express consent, obedience is, at most, prudential, a matter of minimizing risks. In the latter type of case, there is evinced a rather weak kind of "consent", namely, acquiescence or acceptance. Here is found the logic of motivation, rather than that of justification. What it takes for authority to be justified is problematic and, to my mind, not altogether clear. If something is legitimized, is it thereby justified? Can it be justifiable without having received any legitimization? I think the answer to the second question is "Yes"; but I am not sure about the answer to the first, since 'justified' need not mean the same as 'just'. If it does not, then legitimacy and justifiability (alternatively: legitimation and justification) in a political and/or legal sense tend conceptually to coalesce. This category of justification, according to Rawls, consists of three components: a reasonable overlapping consensus, stability for the right reasons, and legitimacy. [11] The decisive factor in all of this is a shared political conception expressing an overlapping consensus incorporating "reasonable comprehensive doctrines". In view of the role of the contractual "original position" in specifying what is basic to justice, the fundamentally regulative principles of a derived constitution are both just and legitimate, even though particular statutes and decisions emanating from the government may be legitimate but not just. [12] It is interesting that justification in the context of the pristine hypothetical contract, as well as in that of political society, is defined by Rawls in terms of consensus. With Habermas, consensus likewise carries (ideal) normative weight of great importance.

The significance of consensus and its dialectical relationship to consent merit particular attention. Schematically and preliminarily, one might say that, conventionally, consent legitimates, whereas consensus "legislates".[13] While perhaps a useful point of departure, such a formulation is indeed tentative and revisable. Given Partridge's detailed classification, cited above, of types of consent, it is possible to say meaningfully, in response to one of the questions raised at the end of the preceding chapter, that one can willingly consent to what one does not consider legitimate; that is, one can accept, or acquiescence in, what is believed to be illegitimate. To the extent that this is so, consent cannot be taken as a clear-cut sign of (bestowed) legitimation, and consent of the governed becomes, in general, acceptance by the governed. As for the other question raised, if consent is construed in a sense stronger than mere acceptance, for example, as active endorsement, then one can knowingly refuse to consent to what one grants is (descriptively) legitimate (or legitimated) as expressed in established law or rule that, however, one considers unjust. Principled civil disobedience is patently an example of this latter situation.

As Christiano notes, some arguments "suggest that individuals indirectly consent to the outcomes of decision procedures when they freely participate in them ... and thereby incur a self-imposed obligation to comply with the outcomes".[14] Consent based upon free participation may well be voluntary consent, yet not informed consent. Often consent of the governed is misinformed consent. Moreover, even where participation, such as voting, might reasonably be taken to betoken a significant degree of legitimization , it nevertheless establishes quite modest control over the activities of those elected. [15]   The obligation to comply is also subject to qualifications. Consent to procedures, as noted above, does not necessarily entail consent to their outcomes -- nor obligated compliance with them -- since one may judge the (legitimate) procedures to have been manipulated or otherwise abused. Further, consent to outcomes (as legitimate) does not necessarily entail a commitment -- even if there is an obligation -- to comply with them, since one may have other commitments that override any presumptive commitment to comply with those outcomes. Commitments sometimes "trump" obligations.

The language of consent tends to be more ceremonial, vindicative and reassuring than descriptive of actual situations and processes. In fact, Partridge maintains that "the vast mass of what a modern government enacts has not in any sense received the prior approval or consent of the electorate".[16] To treat consent as typically after the fact makes it seem somewhat like applause, on the one hand, or, less enthusiastically, acquiescence, on the other. This does not necessarily impugn the credentials of these facsimiles of consent, for one may intelligibly approve of, or assent to, that to which one did not give prior consent. Moreover, much of the "consent of the governed" is related primarily to the society whose perceived favorable functioning is presided over by the government. [17]   It is customary for people to consent to what government does, even if it is not clear what this is, so long as political practices have socially (including economically) endorsable consequences.

With respect to consensus, it seems that consensus implies consent, for example, to procedures and/or outcomes -- but not conversely. Consensus is found in voluntary agreement about something; and to agree "about" (consensus) is not quite the same as to agree "to" (consent). Consent can exist apart from consensus, as in the weak forms of consent catalogued by Partridge. On the other hand, the type of consensus required or expected may be based upon the consent of the individuals who will be involved with it, as in the procedure of majority decision-making. The dialectic of consent and consensus is somewhat intricate. Thus, one may consent to the determining role of a consensus in which one does not share; and there may well be a consensus about the legitimizing role of consent.

It may be said that social cohesion and stability are signs of a (social) consensus. However, this assumption is questionable, since "Many members of a society may regularly conform to established patterns because they are unaware of the existence of possible alternatives; or because they fear that they will be less well off if they deviate; or because they feel themselves to lack the capacity to modify established institutions and modes of behaviour; or because of overt compulsion and constraint such as the pressure of the law and its sanctions." [18] In these cases of conformism as consensus, any "overlapping " character of the latter is, essentially, a reflection of pragmatically or prudentially motivated commonalities of attitude and behavior. Even more, such "consensus" may be merely perfunctory, neither deliberated nor deliberate. In this regard, Partridge contends that the evidence "does not suggest that most citizens of modern industrial societies have either a clear understanding of, or intense or consistent attachment to, the values and principles of democratic political procedures". [19] If this is so, there can be a consensus about the virtues of democracy without much consensus as to just what these virtues are. Often, it seems that a paramount virtue of democracy is that it can "deliver the goods"

Contained in the term 'democratic consensus' is a (non-lethal) ambiguity: it may refer to a consensus about something, a consensus that is reached democratically, or it may refer to a consensus about democracy itself, its nature and value, or both. In any case, as I see the matter, consensus in an authentically democratic context is, on the one hand, a practical expression of the solidarity undergirding democracy as communal empowerment and, on the other, a procedure, more or less satisfied, for implementing this solidarity in problem-solving and decision-making. Although consensus properly pays attention to norms of rationality and impartiality, its driving force is commitment and care. For the quasi- democracy of a nation-state, a minimalist consensus may be sufficient for the purposes of agreement about, and support for, rules, procedures and institutions, a customary consensus that serves important goals of social stability and continuity. This is not to deny that such a consensus can be compatible with the sometimes heated disagreements of adversary democracy, with the oppositions and tensions of "difference", with both virulent criticism of government and political languor; [20] for much consensus expresses not an active and explicit form of agreement about details but, rather, a generalized and diffused agreement about social prospects, which is probably more a form of expectation and hope than principled agreement as such. Even in difficult times, a consensus of expectation and hope can be quite powerful.

For democracy as the communally cooperative practice of positive freedom, the function of consensus is not to inhibit disagreement, criticism or diversity, but to reflect and reinforce the solidarity underlying all of this. Stated differently, consensus is not necessarily about what is to be done but is about the value of communally cooperative relationships, of collaborative projects and of the people who are mutually involved in them.

It has been remarked that where consensus is not forthcoming, say, in the dynamics of adversary democracy -- or even in those of deliberative democracy -- the principle of majority rule may be invoked. On the face of it, majority rule seems reasonable and fair. However, there are problems. [21] In the first place, how is majority rule itself to be justified or legitimized? By an unvalidated appeal to the majority to validate majority rule? By a decision of the majority of a minority to sanction, and possibly to extend the scope of, majority rule (a phenomenon that has probably occurred more than once in the history of political affairs)? By a consequentialist argument on behalf of the beneficial effects of majority rule? These effects might be connected to ensuring the stability of the political system, to maximizing the "efficiency" of the decision-making process, or to satisfying a criterion of "economy" that obviates excessive time, attention or energy devoted to that process. [22] Ideally, and not infrequently in fact, majority rule may be legitimized by a consensus to employ it in cases where a consensus cannot settle extant issues.

In the second place, majority rule may install or perpetuate an entrenched balance of power which is invidious and prejudicial with respect to minorities or, in the case of majority endorsement of elitist rule, which is hardly a manifestation of majority rule proper. Often, of course, it is argued that majority rule is not only consistent with, but does not discourage, shifting or rotating majorities, from which it allegedly follows that this or that minority or set of minorities can become, by means of energetic and deft coalition-building, a new majority. Such an eventuality is theoretically possible; but the claim on its behalf is, I submit, historically naive and politically disingenuous. Some minorities, characterized by particular identities, social status, types of difference or interests, tend to be permanent minorities. [23] Far removed from the kind of minority possessing elite power, these other kinds of minorities usually are relatively powerless. If they are sited within the system of adversary democracy, it may be recommended that they deploy bargaining as a technique for pursuing their interests and objectives. Yet, what do marginalized or subjugated groups have available to them to bargain with? By the way, the relevant question for democratic contexts is not so much whether legitimate decisions displease a minority but whether they disadvantage, or inhibit the empowerment of, a minority. Perhaps here the distinction between offense and harm has some application.

In the third place, the majority rule principle may be judged too strong as well as too weak, that is, sanctioning both too much and too little. On the one hand, there is the hoary problem of the "tyranny of the majority". Different, but still troublesome, is majority endorsement of (centralized) tyranny, rather than actual exercise of tyranny by the majority. In response to the former kind of case, the standard mechanism suggested is a system of rights designed to prevent abuse of power by the majority. However, as argued in an earlier chapter, a system of (human) rights should not only proscribe violations of negative freedom but also prescribe implementation of positive freedom. The obverse of tyranny of the majority is abdication by it of responsibility in the face of domination and oppression suffered by others. With regard to majority assent to tyranny, for example, to dictatorship, neither the concept nor the institution of human rights plays a role in influencing public policy.

On the other hand, majority rule is essentially procedural, a decision-procedure that is considered sound on the strength of its method, not because of outcomes. As Mansbridge observes, "Majority rule ensures equality only in the procedure, not in the result." [24] Whereas majority rule certifies outcomes as legitimate, they may not at all be just. Hence, if justice is an integral element of democracy, then majority rule is not a distinguishing criterion of democracy -- although majority decision-making is probably an important supportive condition for it. Incidentally, "majority rule" is something of a misnomer, since it does not mean that a majority actively rules or controls but that either it selects those who do, in fact, rule or else it approves regulations, laws, etc., that rule or govern.

Another critique of the majority rule principle has been developed in a most pertinent and insightful treatment by Lani Guinier. [25] She recognizes, indeed emphasizes, that in a diversified, heterogeneous society (such as the United States), "the majority may not represent all competing interests. The majority is likely to be self-interested and ignorant or indifferent to the concerns of the minority." [26] Not only that, "While pluralist theories of democracy contemplate minority losses, they do not envision a minority that always loses." [27] As is often the case, equal opportunity is merely formal, with some minority groups having a rather permanent "opportunity" to occupy a socially disadvantaged, exploited status. In the kinds of situations just described, the majority, however much generalized concern or good will it may profess to possess, is, I think it is correct to say, objectively hegemonic and dominating.

In view of the fact that minorities typically do not "circulate" (to become, or to combine to form, a majority) and since a winner-take-all type of majoritarianism means that a simple majority of votes yields a totality of control, Guinier recommends a "principle of taking terms", which "disaggregates" a fixed majority that refuses to cooperate seriously with minorities. [28] To supplement this strategy, she also suggests the use of cumulative voting, under which "voters get the same number of votes as there are seats or options to vote for, and they can then distribute their votes in any combination to reflect their preferences". [29] The former strategy is designed to deter emplacement of a continuing majority that promotes self-serving, parochial interests, the latter to facilitate the development of productive bargaining or coalition-building by minorities. Such development exemplifies the principle that "Consensus must be built, not just located." [30]

Guinier's proposals have been criticized as theoretically eccentric and practically objectionable. However, to my mind, they are sound and relevant, for they reflect, I believe, the standpoint that democracy is not, basically, a technique for managing social contestation by permitting widespread participation in the maldistribution of power but a cooperative program to empower as many people as possible, utilizing, among other things, electoral and legislative mechanisms that are oriented not just on procedural legitimation but on social justice.

II

Earlier, I said that an accepted obligation toward what is legitimate need not presuppose an affirmation of loyalty to it. Another way to put this is to say that an acceptance of obligation under an authority does not itself entail a sense of allegiance to it. In short, obligations may be acknowledged without any involvement of loyalty -- though loyalties inherently imply obligations (to those to whom one is loyal). As mentioned previously, one may voluntarily (accept an obligation to) obey laws of a foreign country that one is visiting without extending loyalty to that country. So also, I contend, one may apply the same principle to the country of one's citizenship. Moreover, one may acknowledge an obligation to comply with a rule or law, not because one considers it justifiably "right" or because one feels allegiance to the authority behind it, but because one thereby shows solidarity with others so obligated, that is, this solidarity constitutes a rejection of special pleading and self-seeking preferment for oneself and, where the obligation imposes a particular burden, expresses sympathy for others so burdened.

The distinction between obligation and loyalty (or allegiance) might be stated schematically in terms of that with which, respectively, they are related: obligation is displayed toward rules or procedures, while loyalty is shown to persons. Some amendments are required here. Whereas obligations can exist in the absence of loyalties to that toward which one has the obligations, obligations to do or to refrain from doing inevitably follow from loyalties. [31]   In addition, fidelity -- rather than loyalty or allegiance as such -- to values or principles also implies an obligation, namely, to support them conscientiously. Provisionally, it might be asserted that obligation is more associated with justice (or, in a weaker sense, with justifiability or legitimacy) and loyalty is more associated with commitment (based, for example, upon caring). Presumably, if a law or rule is legitimate (perhaps even just), there exists an obligation, normatively, to comply with it, since one ought to do what is right (or rightful). However, as the rightness of a rule, law or principle depends upon what it is right for, that is, upon the purpose(s) that it is designed to serve as a means, 'ought' is a logical accessory of 'right', whose use is "justified" by the ends/purposes whose means it normatively prescribes. Thus, moral rules or norms do not have an obligatory character because they are moral, but because they are (prescriptive) rules or norms, which are right insofar as they rightfully, that is, correctly, direct action in accordance with valorized purposes located in the social region known as "morality". To my way of thinking, all of this is consistent with the view that "good" is conceptually, epistemologically and behaviorally prior to "right". [32] Further, by understanding rightness in terms of correctness, it permits rules in general -- whether moral, legal or otherwise -- to be seen, qua prescriptions, as categorially similar, that is, as different parts, functioning in different ways, of a specifically human praxis. Once more, with regard to democracy, this means that its basis lies, not in moral "first principles" or in abstract conceptions of "right" and "justice", but in the values, and the faithful commitment to them, according to which caring human beings, loyal to one another, seek their mutual empowerment, as well as the empowerment of many others who are perhaps only cohorts in various joint projects of social life.

Loyalty to (or solidarity with) some may well take precedence over putative obligations to everyone. Correlated with this is the principle that partiality to some can defensibly override impartiality toward all. A corollary of this principle is that obligation can be universalized, but loyalty cannot. Impartiality involves equal consideration and just treatment. However, when I attempt to consider everyone equally, I find that presiding loyalties (allegiances, solidarities) obtain with some individuals in a way that they do not with others. Furthermore, partiality need not be a manifestation of injustice. Justice requires equal treatment, not in the sense of equal outcomes that one tries to produce, but in the sense of treatment that is differential only when persons or circumstances are relevantly different. For rules and regulations applied, for example, by the state, the kinds of differences that are relevant are one thing; and often there are none. The kinds of differences that are valorized in interpersonal relationships -- kinds reflective of care, commitment, loyalty -- are, however, another thing; and so long as the treatment of persons avoids domination, oppression or exploitation of anyone -- both those to whom one is loyal, as well as anyone else -- this treatment is just. Indeed, the status of persons to whom one has special loyalty or

166

commitment is a relevant difference under the provisions of the formal principle of justice.

It may be thought that partiality toward persons is incompatible with reciprocity between persons. Such, I suggest, is not the case. I may have a (mutually) fair, trusting, even respectful relationship with another person who is not a focus of my particularized loyalty or solidarity, at the same time that I understand myself likewise not to be a focus of that person's loyalty or solidarity. This type of reciprocity is found in social cooperation, which need not embody loyalties and solidarities characteristic of communal cooperation. Further, this type of reciprocity is instrumental, "contractual", a relationship that requires impartiality in the implementation of techniques, procedures and responsibilities agreed upon, but not necessarily in personal affiliations. At a descriptive level, reciprocity is a sociological phenomenon. Normatively, it calls for a mutual moral valorization that, applied "universally", would be abstract, remote and, in practice, uneven.

With regard to the government of the nation-state and its embedded jurisdictions, there are, if these governing bodies are legitimate, therefore legitimated obligations and correlated duties. Recognition and acceptance of such obligations do not necessarily presuppose or manifest allegiance to the authority behind them. This is not because a state has no (legitimate) authority or no "right" to command or rule -- as anarchists not infrequently argue [33] -- but because the nature of the relationship toward (legitimate) authority is not that of allegiance (or loyalty). Part of the anarchist argument is that the state possesses no moral authority. This is true, not because the state possesses no authority but because its authority is not moral. From this it follows that any obligation to obey the state and its directives is not of a moral kind. In that the state is an instrument, obligation toward it is purely instrumental. Even Rawls, in his own way from the standpoint of a political conception of justice, asserts that people as citizens have political rights and duties rather than moral rights and duties. [34] In addition, he

167

claims that, for the liberal conception of justice, "political values and ideals ...
normally outweigh whatever other values oppose them" and thus "allegiance
based on these political values is stronger" than that to "opposing values". [35] Yet,
as I have maintained, "other values" (based upon loyalty and commitment) can
outweigh "political values and ideals" and, moreover, political values are not a
basis for "allegiance". Support (often provisional) for the state to which one is
subject and for the country of which one is a citizen I do not regard as allegiance.
As remarked already, allegiance, like loyalty, should be to persons, not to
impersonal entities such as state or country. Perhaps it will be averred that one
can (or should) feel loyalty, if not to one's country as geopolitical entity, then at
least to all the persons who, as citizens, compose one's country. Such a feeling, I
believe, is neither psychologically possible not practically necessary. Consent to,
that is, acceptance of, dependable forms of social cooperation is sufficient for the
purposes of state and country. National egoism is not required. Pride in one's
country should really be pride, so far as this is justifiable, in the people who
constitute it. A final consideration in this context: one can equally feel loyalty
(allegiance) to various citizens of other countries.

Three consequences (among others, no doubt) related to democratic
practice follow from the preceding discussion of obligation and loyalty. First,
although the state has no moral authority and, hence, there is no moral obligation
to comply with state directives or policies, some of them, at least, may have
"moral" relevance, in accordance with the principle articulated by John Stuart
Mill that the end of human action determines the standard of morality. [36] To the
extent, then, that democratic aims and tasks are, perforce partially, incorporated in
actions of the state, they are, so far forth, morally significant. Even here, though,
citizen obligation is not of a moral kind, since the state itself does not define or
valorize the morally relevant ends of democracy that its actions can, to a very
incomplete degree, promote.

Second, any anarchist rejection of the state is theoretically confused and practically self-defeating. Concerning the former, it may be argued that the state has no authority, since its power is not legitimate or justified. In view of what has been dealt with above, this argument is unsound, for the authority of the state, its institutions, laws and procedures can be legitimized or justified by "consent of the governed". Whether the state and its actions and their results are just is, of course, another matter; but the state and what it does are not necessarily or inexorably unjust. Acknowledged already is the fact that the state has no moral authority. However, it does not follow that the state takes no actions that support, even if inadequately, morally relevant goals. Sometimes anarchists declare rather sententiously and categorically that no one has the right to rule another person. This overstates the matter, for the (legitimized) authority to rule is a bestowed "right" -- and not even a right at that -- conferred and validated by a more or less voluntary agreement. Further, anarchists may argue that, since the rule of the state is irrefrangibly coercive, governance by the state is unacceptable. The issue and the parameters of coercion in democratic contexts have been addressed in a previous chapter. Suffice it to say here that obligatoriness is not itself coerciveness; and if obligation, on the one hand, is voluntarily accepted and, on the other, is not extracted in a heavy-handed, oppressive manner, then it need not be at odds with democratic commitments. What is important is not the (impossible) transcendence of all forms of control but the effectuation of communally cooperative, that is, democratic, forms of control, not the aspiration for (illusory) independence but the realization of mutually caring interdependence.

As a practical orientation, anarchism is, in my opinion, utopian concerning both means and ends -- sometimes a stance of those who can dismantle everything in imagination but do not know how to construct anything in reality or of those who romanticize human nature. Having said this, there is nonetheless merit in the anarchist critique of the state. [37] Yet, radical clearing of the ground so that new types of social growth can develop "spontaneously" is, I contend, fanciful. The task is the perennial one: What is to be done? -- not simply: What is to be undone? Admittedly, authentic democracy, that is, communal cooperation oriented on humanistic values of mutual empowerment, will not exist at the level of the nation-state; but neither will it do so at the level of national society, with or without the state. Communal cooperation, supported by definite loyalties and solidarities, can hardly occur, much less thrive, in very large-scale contexts of complexity, conflict, domination and indifference. To believe that oppressive and disadvantaging relationships would disappear with the abolition of the state is not only to yield to questionable assumptions about the underlying "goodness" of human nature in general but also to presuppose the conventional, and restrictive, use of 'political' criticized much earlier.

Third, and finally, a presumptive obligation to obey the laws and regulations of the state is superseded when sincere, thoughtful loyalties or fidelities call for this. What might be termed "moral" obligations, ensuing from loyalty to persons with whom one is committedly involved in a democratic project of the practice of positive freedom or else from fidelity to values that orient this practice, properly take precedence over strictly statutory obligations. In cases of conflict, the former type of obligations should prevail. Hence, civil disobedience with regard to the latter type of obligations is not excluded. Indeed, the democratic project may well require it on occasion. In these cases, disobedience is "justified" when a law or policy mandates action that is inconsistent with one's commitment to democratic practice and with one's loyalty to those individuals who are integrated into this practice. The "existential" character of civil disobedience is displayed in the fact that sometimes it may not be a central component of a strategic attempt to bring about political/legal change but simply a refusal to comply with anti-democratic or inhumane directives, even if there is no expectation of positive change. Contrary to Habermas's interpretation of civil disobedience, this act of refusal does not, as such, appeal to a sense of justice held by the majority of some social grouping. [38] Indeed, the majority may have a sense of "justice" that is intolerable. Rather, it appeals to commitments that may or may not be shared with others.

NOTES

1. See Partridge, Consent, pp. 113-114.

2. Ibid., p. 9. Consent may bestow or certify "rightful authority", but it is not necessarily the case that the authority is democratic, since consent may be given to undemocratic values, institutions, rules, etc. On the other hand, one may consent to what one does not even consider, or intend to recognize, as rightful authority, on the grounds that the "authority" is illegitimate or unjust, or both.

3. Ibid., pp. 32-36. It is the opinion of Partridge that, in liberal-democratic societies, most citizens consent, that is, assent and conform, in political situations and contexts more from custom and habitual disposition and behavior than from actively held beliefs and values [see ibid., pp. 53 & 56], an orientation that exhibits an "unreflecting adherence to the customary or familiar" [ibid., p. 46]. Hence, "consent of the governed" is likely to be, in fact, in the category of "supportive consensus" or "permissive consensus" [ibid., pp. 150-151].

4. See ibid., p. 22. It should be noted that consent may be an ongoing process, not just a set of discrete events. Where this is so, consent will probably be construed as implicit.

5. See "Reconciliation", p. 122. Clearly, 'acceptable' is being used in the sense of 'ought to be accepted', not 'able to be accepted' -- or at least able to be accepted only under definite normative criteria, namely, those requiring "rational" acceptability [ibid., p. 125].

6. "Reply", p. 175. For Rawls, legitimacy is a weaker idea than justice and imposes weaker constraints. Rawls's formulations also occur in Political Liberalism, pp. 427-428. Incidentally, in view of the difference between 'legitimate' and 'just', I believe it would be correct to say that the so-called entitlement theory of justice articulated by Robert Nozick in Anarchy, State, and Utopia is actually an entitlement theory of legitimacy applied to the concept of ownership.

7. See "Reply", p. 175.

8. See Between Facts and Norms, p. 64. Habermas's type of criticism is perhaps supported by Partridge's charge that political philosophers, who are concerned with the consensual bases of politics and society but who pay insufficient attention to empirical factors and difficulties, sometimes "produce breath-taking over-simplifications" [see Consent, p. 50].

9. In this regard, it is analogous to the conceptual distinction in ethical theory between cultural (or sociological) relativism, which is empirical, and ethical relativism, which is normative.

10. Acquiescent consent to, even enthusiastic endorsement of, authoritarian or totalitarian political regimes is not unheard of [see Partridge, Consent, pp. 23-24]. Cunningham mentions the contention by some of a "possibility of dictatorship in the name of popular sovereignty opened by democracy itself" [Democratic Theory, p. 125]. However, any excesses of popular sovereignty are not "opened" by democracy itself, for, while democracy reinforces communally cooperative, non-exploitative kinds of "rule" of and by the people, it is not defined in terms of whatever popular

"sovereignty" may be pleased to endorse.

11. See "Reply", p. 145.

12. Ibid., pp. 143, 145 & 147.

13. A rather different, yet equally serviceable distinction is presented by Partridge, for whom consent is (normatively) related to political authority, whereas consensus is (descriptively) related to social organization [see Consent, p. 10]. On this account, "Consent has been employed ... in themes about the justification of political authority and in defining the duty of political obedience.... Consensus appears most often in the themes sociologists advance to explain social order or cohesion." [ibid., p. 71] With regard to the latter perspective, consensus has tended to replace consent as the principal factor indicating how (democratic) regimes are supported, especially insofar as active popular participation is considered less decisive than the role of leadership by political elites [see ibid., p. 72].

14. See "Freedom", p. 159.

15. In this connection, Partridge forcefully declares that "in any society there is very little within the complex institutional structure of political authority, and only a small part of what political authorities enact or perform, that can be said to be expressive of the antecedent will of the governed" [Consent, p. 39].

16. Ibid., p. 140.

17. Partridge expresses it this way: "Part of the consent upon which a government relies is rather a reflection of the approval which a large part of the community accords to the more general organization or working of the social system." [ibid., p. 60] Relative satisfaction with the social system redounds to the benefit of the political system.

18. Ibid., p. 76.

19. Ibid., p. 93. Indeed, he adds that it is improbable that "a democratic system rests upon a consensus in support of the values and norms of democracy, if by that we mean a positive attachment to those values and norms manifested by a very large part of the citizen body" [ibid., p. 114].

20. Moreover, it may be argued that consensus can indicate (or generate) too much conformity, a lack of stimulating, fruitful diversity or contestation [see ibid., p. 124].

21. Hardin, by the way, suggests that government is inherently non-majoritarian [see "Public choice", p. 170].

22. On this criterion of "economy", see Dahl, After the Revolution?, pp. 6 & 42.

23. Mansbridge points out that majority rule under adversary democracy "does not usually produce a proportional distribution of benefits, and it can create permanent majorities" [Beyond Adversary Democracy, p. 266].

24. Ibid.

25. The Tyranny of the Majority. New York: The Free Press, 1994.

26. Ibid., p. 3.

27. Ibid., p. 212.

173

28. Ibid., pp. 4-5. This principle incorporates the idea that "votes should not count more than voters" [ibid., p. 12]. Where an electoral paradigm of democracy prevails, the importance of citizens tends to be precisely their role as dispensers of votes. The limitations of this situation, within the context of government decision making, are partially ameliorated by the disaggregative principle, which implies that "Minority empowerment requires a minority legislative influence, not just minority legislative presence", where this influence is made efficacious by "proportionate interest representation" [ibid., p. 55].

29. Ibid., pp. 14-15.

30. Ibid., p. 20.

31. Parenthetically, it should be noted that it makes no sense to speak of a "duty" of loyalty.

32. Habermas claims that, by construing basic rights as primary goods, Rawls assimilates "the deontological meaning of obligatory norms to the teleological meaning of preferred values" ["Reconciliation", p. 114]. Whether or not Rawls would concede that he does this, such an "assimilation" is proper.

33. In his classic In Defense of Anarchism [New York: Harper & Row, 1970, particularly Chapter One], Robert Paul Wolff argued that the moral autonomy of the individual is incompatible with the presumptively legitimate authority of the state. The state asserts a right to command, together with an obligation to be obeyed, but the (self-legislating) individual has an obligation not to be normatively ruled by others. Central to Wolff's argument is the claim that the commands of the state are not, strictly speaking, legitimate, since they lack binding moral force -- an inference, however, that is defective.

34. See Political Liberalism, xlv.

35. Ibid., p. 209. He also refers to allegiance to "a just and enduring constitutional government" ["Reply", p. 149]. I prefer "consent to and compliance with" rather than "allegiance to".

36. See Utilitarianism. Indianapolis: Bobbs-Merrill, 1957, pp. 16 & 49.

37. It was enlightening to be told in an interview in 1988 with Anatoly Butenko, a member of the Institute of Economics of the USSR Academy of Sciences and an influential analyst of problems of socialism, that it is important to rethink and reconsider the anarchist critique of Marxism, authority and dictatorship, including the position of Bakunin.

38. See Between Facts and Norms, p. 383.

CHAPTER 10

THE FAILURE OF CAPITALIST DEMOCRACY AND SOCIALIST DEMOCRACY

Having analyzed and evaluated several models of democracy, along with related conceptions and criteria of its meaningful elaboration, I now wish to examine two historically influential and disparate manifestations of what has been considered real, existing democracy, namely, capitalist democracy and socialist democracy. I will try to show that the former is a contradiction in terms, whereas the latter has been (and may well remain) illusory.

I

It is not infrequently argued either that the principles and social dynamics of capitalism are uniquely commensurate with those of democracy or that capitalist social relations are a precondition for the viability of democracy. From the first perspective, free elections are judged to be a replica of the free market, preference-motivated choices of voters are deemed analogous to those of consumers, the political competition regarding persons and policies is like that regarding products, justice in both contexts is conformity to procedures and not (necessarily) achievement of patterned outcomes, and (negative) liberty is a presiding priority. Fraser puts the matter succinctly: for some people, democracy means "free-market capitalism plus multi-party elections". [1] For both capitalism and democracy, participation in the acquisition and (limited) use of, respectively, material and political values is seen as an accomplishment of sorts, hardly empowerment but, perhaps, a satisfying alternative.

176

Fraser's comment is reinforced by Frank, who states that "American opinion leaders seem generally convinced that democracy and the free market are simply identical". [2] On this view, market mechanisms are inherently democratic, and democratic polity itself expresses a political free enterprise system. The "democracy" of the market is represented as a kind of "market populism", where the market, by its very nature, is seen as "democratic, perfectly expressing the popular will through the machinery of supply and demand, poll and focus group, superstore and Internet". [3] Here the people "rule" through a type of economic "electoralism", in which, by means of their purchases and investments in the context of a multi-brand system, they freely "vote" their preferences. Moreover, the interactive market, facilitated by use of the internet, is thought of, rather grandly, as a form of participatory democracy. [4]

As with many assumed analogies, wherein ostensible correspondences are superficial and/or irrelevant, the assimilation of democracy with the market misses the mark. The "democracy" of the capitalist market is, in its own way, procedural rather than substantive, that is, it emphasizes the range and diversity of choices, of processes of exchange, rather than outcomes making for control or empowerment. Capitalist democracy focuses on the consumerist satisfaction of preferences (alternatively, subjective interests), but not on the production of capacities necessary for the exercise of positive freedom. The market populism of capitalist democracy stresses interactivity instead of collaborative control, "talking to" or "talking back" instead of mutually capacitating communication.

If, as I maintain, democracy is the empowering and empowered practice of positive freedom across multiple areas of human life in accordance with humanistic values, then the logic of capitalism is simply inconsistent with this. Capitalism fails to further positive freedom. It emphasizes, for the masses of people, "having" rather than "doing", accumulation rather than creative production. In addition, it inculcates an acquisitive, adversarial mentality, incompatible with the communally cooperative disposition of democracy.

Not only is the logic of capitalism at odds with that of democracy, the way in which capitalism concretely functions precludes, or at least seriously interferes with, democracy. This factor is brought out by Gould, who declares that those who own property in the means of production are able "to control the conditions of the activity of others who lack property" and, consequently, "It is just this use of private property as a means of social domination and economic exploitation that undermines democracy". [5] Control over the conditions under which people are able to act is, in effect, control over people themselves. Where this control, however mitigated or meliorated, is self-serving and aggrandizing, democratic relationships are inhibited. Hence capitalism, which, generically, uses individuals as means, is hardly likely to be oriented upon their mutual, democratic, humanistic empowerment. On the contrary, as Macpherson notes, a capitalist market society "by its very nature compels a continual transfer of part of the power of some men to others, thus diminishing rather than maximizing the equal individual freedom to use and develop one's natural capacities which is claimed". [6] The presuppositions and the objectives of capitalism and democracy are inconsonant, with the result that, ideologically, they are typically assumed to be situated in different social spheres ("civil society" and "state") and that democracy is construed mainly in formal and procedural ways that accommodate it to basic economic, for example, neoliberal, imperatives.

As mentioned previously, an alternative to the identification of democracy with capitalism is the claim that capitalism is a prerequisite for a democratic polity. Such a claim is ventilated by Dahl, who asserts that modern, democratic-type institutions "have existed only in countries with predominantly privately owned, market-oriented economies".[7] Correlation, however, does not unambiguously bespeak causation. In particular, a capitalist economy is not sufficient for democracy, since the former can exist in political systems that are authoritarian, even totalitarian. To be sure, the economy will be circumscribed by political priorities and production requirements; but capitalist relations can still prevail, including private ownership of the social means of production, exploitation of labor, extraction of surplus value and the private appropriation of profit. Furthermore, a capitalist economy is not necessary for democracy either. Democratic processes and practices have existed for certain periods and in certain spheres of non-capitalist societies, even though their substantive presence at the level of the nation-state has, so far, eluded every kind of society. What is necessary -- though by no means sufficient -- is an "open society", a society that institutionalizes openness and, in general, the characteristics of negative freedom.

Referred to in an earlier chapter was Popper's valorization of the "open society", which he contrasted to the "closed society", the latter constituting a regimented, more or less totalitarian, society that fosters, and relies upon, irrational thinking, tribalistic emotions and utopian expectations, whereas the "open society" is distinguished by individual initiative, critical reason, personal responsibility and a reformist political agenda that focuses upon "piecemeal social engineering". [8] All of this is good as far as it goes; but it does not at all go far enough. An open society is not as such a democratic society. It is simply a (necessary, yet insufficient) component of a democratic society, as negative freedom is a necessary, though not sufficient, condition for positive freedom, that is, freedom as a whole. Incidentally, Popper's fixation on the merely "open society" is accompanied by an emaciated understanding of reform, which permits him to make the following kinds of statements about the situation, for example, in the United States in the 1950s: "Racial discrimination has diminished to an extent surpassing the hopes of the most hopeful" and "we have, in fact, something approaching classless societies". [9] Apparently there is such a thing as the poverty of historical awareness.

It should be recognized that even if the open society is a causal condition of both a capitalist market economy and democracy, this does not entail that capitalism and democracy are themselves causally connected. Indeed, the "openness" of capitalist dominated society may well not conduce to active democratic involvement. Robert W. McChesney goes so far as to claim that "the corporate media system, in conjunction with the broader trappings of a modern capitalist society, necessarily generate a depoliticized society, one where the vast majority of people logically put little time or interest into social or political affairs". [10] Perhaps it is something of an overstatement to say that the society as a whole becomes "depoliticized" -- hardly true at times of significant crisis. Yet, in general, a sense of distance and disconnection from the centers of political power is cultivated, such that citizens are more bemused observers than engaged participants. As argued previously, the politics of distraction, fostered by continually televised "circuses" and by the obsessions of consumerism, play a not insignificant role here.

Some profess to discern elements of democracy within the contours of capitalism. By this, I do not refer to possible modes of "democratic" decision-making among managerial elites. After all, even the Soviet Politburo, except under Stalin, settled matters among themselves in a relatively "democratic" manner. Rather, I refer to such forms of "industrial democracy" as workers' co-participation or workers' cooperatives. The former, in my view, is directed by a corporate desire to enhance worker efficiency in production processes, not by any intention to have workers share ownership or control of the means of production. The latter have problems of their own. For example, Przeworski observes that such cooperatives are constrained by capitalist-type factors of competition and profitability, that cooperatives with larger and more favorable initial endowments will tend to prosper more, and, further, that worker cooperation within enterprises by no means ensures cooperation between enterprises. [11] In short, worker cooperatives (including all forms of worker-owned enterprises) under capitalism must accommodate to its logic and priorities: to maximize profitability, to compete advantageously against businesses with lower wage costs, to borrow needed funds from "bottom-line" oriented financial institutions, to be attractive to investors, and to "rationalize" production, when necessary, by firing "class brothers and sisters". Internally, cooperatives may effect a provisional solidarity; externally, they cannot avoid the competitive and adversarial dynamics characteristic of capitalism.

Under capitalism, democracy is ideologically and structurally limited to the sphere of the state. Democracy is considered inappropriate and irrelevant for the non-state sphere of "civil society", notably for the economy. Coercion, exploitation and oppression in the former sphere are vigorously criticized, but their presence in the latter is either sanctioned or, more likely, denied.

The obfuscatory ideological dynamics in this context have been forcefully censured by Ellen Wood. [12] Thus, she avers that "the differentiation of the economic and the political in capitalism is, more precisely, a differentiation of political functions themselves and their separate allocation to the private economic sphere and the public sphere of the state", a move that constitutes "the privatization of political power". [13] Since the "political" has to do with relations of power and control, then domination and coercion by capitalism can be as socially restrictive as that by government. Whereas dominance by the latter may be more patent and blatant, that by the former is usually more disguised and pervasive. It may be argued that capitalism, with its "free market", does not impose anything like the duties of citizenship or the obligations of the law. Yet, the impositions of capitalism are just as rigorous and unavoidable as those of the state. Indeed, people can opt out of many of the responsibilities of citizenship, including voting (deemed by many a quintessential feature of democracy); but people do not normally opt out of the attempt to satisfy the material exigencies of human existence, such as food, clothing, shelter and medical care, that is, needs whose satisfaction is constrained, sometimes severely, by the capitalist market. The fact is that the "totalizing logic" of capitalism is systemic throughout so-called civil society.

In establishing relative autonomy for the economy, "capitalism has a

181

remarkable capacity to distance democratic politics from the decisive centres of social power and to insulate the power of appropriation and exploitation from democratic accountability".[14] Capitalist democracy should properly be understood, therefore, as capitalism coexisting with (quasi-)democracy, wherein the liberal democratic state somewhat mitigates the deleterious consequences of capitalism for many citizens; and capitalists continually remind us of injurious excesses by the state, particularly those that impact negatively upon their own objectives. Coincident with this social bifurcation is that between class inequality and political equality: "In modern capitalist democracy, socio-economic inequality and exploitation coexist with civic freedom and equality." [15] The latter facilitate involvement but not necessarily empowerment, which is constricted by the former. In Wood's exposition, socioeconomic inequality, however pronounced, is usually considered not germane for democratic practice. In other words, "the balance of class power would in no way represent a condition of democracy", from which it follows that "There would, in effect, be no incompatibility between democracy and rule by the rich." [16] -- at least insofar as the poor were allowed to compete politically with the rich. What one would have, perhaps does have, is a type of plutocratic polyarchy.

"Today", Wood declares, "we have become thoroughly accustomed to defining democracy less (if at all) in terms of rule by the demos or popular power than in terms of civil liberties, freedom of speech, of the press and assembly, toleration, the protection of a sphere of privacy, the defence of the individual and/or 'civil society' against the state, and so on". [17] Here, democracy is understood primarily in terms of negative rights but not positive rights, an open society but not an empowering society, freedom from the coercive arbitrariness of government but not from that of the capitalist regime, social accommodation but not communal cooperation. In my judgment, this kind of capitalist-friendly social formation does not deserve to be considered democracy.

182

II

By contrast to capitalist democracy, socialist democracy is not, in principle, self-contradictory. Not absent from (some) socialist theory is a discernible emphasis upon democracy's encompassing more than state organization and function, upon the importance of positive freedom, and upon the special value of cooperation. [18]   However, whatever the possible theoretical convergence of socialism with democracy, "existing socialism" conspicuously failed to manifest existing democracy. Such a situation may be taken to show the inadequacy of socialist theory, on the grounds that (socialist) practice is a test of (socialist) theory. While this is a sound methodological principle, the democracy-distorting practice of socialist societies demonstrated, I believe, not the defects of socialism, as such or in all respects, but the inability or unwillingness of those societies to implement democracy in anything like the humanistically robust sense that I have envisioned. In the remainder of this chapter, I will make an effort to identify, at least in part, the nature and causes of that failure.

To be sure, other kinds of factors, both internally generated and externally imposed, inhibited the enduringly viable development of a society such as the Soviet Union. Yet, I fully agree with the following comments by Medvedev -- in my opinion, the most astute and insightful interpreter of Soviet and post-Soviet history: "I think that precisely an underestimation of the role and significance of democracy was the chief mistake of Lenin....A disregard of democracy lay at the foundation of all the subsequent deformations of socialist society, socialist consciousness and socialist education." [19]   Apparently, democracy, that is, democratization, was seen as complicating, and interfering with, the tasks of socialist construction. Stated somewhat differently, "the democracy carried along by revolution comes to appear as surplus democracy when revolutions are ended and the permanent institutionalization of politics is begun". [20]   Democratization was a salient rallying cry on behalf of revolution; but, afterwards, it was argued that a thoroughgoing democratization of society must be deferred until socialism

183

had been consolidated. In fact, however, the postponement of such democratization became less and less temporary and more and more permanent, reflecting the all-too-frequent tendency for temporary measures, provisionally necessary "evils", and so on, to take on a life of their own.

Butenko maintains that socialist societies, instead of establishing genuine power "by the people", in fact institutionalized power "in the name of the people", "in the interests of the people" or "for the people". [21] Endorsing this "usurpation" of power, as Butenko designates it, the Hungarian communist philosopher, Kiss, asserted that the correct principle of socialist governance is expressed in the slogan: "for the people, in the name of the people, together with the people". [22] None of this, of course, embodied (democratic) power by the people, but power by the Party, itself constitutionally sanctioned as the "leading and guiding" force of socialist society. Indeed, it was claimed, "The leading role of the Party is ... the fundamental condition and assurance of genuine democracy and of the socialist character of democracy." [23] In this role, the Party authoritatively defined the general objectives and tasks of socialist society, specified guidelines (to be implemented by the state government) for the management of the country's affairs, and "reconciled" conflicting interests in the light of allegedly common interests.

What one has here is a highly skewed version of representative democracy, replete with elitism, namely, a version according to which the Party, purportedly, consistently and profoundly represented the needs and interests of the people. Interestingly, whether or not the Party did, in fact, adequately do so was considered to be a matter to be determined by the Party itself and by organizations subordinate to it. [24] Hence, the Party knew best not only what to do but also whether it had done so.

This "peculiar kind of party egotism", which identified the interests of the Party elite with those of the Party as a whole and, in turn, with the interests of all the people, [25] had its roots in at least two interrelated factors: on the one hand, the interpretation of democracy as class-based and, on the other, the belief that a definitive science of history and society was provided by socialist ideology (magisterially that of Marxism-Leninism, in some contexts emended by Maoism), an ideology most adequately understood and developed by the Party.

With respect to the first factor, Kiss asseverated that "The characteristic features of democracy are linked with the rule of definite classes." [26]   Since, according to Marxist theory, the existence of classes is concurrent with, and a source of, the existence of the state (or some equivalent formation), revolutionary transformations in class power allegedly reshape the nature of state power and thus democracy. Soviet ideology was wont to claim that, as class antagonisms -- even if not classes themselves -- disappeared under socialism, the state came to represent "the whole people". Socialism was not said to be a classless society, but one in which class distinctions were benign and would be eliminated, in the future, in communist society. From this, it supposedly followed that the harmony of class interests under socialism made possible a democracy expressing the will of the whole people. [27]

A serious problem with this formulation lies in determining and elaborating the ostensible will of the people, a problem resolved practically in socialist societies by means of the authoritative hegemony of the Party, sanctioned theoretically by the principle of ideological monism. That is, the Party, claiming to possess, uniquely, knowledge and understanding of proper social and political policies disclosed in accordance with the scientific ideology of Marxism-Leninism, was construed as expertly representing the objective interests of the people. Their preferences and subjective interests might occasionally have had a modest effect on elections to state organizations, either local or national, but not at all on intra-Party elections or on the Party elite and the *nomenklatura*, who ultimately possessed political control and prerogative. By and large, popular elections were acts for the acceptance and/or affirmation of policy (and perhaps sometimes for the expression of a probably sincere sense of solidarity), not for the shaping of that policy.

The thesis of ideological monism asserts that only one ideology, namely, that of Marxism-Leninism, has scientific validity as a social theory applicable, inter alia, to the conception of democracy. Correlated with this affirmation of ideological monism is a rejection of ideological pluralism, the thesis that no one social theory has, or is known to have, a scientific legitimacy giving it principled superiority over other such theories. [28] The rejection of ideological pluralism served to substantiate the associated rejection of political pluralism, understood as legitimation of a plurality of political parties, none of which possesses juridical precedence and each of which may contend with the others on officially equal terms in the attempt to promote certain interests and to influence public policy. Multiple political parties did, indeed, exist legally in some socialist countries; but the role of the noncommunist parties was essentially advisory and informational.

If socialist ideology (in its Marxist-Leninist form) is an objectively correct social theory, if, moreover, this theory, as ideology, most adequately reflects progressive human interests, needs and values, and if, finally, a communist party has an unsurpassed (and unsurpassable) knowledge and appreciation of this ideology, then such a party is the objectively privileged determiner and arbiter of what is required for public (including democratic) policy. According to Kiss, the Party has the highest level of socialist consciousness and knows most satisfactorily the interests and needs of the people, who, in general, have a substantially lower level of socialist consciousness. [29] As the Party, through the mediation of the state, expertly directs the affairs of society, the people can participate by supporting and helping to implement Party directives. If the overall arrangement described qualifies even remotely as a form of "democracy", it was a rather egregious type of elitist democracy, a democracy for the few, with unstable kinds of paternalism above, coupled with lack of accountability to the people, and not infrequent manifestations of cynicism and opportunism below. [30] In any case, the features of democracy as I have emphasized them were essentially lacking : democratization, at best nominal, was restricted to the sphere of the state; social welfare, often uneven and inadequate, took the place of social empowerment; and social cooperation was basically the willingness of those commanded to do what was ordered -- although it seems that a fair amount of real cooperation among people occurred in the interstices of what passed for civil society.

The official substantiation of historically existent socialist democracy by means of appeal, theoretically, to ideological monism was only part of its rationale. In my opinion, the no doubt sincere belief in the epistemic superiority of socialist theory was reinforced by, as much as anything, a deep-seated apprehension that ideological or political pluralism might destabilize the dependable inclinations of popular consciousness, rendering control by the Party less routine and reliable and, possibly, jeopardizing the perpetuation of the social system. [31] Furthermore, the apathy, passivity and indifference bred by the lack of opportunity for effective participation by either rank-and-file Party members or the people in general were useful to the Party elite, facilitating an affectedly benevolent and dissimulative disregard. [32]

Compounding psychological factors such as these were structural deformations, with bureaucracy constituting a prime example. As with capitalist democracy, so with socialist democracy, bureaucracy is a debilitating element. Medvedev has explicitly asserted that bureaucracy was "the principal enemy of socialist democracy". [33] To be sure, this "caste system" can be found prominently under capitalism; but the pervasive role of the state under socialism meant that governmental bureaucracy was more ubiquitous and prominent. For capitalist society, governmental bureaucracy is more demarcated. However, the bureaucracies of capitalist enterprises can rival those of the state in terms of complexity, obscurantism and self-aggrandizement. Bureaucracy objectively disempowers people and subverts the development of positive freedom, hence democracy. In passing, I would suggest that a major problem with bureaucrats is often not, so much, overweening ambition or malicious intent as unacknowledged incompetence.

Other factors might be cited as contributing to the deficiency of socialist democracy. For example, whereas capitalist societies have usually failed to institutionalize the democratically empowering conditions afforded by social and economic rights, socialist societies were gravely remiss regarding civil and political rights. Further, the "unity" of socialist societies characteristically reflected, not strains of communal cooperativeness, but, at best, what might be called solidarity by default, reinforced by opportunistic accommodations and probably cynical hopefulness. [34] Beyond this, the lack of democracy in gendered relationships -- also noticeable in capitalist societies -- rendered the scope of democracy even more exiguous.

The viewpoint that, in socialist society, the expansion of democracy should be directed and controlled by the Party, [35] combined with the mentioned disinclination of the Party to emphasize democracy in gendered contexts, meant that the democratization of marriage and, where feasible, of family life was infrequent and not deemed an urgent matter. In place of thoroughgoing democratization, as such, one of its constituents, namely, equality, was highlighted, in particular with regard to occupational roles. Women were treated with a fair degree of equality in the workplace, though not in the councils of state, much less in the Party. By comparison, capitalist democracy has been more receptive to women's roles in the state apparatus, although male domination is still pronounced in many of the interpersonal relationships of civil society.

Hegemonic, anti-democratic patriarchalism has distinguished both socialist societies and capitalist societies, showing that a regulative class analysis of social relations is, if not "reductionist", at least oversimplified. Incidentally, it is worth noting that, although the historical advent of socialism involved a socialization of the forces of production under state auspices, it produced only a partially democratic socializing of the conventionally understood relations of production -- excluding, by and large, democratization of the "production" relations resident in marriage and family life. In addition, since the collapse of socialist societies and the enfeeblement of communist parties in the European space, it is questionable whether socialist democracy was replaced by substantially richer forms. With respect to Russia, Kagarlitsky avers that "In place of the power of the party we had the power of a political elite, resting on laws which it drafted itself in order to serve its own goals", adding that "in the course of two years [during the early 1990s] the Russian ... democrats had managed to compromise the idea of democracy almost as thoroughly as the Communists compromised the idea of socialism in seventy years".[36]

Concerning gender issues as "issues of democratic theory and political power", Funk remarks that "While there is no doubt that GDR family and social policy was immeasurably better disposed toward women ... than the current legislation of the united Germany, it was based on paternalistic and patriarchal premises." [37] Recognizing this, many in the women's movement in the GDR, from 1989 onwards, insisted that "democratization meant not only the creation of rule by law and the division of power but also the transformation of the political structures and the hierarchy of gender relations". [38] However, the centrality of this task for the democratization of human relationships was often officially disregarded or disdained; and Funk refers to various attitudes and statements expressed -- sometimes by noted anticommunist defenders of "freedom", "democracy", etc., etc. -- that belittled the democratic aspirations of the women's movement. [39] In the face of factors such as suspicion about, or contempt for, women's equality due to its nominal association with discredited socialist ideology, the desire to limit competition from women workers at a time of rising unemployment, and the enduring dynamics of male chauvinism (a truly multicultural phenomenon), the skepticism manifested in the following comment by Funk is apposite: "It remains very uncertain whether newly emerging parliamentary democracy can in itself guarantee women's rights and freedoms .... the societal transformation does not imply a reduction of arrogance, discrimination, and neglect with respect to women: quite the contrary." [40]

In fact, the interpretation of democracy mandated earlier in accordance with the ideology prevailing in the countries of erstwhile socialism fostered a severely truncated understanding of democracy that facilitated, by simplistic contrast, subsequent acceptance in post-socialist conditions of a capitalist paradigm of democracy, with its relatively more "open" character, its consumer blandishments and its attribution of socially systemic problems to failures of previous state policy. [41]

Historical changes are often propelled as much by what is being rejected as by what is believed to be gained as a result. Many, early in the twentieth century, thought that what replaced, or was replacing, state-sponsored capitalism was assuredly socialism. Likewise, many, late in that century, believed that what replaced, or was in the process of replacing, socialism was real democracy grounded in a capitalist social order. In my opinion, both expectations have proved to be largely illusory. At the beginning of this chapter, I suggested that capitalist democracy is self-contradictory, whereas socialist democracy has turned out to be, in fact, self-defeating. Przeworski proffers a variation on this theme: "Capitalism is irrational; socialism is unfeasible." [42] Whatever may be the most pertinent formula, neither capitalist democracy nor socialist democracy has systematically empowered citizens in general or established objective conditions for the manifold democratization of social, interpersonal life in line with humanistic values. Is substantive democracy, as I have tried to characterize it, then, an illusion or a futile hope? In the next, and final, chapter, I will address this issue.

NOTES

1. "Equality", in Trend, Radical Democracy, p. 197.

2. One Market, p. 15.

3. Ibid., p. 29.

4. Ibid., p. 60.

5. Rethinking, p. 175.

6. Democratic Theory, pp. 10-11.

7. After the Revolution?, p. 80. He adds that historical evidence indicates that predominantly state-owned, centrally directed economies are incompatible with democracy [p. 81]. Later in this chapter, I will try to identify a fundamental problem in this regard.

8. See The Open Society, pp. 121 & 124.

9. See Conjectures and Refutations. London: Routledge & Kegan Paul, 1963, pp. 370-371.

10. Rich Media, Poor Democracy. New York: The New Press, 2000, xxxi. Significantly contributing to this is the fact that the mass media often oversimplify or misrepresent complex matters, in the process ignoring or obscuring relevant facts, data and perspectives. This is compounded by their role in "reinforcing existing viewpoints and helping to set the outer limits of respectable discourse" [see Domhoff, Who Rules?, p. 107].

11. See Democracy, p. 130.

12. In her opinion, this obfuscation has frequently been abetted by "left" intellectuals who, avoiding an explicit critique of capitalism, instead "seek out the interstices of capitalism, to make space within it for alternative 'discourses', activities and identities", much of which simply gives rise to the "radicalization of liberal pluralism" [Democracy, pp. 1-2]. She comments trenchantly that "There may never be a revolutionary reconstruction of society, but there can always be a ruthless deconstruction of texts." [ibid., p. 10]

13. Ibid., pp. 31 & 37.

14. Ibid., p. 275.

15. Ibid., p.201. Wood remarks that capitalism "makes possible a form of democracy in which formal equality of political rights has a minimal effect on inequalities or relations of domination and exploitation in other spheres" [p. 224]. Briefly, "liberal democracy leaves capitalist exploitation essentially intact" [p. 271].

16. Ibid., p. 223. The individualization of success and failure can be used to rationalize an elitist

type of democracy that, at the same time, valorizes capitalism on the grounds that elite decision-makers are those most adept at playing according to the rules of the capitalist social game.

17. Ibid., p. 231.

18. On democracy in the workplace, marriage and the family, see Holt's discussion of Alexandra Kollontai in the Introduction to Selected Writings; on the importance of positive freedom, see The Holy Family by Marx and Engels, in MECW, Vol. 4, p. 131; and on the value of (cooperative) community, see The German Ideology by Marx and Engels, in MECW, Vol. 5, p. 78.

19. *Russkaja revoljutsija 1917 goda: pobeda i porazhenie bol'shevikov.* Moskva: *Izdatel'stvo "Prava cheloveka",* 1997, s. 114.

20. Wolin, "Fugitive Democracy", in Benhabib, Democracy, p. 39. The post-revolutionary (socialist) state tended to rely, non-democratically, upon elites, a practice carried over, in large measure, from the habits of its prerevolutionary past [see Fisk, The State, p. 324]. Further reinforcing this neglect of democracy was the attitude evinced by communist officials that "basic economic problems should be solved before attention is paid to the question of democratization" [Medvedev, On Socialist Democracy, p. 231].

21. See *"Marksistsko-leninskaja ideja",* pp. 15-17.

22. Marxism and Democracy, p. 216. Kiss added that the Party, the leading and guiding force of socialist society, should not let itself be led by the masses, otherwise it "renounces the opportunity of pursuing a principled policy and this inevitably leads to spontaneity" [ibid., p. 217]. He also managed to claim, rather disingenuously or dishonestly, that "in the socialist system power belongs to the workers" [ibid., p. 148].

23. Ibid., p. 293.

24. See ibid., p. 280.

25. See Medvedev, On Socialist Democracy, p. 75. Anticommunist successors to political leadership in post-socialist countries have not been immune to their own varieties of elitism. For example, John Feffer quotes Lech Walesa, who, likening his role to that of a bus driver, declared that "There's no place for democracy when you are driving a bus." [Shock Waves: Eastern Europe after the Revolutions. Boston: South End Press, 1992, p. 124]

26. Marxism and Democracy, p. 152.

27. The idea that the state, the allegedly paradigmatic province of democracy, "withers away" under communism seems to have prompted Lenin to suggest that democracy itself likewise does so. Perhaps he was referring to the superseding of adversarial democracy; but it is not clear what other type of democracy should takes its place [see The State and Revolution, in Collected Works, Vol. 25, pp. 460-461. Moscow: Progress Publishers, 1964]. Imprecise and not altogether consistent discussions are not redeemed by polemical vigor; and Medvedev is surely correct when he charges that statements by Lenin on democracy are often one-sided, limited and open to question [see On Socialist Democracy, p. 327].

28. Ideological monism (and what it implies) has been defended, for example, by A. V. Momdzhjan, *Pljuralizm: istoki i sushchnost'.* Moskva: *Izdatel'stvo "Nauka",* 1983; by Jürgen Reusch, *Pluralismus und Klassenkampf.* Frankfurt am Main: *Verlag Marxistische Blätter,* 1982; and by Assen Kozharov, Monism and Pluralism in Ideology and in Politics. Sofia: Sofia Press, n.d. Kozharov argued that epistemological pluralism is the methodological basis for ideological pluralism [see ibid., p. 21].

29. See Marxism and Democracy, pp. 294-295 & 299.

30. Kiss even asserted that democracy under socialism was a form of direct democracy, in that "The workers' initiative, attitudes and actions have far-reaching influence on the government." [ibid., p. 256] Of course, ensconced rulers are, pragmatically, attentive to such factors, so as to be prepared to react, paternalistically or repressively, according to what is judged necessary.

31. Kiss declared that socialist discipline is "the goal and meaning of socialist democracy" [Marxism and Democracy, p. 262].

32. See a related comment by Medvedev [On Socialist Democracy, p. 111 & fn. 5, p. 365].

33. Ibid., p. 290. He defined bureaucracy as "a structure whose main characteristic is the absence of accountability from the top down, i.e., an authoritarian system of administration" [p. 291].

34. Boris Kagarlitsky maintains that, during Stalin's regime, "society itself was declassed, marginalized and atomized. The regime was the only organized, unifying force in the country. In this, and not in the terror, lay the astonishing stability of the Stalinist system despite its catastrophic failures." [The Disintegration of the Monolith. London: Verso, 1992, p. 43]

35. See Kiss, Marxism and Democracy, p. 246.

36. The Disintegration, pp. 83 & 110. The political chicanery of the Yeltsin administration is astutely detailed by Medvedev in Post-Soviet Russia. New York: Columbia University Press, 2000, while its complicity in economic corruption is laid out by Paul Klebnikov in Godfather of the Kremlin. New York: Harcourt, 2000.

37. Nanette Funk & Magda Mueller (eds.). Gender Politics and Post-Communism. New York: Routledge, 1993, p. 142.

38. Ibid., p. 153.

39. See ibid., p. 234 [on Hungary], p. 263 [on Polish Solidarity], p. 285 [on exiled Soviet dissidents], p. 288 [on "democrats" in Russia], and p. 314 [on Vaclav Havel in the Czech Republic].

40. Ibid., p. 27.

41. On this type of development, see Boris Kagarlitsky. New Realism, New Barbarism. London: Pluto Press, 1999, pp. 143-144. In Shock Waves, Feffer provides another graphic example. As he explains the matter, in the last days of the German Democratic Republic, "reunification" was widely preferred to any "Third Way" [between orthodox socialism and Western-style capitalism], since the former was perceived as more explicit, tested, proximate and alluring than the latter. Feffer remarks: "New Forum [a *Dritter Weg* grouping] called on East Germans to rebuild their society; the [successful] Christian Democrats called on West Germany to do the same job. Stated another way, the CDU offered things while New Forum offered ideas." [p. 75] Furthermore, New Forum, which "wanted to create a different kind of political system, one that valued civic participation over party professionalism, democratic accountability over administrative efficiency, *ethike* (ethical conduct) over *techne* (technical expertise", lost the support of East German citizens, who preferred the reunification promise of economic benefits and a prompt return to stability [ibid., p. 79].

42. Democracy, p. 122.

CHAPTER 11

CONCLUSION

In preceding chapters, I have sought to address and constructively clarify a variety of factors that bear upon an explication of democracy, factors such as the public-private distinction, representation (elitist and otherwise), participation, majority rule, justice and equality, legitimation and obligation. Whether or not my analyses are persuasive, they at least serve to define the content of the conception of democracy that I propose. The conceptual framework is, to be sure, not altogether complete, the factors mentioned (together with others discussed) might be worked out in greater detail, and additional objections could be confronted. However, appealing to the principle that it is not unreasonable to say something even where one cannot say everything, I believe that a fairly coherent model of democracy has been outlined herein. Perhaps my interpretations of matters such as the political, interests, values, needs, rights, freedom, cooperation, and so on, may be deemed problematic. Nevertheless, they focus the specific orientation that I have adopted.

I

In addition possible misgivings regarding my use of various concepts, problems having to do with the practicability of my conception of democracy will likely intrude. In particular, the difficulty, indeed the practical impossibility, of implementing this conception for contexts of quantitatively and qualitatively significant scale, such as that of the nation-state, may be judged to render this conception irrelevant, since it is in the latter context that, it seems, democracy is most needed. Granted, a communally cooperative model of democratic empowerment (the practice of positive freedom oriented on humanistic values) can hardly be realized institutionally where large-scale structures and processes prevail that embody great complexity, frequently antagonistic interests, distorted and/or inadequate information, incommensurable discourses, and entrenched relations of subordination. However, the inapplicability of my proposed conception of democracy as a workable model for the nation-state does not at all impugn its pertinence for other, equally important social contexts, a fact that I hope to make explicit subsequently. For the present, I will recall my previous argument that democracy at the national level can only be a kind of quasi-democracy, adversarial in disposition, socially contractual in strategy, limited in effective popular participation, often elitist in governance, and much more likely to generate forms of satisfied accommodation than creative empowerment.

Of course, it may be that citizens, generally, find the contours and possibilities of adversarial quasi-democracy relatively agreeable, an attitude based not only upon a prudent assessment of the seemingly intractable realities of modern society but also upon an inclination to engage in political activity primarily because it is believed to protect what one has or hopes to have. Bargaining, whether from positions of strength or weakness, may function to provide acceptable degrees of social stability and continuity, especially when complemented by a politics of aggrandizement for the dominant and a politics of distraction for the subordinate. Cynicism and/or apathy can play a non-disruptive role here in the management of public life; and, in general, they are compatible with the de facto elitism of adversary democracy and do not constitute a challenge to it. Furthermore, they can be rather readily disengaged and transcended when the public perceives that it should stand together against a common threat.

It is by no means appropriate to go as far as does Nietzsche when he casts aspersions on democracy as a decadent expression of "herd" mentality. [1] Still, however much the people are well intentioned and however much they criticize the illusions of politics -- without agreeing just what these are -- interrelationships and interactions at the level of the nation-state do not encourage communally cooperative engagements of positive freedom in line with humanistic values secured by the mutuality of a genuinely caring solidarity. Some, influenced by a communitarian-type ideology, will aver that the nation-state can be a communally cooperative society of deeply embedded loyalties, a type of society that it once was and that it can be again. Having already criticized the communitarian outlook, I will merely state here that, in my judgment, its postulation of a historically earlier manifestation of national community is a piece of nostalgic fabrication and its expectation that a community of this sort can be retrieved and renewed is evidence of illusionary naiveté.

Adversary democracy "works" at the national level because it abjures communitarian fancies, because its democratic objectives, albeit worthwhile, are relatively modest, because it accommodates self-interests through a combination of permitting their competitive struggle and, at the same time, ensuring the stabilizing dominance of some of them, and because it reduces "democratic" tasks for most citizens to largely perfunctory, not overly demanding, maneuvers. This model of democracy, essentially comprising competitive electoralism and constitutional proceduralism, is normally able to furnish instrumentally adequate management of public affairs, taking into account the ascendant predilections of citizens for material satisfactions (a repertoire of official explanations is available to show why these are frequently unattainable by some citizens), for only partial political involvement (citizen "free-riding" is not so much a problem when the "driving" -- and choice of route -- is left to others), and for vicarious empowerment by means of chauvinistic identification with national power.

I do not wish to suggest that "human nature" is inveterately uncongenial to democratic values and practices. Human motivation and behavior are congruent, to a considerable degree, with what is required, at least minimally, for democratic arrangements. Yet, even on the most sanguine assessment, democracy as communally cooperative empowerment is unlikely to win through at the national level, where loyalties are divided (often antagonistic), solidarity is episodic, tentative and frequently factitious, the valorized egoism of economic life contradicts the honored collective spirit of the citizen, and cooperation is tantamount to coordination by whatever means necessary. Of course, it may be, as it has been, argued that propitious social conditions, including the endeavor to put them into place, will create a "new type" of individual, disposed to develop a more advanced or progressive national society and culture. This "revolutionizing praxis", I submit, has a most dubious prognosis at the national level with respect to the conditions of my proposed model of democracy; and, moreover, it is instructive that twentieth-century experiments designed to produce a new type of individual were catastrophic when the objectives were pernicious and abortive when they were not.

Apart from the obstacles to mutual empowerment (positive freedom) as a project for large-scale politics, apart from the elusiveness of community at the level of the nation-state, and apart from the recurring "depoliticization" of many citizens, there will likely exist doubt about the probability of a broadly sustained commitment to what I have called "humanistic" values. In addition, theoretical objections may well surface concerning the absence of "foundations" for my conception of democracy. On the latter point, a demand for strict foundations is characteristically irrelevant or imprecise. On the one hand, foundations are neither epistemologically nor psychologically requisite. As remarked already, a sufficient basis for orienting the conception of democracy can lie, epistemologically, in a naturalistic understanding of values and, psychologically, in an existentially committed affirmation of certain of them. Mandates for foundations are not infrequently vague. With respect to democracy, emphasis is usually directed to the issue of the theoretical justification of democracy itself, often accompanied by efforts to demonstrate that the conception of democracy preferred is feasible in practice. In my view, democracy can be "justified" only in the sense, and to the extent, that reasons can be given to show that it is a necessary condition for the effectuation of objectives or ends validated because valorized. If the meaningful (creative, non-exploitative) enhancement of human life is affirmed as an enduring goal, then the communally cooperative empowerment of as many people as possible pursuant to humanistic values is presupposed. The "foundations" for democracy consist partly in the orientation provided by this commitment and partly in the plausibility of the basic ideas that specify the content of the conception of democracy. It is upon these two kinds of factors that my conception of democracy is based. Additionally, the practice of democracy, that is, the actual democratization of life in various spheres of human existence, is based upon the presence of social and other conditions objectively supporting this democratization. If such practical "foundations" are lacking or severely restricted, then the theoretical model of democracy constitutes, at most, a kind of manifesto whose relevance is highly problematic. For these reasons, my own interpretation of democracy is influenced by the paucity of conditions that would invest it with practicability for large-scale contexts. Surrogates for democracy in these contexts should be tended and improved; but, as I see it, they do not, strictly speaking, merit the label of 'democracy'.

II

If my proposed conception or model of democracy is not really feasible at the level of the nation-state, where affairs of great public and political moment transpire, one may understandably wonder what is the point of elaborating it at all. To this skeptical query, several types of rejoinder can be offered, here summarized and subsequently discussed more fully: the proposed model is valuable, without diminution, when and where it can, in fact, be realized; it brings into focus the deficiencies of (adversary) democracy extant in the nation-state; its presence in smaller contexts is necessary for the development of a democratic culture of attitudes, behavior and habits that is able to achieve some resonance at the level of the nation-state; and it expresses the view that democracy is situated in democratization of the manifold interactive social relationships of human life.

That something of value for human life may not prevail as widely or as assuredly as might be wished or hoped does not thereby detract from its value. To be sure, limits and uncertainties present themselves; but whatever the scale of the greatest (aggregated and distributed) good, that which is valorized as good remains so. For example, the value of friendship, kindness, caring, etc., is not called into question by the patent fact that their existence is not as extensive and deeply rooted as one would like. Kindness is still a good thing, however infrequently it may be displayed. If democracy, as communally cooperative empowerment, is more likely to exist in contexts such as marriage, friendship, the workplace, associations of like-minded individuals committed to commonly significant tasks and objectives, and so on -- voluntarily "chosen" communities, in Friedman's terminology -- than in the sphere of the nation as a whole, this hardly diminishes the importance of democracy for those contexts where it can be, and often has been, realized. These contexts are as existentially meaningful for human beings as the national sphere, even though policies and actions in the latter will frequently be more consequential for the public in terms of overall and long-term effects. At the same time, the quotidian contexts in which democratization can take hold are precisely those in which human life is lived most immediately and intensively.

Because of considerations such as the foregoing, my conception of democracy, I submit, is neither merely abstract nor utopian. In the first place, it specifies criteria that can be satisfied concretely in a variety of contexts other than the nation-state. For the latter context, these criteria at least underline admittedly ideal possibilities that serve to mark out the actuality of substantive, persisting limitations. Identification of these limitations might help to point the way toward a partial improvement of quasi-democracy in its role as a regulatory, stabilizing mechanism that, among other things, gives citizens a more or less satisfying sense of participation in public affairs. One such improvement, discussed previously and acknowledged to be elusive, would be legal mandates for socioeconomic rights or entitlements that were seen not simply as compensatory but as necessary conditions for the practical empowerment of citizens as agents of cooperative self-development. Furthermore, honest recognition of the limitations of adversarial quasi-democracy could function as an appropriate counterweight to the self-congratulatory illusions promulgated officially, and often entertained popularly, regarding the virtues and the successes of democracy at the national level.

In the second place, the realizability of democracy within the kinds of contexts cited demonstrates that humanistically oriented cooperation for the sake of mutual empowerment, in short, democracy, is not idealistically visionary. It is, in various spheres of life, a discernible fact. By contrast, in my opinion, rather extravagant claims are made on behalf of the progressive achievements, superlative virtues and humanizing practices of quasi-democracy (Dahl's "polyarchy). Indeed, it seems to me that what one finds here is a type of utopian valorization of the present political system, [2] which tends to reach its apogee at times of national crisis and challenge, particularly by the "Other". In all of this, however, symbiosis of the individual with collective political power is quite different from cooperation for mutually social, hence personal, empowerment.

The practice of democracy, as I understand it, can be embodied in the lives of many individuals and groups of individuals. That real democratization of human relationships is substantially, perhaps permanently, unattainable elsewhere -- especially in large-scale contexts -- does not imply that democracy is a hopeless enterprise in general or that it is spurious where it does exist. Indeed, democratization of everyday relationships is all the more important in light of the fact that such democratization will not likely materialize in domains of much broader scope and structural complexity. Democratic relationships can be engendered and nourished in a world that itself is anything but democratized -- a principle that is applicable to many things of human value. Besides it is precisely the relatively local contexts of daily relationship and activity that can constitute the most efficacious "school" for understanding and appreciating the significance of democracy, including its flawed and uncertain manifestation in the nation-state.

The model of democracy that I have presented functions to specify criteria or standards - as well as interpretations of concepts basic in this model -- for the assessment of democracy in the world of reality, not in that of imagination or assumption. In this sense, with respect to the nation-state, my model stands primarily as critique, with only occasional attention to recommendations for positive change in adversary quasi-democracy. Given differing structures, dynamics and parameters for different spheres and dimensions of democracy, improvements would involve dissimilar expectations and arrangements. For example, democratization of marriage, friendship and voluntary association would include patterns and processes that could not be replicated in the public affairs of the nation-state. Democracy in the latter will always be, it seems to me, an unfulfillable aspiration, doubtlessly to be celebrated honorifically as an ideal and disingenuously as a fact.

As conventional quasi-democracy generally valorizes negative freedom over positive freedom, much of its utility lies in "negating" the probability of permanently disruptive social inequalities, intolerably flagrant abuses of governmental power, sustained political alienation of the majority of citizens, and systemically debilitating conflicts of interests not amenable to stabilizing resolution by means of strategic compromises guided by elitist management. Further, although national quasi-democracy is not at all an empowering form of democracy, it can at least permit possibilities that will not hamper the development of communally cooperative, empowering democracy in other, interior contexts. Of course, though people may be politically involved in, even inspired by, the aims and practices of national quasi-democracy, they will not be equally and mutually empowered by it, either as citizens or as individuals. This is not to gainsay the value of whatever degree of democracy that may be able to exist at the level of the nation-state. However circumscribed and truncated, more

201

democracy is better than less; and some is surely better than none.

In an earlier chapter, other types of democracy, such as unitary democracy and deliberative democracy, were distinguished and discussed. Whereas there are elements and emphases in each that are relevant for my own model, the relevances are but partial. Thus, the focus on community in unitary democracy, for example, by communitarians, tends to treat community as socially and/or psychologically homogeneous, to define identity by means of "found" commonalities, to make loyalty a duty rather than an existential commitment, and to ignore forms of what I call "experimental solidarity". By this term, I designate a type of practical, contingent, defeasible communality that involves people who, whether or not they have anything like deep moral respect for one another, are at least prepared to trust each other so as to make (effective) cooperation possible.

For its part, deliberative democracy adopts a more informed view concerning the role of democracy, the need for dialogue, the importance of considerate thoughtfulness, and so on. Yet, its expectations, even within the framework of what approximates communally cooperative relationships, are, I think, overly optimistic, particularly with regard to the extent that reason and (good) reasons will prevail. Moreover, deliberative concord, grounded in discourse-theoretic presuppositions, does not itself constitute empowerment -- or, at most, it is only the "empowerment" of being listened to and taken seriously. Of course, to be valorized and respected as a reasonable participant in discourse is, in its own way, a degree of empowerment. However, it is but a prelude and precondition for that richer kind of empowerment that gives democracy its meaning as the enabling practice of positive freedom under humanistically delineated conditions.

Neither unitary democracy nor deliberative democracy is feasible under the social conditions and political requirements of the nation-state. Each promises in principle considerably more than it could deliver in practice. The extended national community espoused by communitarians is as elusive as the universalized deliberative arena projected by liberal theorists. While it is no doubt true that "members of a community ... act to embody values in their daily practices and projects" [3] and do not, in general, engage in habitual reflection on, or reconsideration of, them, the acts of members of the national society, that is, citizens, given this society's plethora of disparate interests, ideologies and valuations, embody something substantially different from communally shared values. Socially coordinated, perhaps, but not communally shared. To be sure, politicians and others may declaim about "all that we have in common"; yet this is more likely to be true of common obligations and tasks than of common values. Referring to one's country as a whole, Charles Taylor announces that a democratic society "requires not only a commitment to the common project, but also a special sense of bonding among the people working together". [4] Communally cooperative democracy does indeed require "bonding", in other words, commitment, care, solidarity and loyalty; but these factors are hardly to be found distributed widely at the national level. Moreover, even if communitarian aims might be advanced in the national pseudo-community by means of "civic education and public rituals",[5] assuming that these do not coercively prescribe thinking or behavior, they are not themselves explicitly conducive to the substantive democratization of human life. On this point, it is interesting to note that communitarians are often gravely concerned that some ideals and valued forms of life may not survive the "atomization" and the allegedly official moral indifference of contemporary society unless they are preferred and actively supported by the authority and resources of the state. [6]   However, if community, in general, is threatened by divisiveness and fragmentation, democratic community, in particular, cannot be secured by coercion, even if benevolent, by cajolery or by collectivization of the psyche.

Republicanism, too, incorporates a few themes that, broadly speaking, are not altogether dissimilar from those ingredient in my conception of democracy, for example, solidarity and an orientation to what is misleadingly termed the common good. These sources of social integration are, however, not operative at the national level. The purported solidarity of all or even most citizens is exigent and not enduring; and, in any case, it does not embody very much in the way of principled loyalty to, and care for, persons. Furthermore, a common good for the nation is an idea both abstract and largely evocative, often nothing more than an "idol" of the tribe. Also, at the national level, there is no "shared form of life or collective identity". It is relevant to note here that democracy involves the former factor, but definitely not the latter. In addition, one's role as a citizen is not normatively superior to, or socially more important, than one's role as a member of a communally cooperative community wherein democratized life can flourish. Certainly, it is eminently appropriate to be concerned about the destiny of one's country of citizenship and to take seriously one's legal obligations to it; but this does not require the valorization of national society over, or at the expense of, genuine communities.

As for deliberative democracy, I contend that, except for rather limited contexts, it is unrealistic to expect occurrence of "the free and unconstrained public deliberation of all about matters of common concern".[7] It is not likely that, within the framework of the nation-state -- or of many less extended spheres of political or social activity -- deliberation would or could be carried on by "all" in an "unconstrained" mode. The principle that "only the freely given assent of all concerned can count as a condition of having reached agreement in the discourse situation"[8] is, if stipulated for contexts of considerable scale and complexity, just as hypothetical a position as is Rawls's "original position". It may be argued that the former position helps to elucidate the normative presuppositions behind democratic theory and is, therefore, not itself concerned with "institutional specifications and practical feasibility". Instead, this normative model functions to define "test cases", with respect to which existing democracy can be assessed.[9] However, in my judgment, the existing democracy of the nation-state will perennially fall quite short when evaluated according to such "test cases". Deliberations at this level tend to exhibit much more in the way of agonistic encounters, strategic bargaining, contractual compromises, and purely instrumental rationality than the respectful and refined discourses posited by deliberative democracy would countenance. To put the matter in other words, the deliberative theory of democracy does not so much reflect principles "implicit" in existing democracy as it imputes what might be called "participation" by the latter in an ideal form of democracy.

Not all theorists of deliberative democracy consider the discourse-deliberative model relevant only for the nation-state as such. Thus, it is assumed that society can contain an interlocking network of associations of deliberation. [10] This notion of an "interlocking network" is vague. It matter much whether the interlocking is adventitious or deliberate, whether interactions within the network are fruitful, whether some of the associations are marginalized or otherwise at a disadvantage, and whether results springing from the deliberative network have perceptible influence on the formulation and conduct of public policy. While the deliberative model identifies several important elements of the kind of communal and cooperative democracy that can, in fact, materialize in certain contexts, I believe that deliberative theorists are simply unrealistic about the more general prospects of their model.

Unrealistic expectations, in my judgment, have also been associated with what has been designated as direct, participatory, self-managing democracy, not yet discussed herein as such. To be sure, the conceptual model has many features in common with the model of communally cooperative, mutually empowering democracy that I recommend. However, I maintain that self-managing democracy, like my own model, cannot be successfully extended to national society as a whole.

Pateman has dealt at length with the nature of (political) obligation as something properly self-assumed in a collective manner by free and equal citizens, who see these obligations as binding them to each other rather than to the state, a union that helps to constitute the conditions of direct, participatory democracy. [11] All of this is admirable and desirable so far as it can go; but, contrary to Pateman, I contend, once again, that it cannot go as far as the scale of national society, that the "self" in self-managing democracy would always be of considerably lesser proportions. Pateman would not be deterred by such reservations, for she argues that serious consideration should be given to the transformation of the state into a "self-managing, non-statist form of democracy",[12] one which "presupposes a non-statist political community as a political association of a multiplicity of political associations. The members of the community are citizens in many political associations, which are bound together through horizontal and multifaceted ties of self-assumed political obligation." [13]

Problems remain, I submit, that will not go away. It is not at all clear how more or less localized "participatory democratic associations" are to be operationally conjoined and coordinated so as to make possible the "self-management" of society at the national level. In addition, I believe that some of the manifold associations will be more important to individuals than will others, such that the strength of "horizontal and multifaceted ties" will vary substantially. Moreover, as I see the matter, it is a mistake to speak of "community" as existing at a national (or even approximately national) level. Community involves much more than "self-assumed" obligation; it is based also, in particular, upon commitment, care, loyalty and solidarity, none of which, I maintain, can extend to the scale of national society.

Advocates of participatory, self-managing democracy, such as Pateman, do acknowledge difficulties associated with its implementation on a national scale: problems of resource allocation and of coordination generally, differences of opinion and interest, questions of efficiency, the greater attention of citizens to more proximate concerns, etc. [14] At the same time, these advocates "say very little about fundamental factors such as how, for instance, the economy is actually to be organized and related to the political apparatus, how institutions of representative democracy are to be combined with those of direct democracy, how the scope and power of administrative organizations are to be checked....Moreover, their arguments pass over the question of how their 'model' could be realized, over the whole issue of transitional stages." [15]

Several decades ago, many proponents of self-managing democracy were enthusiastic about developments in Yugoslavia, which seemed to exhibit auspicious innovations in democratic control of horizontally associated workplaces. Against this optimistic assessment, it has been averred that self-management in Yugoslavia "was a short-lived propaganda triumph and a long-lived economic catastrophe. In the artificial prosperity of the 1960s and 1970s its deficiencies could be hidden. Later, when it was too late, they could not. Self-management gave Yugoslav socialism a global reputation for enlightenment it did not deserve." [16] Of course, the failure of practical construction may not dissuade from theoretical reconstruction, the latter a recurring endeavor that can be rationalized by treating an aim not as a concrete task but as a guiding, albeit elusive, ideal.

If my model of communally cooperative, mutually empowering democracy is not feasible at the national level, as is the case also with unitary and deliberative models, then one must make do the best one can therein with adversary quasi-democracy. Is this prognosis disappointing? It depends upon what it is reasonable to expect. On one hand, it is, I suppose, somewhat sobering, perhaps frustrating, to realize that public political affairs and institutions of the nation will, in all probability, never be democratized to any significant degree. Strategic cooperation, supplemented by top-down political management and bottom-up political busywork, is quite practicable and is, moreover, useful for purposes of social stability and continuity. Here is a national environment in which one can live with minimal illusions and with generally reliable, so long as not unrealistic, expectations. On the other hand, coming to terms with the ineluctable obstacles to any substantive nation-wide democracy frees one from the vain (and frequently vainglorious) attempt to fabricate or simulate one, so that one's efforts might be directed both to fostering a more open and considerate national society and to creating within it cooperative and empowering communities in the various dimensions and spaces of social life. It is precisely in such communities that prospects for the practice of democracy are most auspicious.

In sum, since I do not believe that an authentic type of democracy can exist at the level of the nation-state, the objective remains to improve, if possible, the structures and procedures of its quasi-democracy, for example, in the following ways. Elitism in government should be inhibited, accompanied by the understanding that the task of ostensible experts is to elaborate means, not to define ends. Greater opportunities for citizen participation in public discourse and deliberation should be developed, opportunities that go beyond occasional, transient involvement in electoral procedures. The self-aggrandizing influence of economic power upon public affairs should be severely curtailed. The (non-exploitative) interests of assorted difference and identity groups should be given more serious attention in the processes of public decision making. Positive (socioeconomic) rights should be endorsed and, if at all possible, accorded institutional support. Open government should be treated as an inseparable concomitant of the open society. Ideological and/or moral unity should be neither expected nor mandated; rather, there should be consistent encouragement of civic friendliness and of a disposition toward mutually advantageous social cooperation. In general, where citizens cannot effect these kinds of changes in the system, they can at least criticize and contest the system itself.

Communal cooperation is, however, more than social, collective cooperation -- as useful as the latter may be. It is the former that is indispensable to the fuller meaning of democracy, that is, the mutually beneficial empowerment of various types of communities of individuals who are interrelated through commitment, care, loyalty and solidarity and whose common tasks and activities are consistent with humanistic values. Perhaps it might be helpful to look upon the nation-state (and beyond) as a social environment that is analogous, in certain respects, to the environment constituted by nature as a whole. Each environment may be experienced as indifferent, remote, inscrutable, recalcitrant to many human purposes, a context evincing ambiguities and uncertainties. To be sure, nature itself has no hidden agendas, no special interests to serve. Nature is neither incompetent, mendacious nor malicious. Moreover, it would make no sense to criticize or blame it for being what it is. In contrast, the ambience of the political state does manifest human mischief, ineptness, callousness -- and worse; and all of these deserve to be criticized and challenged. Yet, the analogy does contain, I think, a relevant point of comparison. As human beings can locate enriching aspects of their existence in shared experience occurring in this or that sector of nature, however much the totality of nature may compose a rather obscure, though determinative, background, so they can find enriched dimensions of existence in democratized contexts of communally empowered life that are accessible within the social totality of the nation-state and its perimeters. This "existential" meaning of democracy is not the stuff of political sound-bites, campaign posturing or grand schemes. It is, however, the substance of a more creatively satisfying life together.

Nothing that I have said is intended as an admonition to restrict the horizons of one's concerns to the more immediate forms of interpersonal life or to adopt an attitude of aloof indifference to that which affects others but not oneself. Thus, democracy should be encouraged and supported anywhere, even though there will be striking differences in the extent of its realization. This applies, importantly, to the nation-state, where inexorable and appreciable limitations on democratization cannot be superseded. Nevertheless, this does not imply that the development of national quasi-democracy should be left to proceed by default. Conscientious citizens will do what they can to improve its practice, understanding, it is hoped, that this practice will never live up to what is usually claimed on its behalf. At the same time, conscientious human beings will create and develop mutually empowering forms of communal life, in which democracy, as the humanistically meaningful practice of positive freedom, can be made manifest.

210

NOTES

1. See _Nachgelassene Fragmente_, in WKG, VII.3, 37, §11 and VIII.2, 10, §77.

2. Whereas adversary quasi-democracy yields to pseudo-utopian valorization of what does exist, both unitary democracy and deliberative democracy engage in utopian expectation about what is supposed to exist.

3. Etzioni, "Old Chestnuts", p. 26.

4. "Why Democracy Needs Patriotism", in Nussbaum, For Love, p. 120.

5. See Spragens, "Communitarian Liberalism", p. 51.

6. See Stephen Mulhall & Adam Swift. Liberals and Communitarians, Second Edition. Oxford: Blackwell, 1992.

7. Benhabib, "Toward a Deliberative Model", p. 68.

8. Ibid., p. 79.

9. Ibid., p. 70.

10. See ibid., p. 74.

11. See The Problem of Political Obligation. Chichester: John Wiley & Sons, 1979.

12. Ibid., p. 96.

13. Ibid., p. 174. This is not an endorsement of anarchism, since Pateman declares that anarchists, as radical individualists, "fail to deal coherently with the mutuality and reciprocity of social relationships" [p. 135]. Likewise, I think that her (implicitly national) "political association of a multiplicity of political associations" has anything to do with anarcho-syndicalism. Instead, it seems to suggest a reconstitution of political power as social power, somewhat like that envisioned by Marx [see ibid., p. 192, fn. 22].

14. See Held, Models, p. 260.

15. Ibid., p. 263. Thus any radical reconstruction of the state along the lines of a "non-statist" form of democracy is not plausible: "Institutions of direct democracy or self-management cannot simply replace the state; for...they leave a coordination vacuum readily filled by bureaucracy." [ibid., p. 257].

16. Brown, Surge, p. 222. Fragmentation, rather than coordination, becomes ascendant [ibid., p. 223]. See, also, Feffer, Shock Waves, p. 100.

BIBLIOGRAPHY

Ali, Tariq (ed.). <u>Masters of the Universe?</u> London: Verso, 2000.

Axelrod, Robert. <u>The Evolution of Cooperation</u>. New York: Basic Books, 1984.

Bell, Daniel. <u>Communitarianism and Its Critics</u>. Oxford: Clarendon Press, 1995.

Benhabib, Seyla (ed.). <u>Democracy and Difference</u>. Princeton: Princeton University Press, 1996.

Berlin, Isaiah. <u>Four Essays on Liberty</u>. New York: Oxford University Press, 1970.

Boucher, Douglas H. (ed.). <u>The Biology of Mutualism</u>. New York: Oxford University Press, 1985.

Brecht, Bertolt. "*Die Lösung*", *Gesammelte Werke in acht Bänden*, IV. Frankfurt am Main: Suhrkamp Verlag, 1967.

Brown, J. F. <u>Surge to Freedom</u>. Durham, NC: Duke University Press, 1991.

Butenko, A. P. "*Marksistsko-leninskaja ideja samoupravlenija naroda i ee istoricheskoe razvitie*" ["The Marxist-Leninist Idea of Self-Government of the People and Its Historical Development"], <u>Sovetskoe gosudarstvo i pravo</u>, 3, 1986.

_____. <u>Vlast' naroda posredstvom samogo naroda</u>. [<u>The Rule of the People by Means of the People Themselves</u>]. Moscow: "*Mysl'*", 1988.

_____. Personal Interview. Moscow, 17 June 1988.

Childs, David. <u>The GDR: Moscow's German Ally</u>. London: Unwin Hyman, 1988.

Christiano, Thomas. "Freedom, Consensus, and Equality in Collective Decision Making", <u>Ethics</u>, 101, October 1990.

Copp, David <u>et al.</u> (eds.). <u>The Idea of Democracy</u>. Cambridge: Cambridge University Press, 1993.

Crocker, Lawrence. <u>Positive Liberty</u>. The Hague: Martinus Nijhoff, 1980.

212

Cunningham, Frank. Democratic Theory and Socialism. Cambridge: University Press, 1987.

Dahl, Robert A. After the Revolution?, Revised Edition. New Haven: Yale University Press, 1990.

_____. Democracy and Its Critics. New Haven: Yale University Press, 1989

Davis, Morton D. Game Theory. New York: Basic Books, 1983.

Dewey, John. The public and its problems. Athens: Ohio University Press, 1954.

Domhoff, G. William. The Powers That Be. New York: Random House, 1978.

_____. Who Rules America Now? Englewood Cliffs, NJ: Prentice-Hall, 1983.

Etzioni, Amitai (ed.). New Communitarian Thinking. Charlottesville: University Press of Virginia, 1995.

Feffer, John. Shock Waves: Eastern Europe after the Revolutions. Boston: South End Press, 1992.

Feinberg, Joel. Rights, Justice, and the Bounds of Liberty. Princeton: Princeton University Press, 1980.

_____. Social Philosophy. Englewood Cliffs, NJ: Prentice Hall, 1973.

Fisk, Milton. The State and Justice. Cambridge: Cambridge University Press, 1989.

Frank, Thomas. One Market Under God. New York: Doubleday, 2000.

Friedman, Marilyn. "Feminism and Modern Friendship: Dislocating the Community", Ethics, 99, January 1989.

Fritzsche, Peter. Germans into Nazis. Cambridge: Harvard University Press, 1998.

Funk, Nanette & Magda Mueller (eds.). Gender Politics and Post-Communism. New York: Routledge, 1993.

Gould, Carol C. Rethinking Democracy. Cambridge: Cambridge University Press, 1988.

Gray, Tim. Freedom. Atlantic Highlands, NJ: Humanities Press, 1991.

Guinier, Lani. The Tyranny of the Majority. New York: The Free Press, 1994.

213

Habermas, Jürgen. Between Facts and Norms. Cambridge; MIT Press, 1996.

_____. "Reconciliation through the Public Use of Reason", Journal of Philosophy, XCII, No. 3, March 1995.

Hardin, Russell. "Political Obligation", The Good Polity: Normative Analysis of the State, ed. Alan Hamlin & Phillip Pettit. Oxford: Basil Blackwell, 1989.

Hare, R. M. "Justice and Equality", Justice, ed. James P. Sterba. Belmont, CA: Wadsworth, 1999.

Hatab, Lawrence J. A Nietzschean Defense of Democracy. LaSalle, IL: Open Court Publishing Co., 1995.

Held, David. Models of Democracy. Stanford: Stanford University Press, 1987.

Herzog, Don. Happy Slaves: A Critique of Consent Theory. Chicago: University of Chicago Press, 1989.

Holden, Barry. The Nature of Democracy. New York: Barnes & Noble, 1974.

Holt, Alix (ed.). Selected Writings of Alexandra Kollontai. London: Allison & Busby, 1977.

Kagarlitsky, Boris. The Disintegration of the Monolith. London: Verso, 1992.

_____. New Realism, New Barbarism. London: Pluto Press, 1999.

Kershaw, Ian. The Hitler Myth. Oxford: Oxford University Press, 1989.

Kiss, Arthur. Marxism and Democracy. Budapest: Akadémiai Kiadó, 1982.

Klebnikov, Paul. Godfather of the Kremlin. New York: Harcourt, 2000.

Korten, David C. When Corporations Rule the World. San Francisco: Berrett-Koehler Publishers, 2001.

Kozharov, Assen. Monism and Pluralism in Ideology and in Politics. Sofia: Sofia Press, n.d.

Lenin, V. I. The State and Revolution, in Collected Works, Vol. 25, pp. 460-461. Moscow: Progress Publishers, 1964.

Lewis, Michael. The Culture of Inequality. New York: New American Library, 1978.

MacCallum, Gerald C., Jr. "Negative and Positive Freedom", Philosophical Review, LXXVI, 1967.

Macpherson, C. B. Democratic Theory. Oxford: Clarendon Press, 1973.

Malov, Yuri. The Communist Party in Socialist Society. Moscow: Progress Publishers, 1987.

Mansbridge, Jane J. Beyond Adversary Democracy. New York: Basic Books, 1980.

Marcuse, Herbert. One Dimensional Man. Boston: Beacon Press, 1991.

Marx, Karl. Critique of the Gotha Programme, in Karl Marx & Frederick Engels. Collected Works [MECW], Vol. 24, p. 87. New York: International Publishers, 1989.

Marx, Karl & Frederick Engels. The German Ideology, in MECW, Vol. 5, p. 78. New York: International Publishers, 1976

_____. The Holy Family, in MECW, Vol. 4, p. 131. New York: International Publishers, 1975.

McChesney, Robert W. Rich Media, Poor Democracy. New York: The New Press, 2000.

Medvedev, Roy. Let History Judge. New York: Columbia University Press, 1989.

_____. On Socialist Democracy. New York: W. W. Norton, 1977.

_____. Post-Soviet Russia. New York: Columbia University Press, 2000.

_____. Russkaja revoljutsija 1917 goda: pobeda i porazhenie bol'shevikov [The Russian Revolution of 1917: Victory and Defeat of the Bolsheviks]. Moscow: Izdatel'stvo "Prava cheloveka", 1997.

Mill, John Stuart. Utilitarianism. Indianapolis: Bobbs-Merrill, 1957.

Momdzhjan, A. B. Pljuralizm: istoki i sushchnost' [Pluralism: Sources and Essence]. Moscow: Izdatel'stvo "Nauka", 1983.

Mulhall, Stephen & Adam Swift. Liberals and Communitarians, Second Edition. Oxford: Blackwell Publishers, 1992.

Nietzsche, Friedrich. Werke. Kritische Gesamtausgabe [WKG], hrsg. von Giorgio Colli & Mazzino Montinari. Berlin: Walter de Gruyter, 1967- .

Nozick, Robert. Anarchy, State, and Utopia. New York: Basic Books, 1974.

Nussbaum, Martha et al. For Love of Country. Boston: Beacon Press, 1996.

Okin, Susan Moller. "Gender, the Public and the Private", <u>Political Theory Today</u>, ed. David Held. Stanford: Stanford University Press, 1991.

_____. <u>Justice, Gender, and the Family</u>. New York: Basic Books, 1989.

Parenti, Michael. <u>Democracy for the Few</u>, Fifth Edition. New York: St. Martin's Press, 1988.

Partridge, P. H. <u>Consent and Consensus</u>. New York: Praeger Publishers, 1971.

Pateman, Carole. <u>The Disorder of Women: Democracy, Feminism and Political Theory</u>. Stanford: Stanford University Press, 1989.

_____. "Feminism and democracy", <u>Democratic theory and practice</u>, ed. Graeme Duncan. Cambridge: Cambridge University Press, 1983.

_____. <u>The Problem of Political Obligation</u>. Chichester: John Wiley & Sons, 1979.

_____. <u>The Sexual Contract</u>. Stanford: Stanford University Press, 1988.

Phillips, Anne. <u>Democracy and Difference</u>. University Park, PA: Penn State University Press, 1993.

Popper, Karl. <u>Conjectures and Refutations</u>. London: Routledge & Kegan Paul, 1963.

_____. <u>The Open Society and its Enemies</u>. New York: Harper & Row, 1963.

Przeworski, Adam. <u>Democracy and the market</u>. Cambridge: Cambridge University Press, 1991.

Rawls, John. "Justice as Fairness: Political Not Metaphysical", <u>Philosophy and Public Affairs</u>, Vol. 14, no. 3, 1985.

_____. <u>Political Liberalism</u>. New York: Columbia University Press, 1996.

_____. "Reply to Habermas", <u>Journal of Philosophy</u>, XCII, No. 3, March 1995.

_____. <u>A Theory of Justice</u>. Cambridge: Harvard University Press, 1971.

Reusch, Jürgen. <u>*Pluralismus und Klassenkampf*</u>. Frankfurt am Main: *Verlag Marxistische Blätter*, 1982.

Sen, Amartya. <u>On Ethics and Economics</u>. Oxford: Blackwell, 1987.

Talmon, J. L. The Origins of Totalitarian Democracy. New York: Frederick A. Praeger, 1960.

Trend, David (ed.). Radical Democracy. New York: Routledge, 1996.

Watson, Peggy. "The Rise of Masculinism in Eastern Europe", New Left Review, March/April, 1993.

Wilson, William Julius. The Truly Disadvantaged. Chicago: University of Chicago Press, 1987.

Wolff, Robert Paul. In Defense of Anarchism. New York: Harper & Row, 1970.

Wood, Ellen Meiksins. Democracy Against Capitalism. Cambridge: Cambridge University Press, 1995

Woods, Roger. Opposition in the GDR under Honecker, 1971-1985. New York: St. Martin's Press, 1986.

Young, Iris Marion. Justice and the Politics of Difference. Princeton: Princeton University Press, 1990.

INDEX

Pateman, Carole, 20, 21, 22, 205, 210
Criticism of Rawls, 87-89
Self-managing democracy, 205
Social contract, 87-89
Personal and political, 7-8
Phillips, Anne, 21, 22, 37, 110, 111, 144, 145
Class difference, 96
Disruptive difference, 104
Equality and gender, 90
Exclusivism, 100
Politics of presence, 27-28
Politics of distraction, 30
Popper, Karl, 21, 178
Przeworski, Adam, 36, 68, 109, 123, 130, 179, 189
Public and private, 9-11

R
Rawls, John, 67, 77, 85, 86, 87, 89, 108, 109, 131, 132, 138, 139, 140, 143, 146, 147, 148, 149, 153, 154, 156, 166, 171, 173
Redeker, Robert, 146
Representation, 25-27
Republicanism:
Critique, 118-120, 202-203
Model of democracy, 117-118
Reusch, Jürgen, 191

S
Schumpeter, Joseph, 31-32
Sen, Amartya, 51, 75, 79, 149
Socioeconomic inequality, 55-57
Spragens, Thomas A.,143, 210

T
Taylor, Charles, 202

U
Unitary democracy:
Critique, 115-120, 201
Nature, 114-120

W
Watson, Peggy, 20
Weber, Max, 31-32
Wilson, William Julius, 78, 95
Wolff, Robert Paul, 173
Wolin, Sheldon, 21, 22, 51, 191
Wood, Ellen Meiksins, 36, 110, 190
Class difference, 105-106
Critique of capitalist democracy, 180-181
Woods, Roger, 36

Y
Young, Iris Marion, 21, 108, 110, 111, 143, 144, 147, 148
Assimilationist ideal, 98-99
Criticism of deliberative democracy, 97, 130-131
Critique of community, 136
Justice and difference, 89-90
Representation, 99

PROBLEMS IN CONTEMPORARY PHILOSOPHY